3/94

UNIVERSIT...
WOLVE...

KT-384-741

Dudley Campus Library

Castle View
Dudley DY1 3HR

Wolverhampton (01902) 323559
321333

M

This item may be recalled at any time. Keeping it after it has
been recalled or beyond the date stamped may result in a fine.
See tariff of fines displayed at the counter.

-9 FEB 1996	-2 APR 1998	2 8 SEP 2007
21 JUN 1996	-1 MAY 1998	2 4 APR 2009
13 NOV 1996	-8 JAN 1999	
18 APR 1997	2 8 FEB 2000	
-1 DEC 1997	12th April	
	6/10/03	
	2 3 MAR 2004	

WITHDRAWN

WP 0867829 4

Cross-Cultural Perspectives on Women

General Editors: Shirley Ardener and Jackie Waldren, for The Centre for Cross-Cultural Research on Women, University of Oxford

Muslim Women's Choices

Religious Belief and Social Reality

Edited by

Camillia Fawzi El-Solh and Judy Mabro

UNIVERSITY OF WOLVERHAMPTON
LIBRARY

Acc No. 867829

CLASS

CONTROL
0854968350

305.
42088

DATE
-6. JUN. 995

SITE
04

297
MUS

BERG
Providence/Oxford

English edition
first published in 1994 by
Berg Publishers

Editorial offices:
221 Waterman Road, Providence, RI 02906, USA
150 Cowley Road, Oxford, OX4 1JJ, UK

© Camillia Fawzi El-Solh and Judy Mabro

All rights reserved.
No part of this publication may be reproduced in any form or by any means
without the written permission of Berg Publishers Limited.

Library of Congress Cataloging-in-Publication Data
A Catalogue record for this book is available from the Library of Congress

I. El-Sohl, Camillia Fawzi
II. Mabro, Judy III. Series 305. 420917671
ISBN 0-85496-836-9 (paper)
        0-85496-835-0 (cloth)

British Library Cataloguing in Publication Data
Muslim Women's Choices – (Cross-cultural Perspectives on Women Series)

ISBN 0-85496-836-9 (paper)
        0-85496-835-0 (cloth)

Printed in the United Kingdom by Short Run Press, Exeter.

Contents

Preface

This book arose from a seminar series on Women in Muslim Communities: Religious Belief and Social Reality, organised in 1991 by the Centre for Cross-Cultural Research on Women, University of Oxford (though the paper by Gillian Tett was subsequently commissioned). The aim of this volume is to contribute to the on-going, exciting and controversial debate on Islam in the contemporary world.

The contributions provide us with insights into the complexity of Islam and the diverse lives of Muslim women, which will be of interest to social scientists concerned with gender and ideology. The book will also be of relevance to those working towards a greater understanding of non-western cultures and societies, an understanding which should aim to explain without being apologetic, and to be critical without being patronising.

Several people were kind enough to read and comment on the first draft of this introduction, and we would like to thank them all: Sara Ahmed, Derek Hopwood, Nahla Khalifeh, Robert Mabro, Marion Farouk Sluglett, Cecillie Swaisland. Particular thanks go to the series editors, Shirley Ardener and Jackie Waldren, for their support and encouragement.

Notes on Contributors

Tamara Dragadze is a Research Fellow at the School of Slavonic and East European Studies, University of London. She was born in Oswestry, Shropshire of Georgian descent, and has done research on the Caucasus since 1969. Her D.Phil. from the University of Oxford was entitled 'The Domestic Unit in Rural Soviet Georgia'. She has published extensively on the Caucasus and nationalism.

Camillia Fawzi El-Solh is a Research Associate at the Centre for Cross-Cultural Research on Women, University of Oxford and a freelance consultant on gender and development in the Arab region. She is also interested in the field of migration and has carried out fieldwork on Egyptian peasant families in Iraq and, more recently, on Arab communities in Britain, a subject on which she has published. Together with Soraya Altorki she has edited and contributed to *Arab Women in the Field: Studying your own Society* (Syracuse University Press, 1988).

Naila Kabeer is a Fellow at the Institute of Development Studies at the University of Sussex, doing research and training on gender, poverty, population and health issues. She is a Director of the IDS short course 'Women, Men and Development'and is at present completing a book called *Reverse Realities: Gender Hierarchies in Development Thought*, which will be published by VERSO in Spring, 1994.

Judy Mabro works as an editor and is the author of *Veiled Half-Truths: Western Perceptions of Middle Eastern Women* (London: I.B. Tauris, 1991).

Ziba Mir-Hosseini received her Ph.D. in Social Anthropology from the University of Cambridge, where she is currently a research fellow at Girton College. Her initial research was on family and change in rural Iran: she has also done fieldwork in urban Iran and Morocco, and most recently on a mystical sect in Kurdistan. She has published several articles and a book *Marriage on Trial: A Comparative Study of Islamic Family Law in Iran and Morocco* (I.B. Tauris, 1993).

Rosemary Ridd is a social anthropologist. Her doctoral research was on an inner-city area in South Africa where women had a dominant role in the community as a response to racial oppression. She is interested in inter-religious dialogue. With Helen Callaway she has edited *Caught up in Conflict: Women's Responses to Political Strife* (London: Macmillan, 1986). She is currently in South Africa carrying out further research.

Jacqueline Siapno is a PhD. candidate in the Department of South and Southeast Asian Studies, University of California, Berkeley. She is writing her dissertation on the social, political and noetic relations between Aceh and Sulu, areas of the Malay world which have now become parts of Indonesia and the Philippines respectively.

Cornelia Sorabji teaches Social Anthropology at the School of Culture and Community Studies, University of Sussex. A graduate of Cambridge University, she has also held a British Academy research fellowship at the School of Oriental and African Studies, University of London.

Gillian Tett recently spent two years in the Soviet Union, carrying out field research for a PhD. in Social Anthropology and working as a foreign correspondent. She is now completing her PhD. at Cambridge University, before taking up a job as a journalist with the *Financial Times*.

Gloria Thomas-Emeagwali has lectured at the Ahmadu Bello University, Zaria; the Nigerian Defence Academy, Kaduna; and the University of Ilorin, Nigeria. She has served as a visiting scholar at the University of the West Indies, and more recently Oxford University, where she was a Visiting Fellow and Senior Associate Member. She is an Associate Professor at the Central Connecticut State University, USA. Dr Emeagwali was a founding member of *Women in Nigeria* (WIN), an activist women's organisation established in 1982. She is also a member of Development Alternatives with Women for a New Era (DAWN).

Helen Watson is a Lecturer in Social Anthropology and Fellow of St John's College, Cambridge. She is the author of *Women in the City of the Dead* (London: Hurst & Company, 1992). Her interests include Arab-Muslim society, gender and power inequalities. She is currently working on conflict in Ireland.

Introduction: Islam and Muslim Women

Camillia Fawzi El-Solh and Judy Mabro

The Muslim women presented in this book live in a variety of societies and communities where legislation, customs and traditions, affected or inspired by interpretations of the Qur'an and the Shari'a,[1] combine to define concepts of female roles and status. It is clear that, within a specific Muslim society, these concepts may vary from one class or generation to the other as well as over time, just as they may differ from one Muslim country to another. In addition, Muslim women's lives and the choices they face are influenced as much by patriarchal social arrangements as they are by religious ideology. This confirms Shirley Ardener's observation that we 'need to be wary in cross-cultural comparisons of women's status (since) giving a weighting to the value of each variable for each society . . . is impossibly complex' (1992a: 6).

Moreover, in the same way as women in non-Muslim societies, Muslim women tend to be 'divided over the definition of their gender interests, over the nature of social arrangements which best serve them and over their visions of a better society' (Kandiyoti, 1991a: 18). This divergence of views on women's social position is reflected by the different Muslim discourses depicting modernist, traditionalist and fundamentalist trends. It is also reflected by the reality that not all Muslim women feel compelled to resort to dress or other symbolism to signal their adherence to Islam and to the Muslim component of their identity.

Stereotyping Islam

Public opinion in the West generally ignores this diversity and is largely influenced by deep-rooted assumptions that Islam is a monolithic religion controlling all aspects of its adherents' lives. A tendency to explain it solely in terms of the Qur'an and/or other Islamic sources all too often taken out of context, ignores the fact that, like other world religions,

1

Islam has been subject to growth and development, adaptation and change (Stowasser, 1987a: 262; cf. Esposito, 1984). Over the centuries since its revelation, Islam has been permeated by a succession of cultural accretions reflecting the complex ways in which religious belief and social reality accommodate one another. There is of course a unifying framework which is provided by the Qur'an as the quintessential source and language of the faith, as well as through the five pillars of the creed – *shahada* (proclaiming the faith), *salat* (prayer), *zakat* (almsgiving), *sawm* (fast) and *hajj* (pilgrimage to Mecca). Nevertheless, this unity is accompanied by a multitude of diversities which need to be taken into account in any discussion of Islam and its practice by Muslims.[2]

The furore which erupted in Britain over the publication in 1988 of Salman Rushdie's book *The Satanic Verses*, which some Muslim groups considered to be blasphemous, also revealed in the West the limited nature of knowledge about Muslims in geographically remote areas as well as the biased perception which mainstream societies hold of Muslim ethnic communities living in their midst (cf. Ruthven, 1991). Similar stereotyping occurred in France in 1989 during the crisis over whether three North African girls should be allowed to wear headscarves (*le foulard islamique*) in school.[3] In both countries, communities which had previously been identified as Pakistani, Yemeni, Algerian and so on, were suddenly referred to as 'the Muslims' in the popular press. This categorisation ignored the fact that Islam is just one part of a composite identity influenced by country of origin, socio-economic status, sectarian and political affiliations, language and dialect, age group, gender as well as history of settlement in the West. This diversity is, for instance, illustrated by Giles Keppel who interviewed Muslims living in France, among which,

> there were young Algerians born in France and knowing no Arabic, Turkish workers speaking no French, Moroccan housewives, Senegalese *marabouts*, those who were literate and those who were illiterate, those who were fighting for various causes and those who had retired into themselves, there were French citizens and a variety of nationalities (1991: 27; transl. by editors).

Tensions involving Muslim immigrant communities settled in the West have partly been exacerbated by, for example, the demand in Britain by some Muslim groups for state-funded schools for Muslim girls, the proclamation of the Muslim Parliament of Great Britain, or the questioning of British Muslims' loyalties during the 1991 Gulf War, all of which points to the uncertainties related to the place of Islam in mainstream British society.[4] In addition, the crisis in France revealed the xenophobia of groups seeking a scapegoat for the economic and social ills of the country – indeed, in November 1989, there were demonstrations against 'the Islamisation of France'.[5]

Although the reluctance of some Muslim ethnic communities to bridge the cultural divide, and the fact that some Muslims may hold equally bigoted views of Westerners, should not be ignored,[6] the problem of integration into mainstream western societies is further exacerbated by overt and subtle manifestations of racism, as well as by the tendency to view Islam as an intrusion into western culture. As a recent volume on Islam in North America puts it, Muslims tend to be described and interpreted by the West as 'other', 'non-us', or 'them', with Islam 'held up as an alien religion against an idealized, ahistorical Judeo-Christian mirror' (Waugh et. al., 1991: xi; cf. Hourani, 1991). In addition, in the current political climate, fundamentalist Islam tends to be represented as 'universal, irrational, terrifying and mad', with a central political role in Muslim cultures and societies. By contrast, fundamentalist Christian sects are generally depicted as 'minor abberations' of 'restricted political significance' (Marcus, 1992: 92).

This view of Islam has been inadvertently caused by the widespread religious revival sweeping much of the Muslim world over recent decades, a resurgence generally associated with the 1979 Iranian Revolution with its images of turbaned, bearded clergymen and women covered in black from head to foot (cf. Azari, 1983). From North Africa to Pakistan and down the geographical map to Indonesia, Islam has become a political and social force increasingly impinging upon the consciousness of western societies (cf. Roff, 1987). All too often, the West gives little thought to the economic, social and cultural context in which the Islamic movement operates, or the reasons why Islam is held up as an alternative political model to the one enforced by the ruling elite (cf. El-Guindi, 1981; Eickelman, 1987). Moreover, as participants in the International Workshop of Women from Muslim Countries (held in 1986 in Lahore, Pakistan) concluded:

> Islam and Islamic culture are a complex reality. This complexity is distorted by the West in terms of the way the West views Islam. But the West also has a contradictory position on Islam. On the one hand, it operates an active anti-Islamic campaign, and on the other, it supports fundamentalism. In both cases, however, it does this for its own political purposes (Matsui, 1991: 97).

More recently, post-independence developments in Muslim Central Asia have been raising questions about the role of Islam in filling the political vacuum left by the demise of communism in these newly independent states. Here again the western preoccupation with Islam lurks between the lines, seen, for example, in the questioning of the effects of closer political and social ties between these newly independent states and Muslim countries south of their borders.[7] To which one may add the civil war in the former socialist republic of Yugoslavia, which has served to remind Westerners of the existence of Muslims on Europe's eastern periphery.[8]

A Quintessential Muslim Woman?

At the forefront of concerns over Islamic revivalism in different parts of the world is an abiding western interest in Muslim women. In the western mind, Muslim women all too often tend to conjure up 'a vision of heavily veiled, secluded wives, whose lives consist of little more than their homes, their children, and the other women in the harem or immediate kinship circle' (Gerner-Adams, 1979: 324). While this description may have been true in the past or, more accurately, it may have been true for certain groups in certain Muslim societies, and though it may continue to be partly true for some present-day Muslim communities, it is of limited relevance to understanding the lives of the majority of contemporary Muslim women. In effect, the prejudices generally associated with earlier western travellers to the Muslim world – who imagined native women as either ignorant heathens, or exotic beings whose allures were tantalisingly hidden by layers of clothing – largely continue to colour contemporary western perceptions of Muslim women (cf. Mabro, 1991). Indeed, such perceptions prevail despite the fact that in many western as well as non-western societies Muslim women are to be found engaging in a wide variety of economic activities.

Thus, the word Muslim tends to be used as a label which ignores a multitude of factors contributing to the definition of women's status in Muslim societies, both past and present. Partly this is due to the deduction that

> since gender relations are rather strictly formalized in the *Qur'an*, in the *hadiths*, and in *shari'a*; and since these religious and legal doctrines are seen by many Muslims as eternal and universal; and since women are unequal under these theological and legal doctrines, women are seen as enduring a universal and uniform state of subjugation (Hale, 1989: 247).

But as Fatima Mernissi points out, Islam is, in itself, 'no more repressive than Judaism or Christianity' with regard to the position of women (1991: vi, vii).[9] Neither of these three world religions can be adequately understood without taking the patriarchal social systems which spawned them into account. In fact, the widespread patriarchy beneath the veneer of western secular societies is well captured in a recent book on the role of Christian women in contemporary British society (Lees, 1991). Thus one contributor to the volume – incidentally a woman – extols the Christian wife as 'a helper to her husband physically, emotionally, mentally and spiritually', perceiving her as 'someone who runs her family and household so efficiently that her husband is free to take his place as a leader in the outside world' (Catherwood, 1991: 24).

With respect to Islam, though Shari'a-based personal status law obviously has an important impact,[10] the combined weight of pre-capitalist ideologies and patriarchal kinship arrangements has also had, and continues to have, implications for Muslim women's status in countries of the Muslim world (cf. Moghadam, 1990). However, one needs to keep in mind that just as there is no universal interpretation of Islam, there is no universal system of patriarchy. Hence,

different systems of male dominance, and their internal variations according to class and ethnicity, exercise an influence that inflects and modifies the actual practice of Islam as well as the ideological constructions of what may be regarded as properly Islamic (Kandiyoti, 1991b: 24).

A clearer understanding of these systems of male dominance may be gained by considering the measures women adopt in different situations. For example, in the West African Sahel, Muslim women challenge male dominance through 'a kind of obstinate, refractory struggle for a continuation of certain pre-Muslim and non-Muslim elements' which they believe gives them greater autonomy in their lives (Bovin, 1983: 90). As Jean O'Barr also argues, women in many African societies use paths to political participation which will not be understood without moving beyond western ideas of parliamentary democracy. It is important to recognise the amalgamation of politics and other aspects of social life when analysing the role and status of women in their societies (1984: 140).

By contrast, in 'classic patriarchy', as Deniz Kandiyoti calls it, that is in the Middle East, South and Southeast Asia, 'the cyclical fluctuations of [women's] power position, combined with status considerations, result in their active collusion in the reproduction of their own subordination' (1991b: 34). However, this generalisation should not overlook the reality that class and educational level, for example, may undermine the impact of 'classic patriarchy'. Thus women in those cultural areas are becoming increasingly vocal against a number of oppressive aspects of the system within which they live, even though there may not necessarily be a consensus over the means to achieve change. This is well expressed, for example, in interviews with Egyptian, Moroccan and Tunisian women discussing their attempts to place the 'woman's question' on the national agenda in their respective countries (Dwyer, 1991: 182–207).

Hence, as pointed out at the beginning of this chapter, to characterise all women subject to Islamic law as *ipso facto* subservient beings is to disregard the fact that religious sources have been subject to changing interpretations (cf. Esposito, 1982). Accordingly, there will be discernible differences in the ways in which, for example, traditionalist, modernist or fundamentalist Muslims perceive these sources. Traditionalists believe that the injunctions laid down in the Qur'an and in the different schools of Islamic jurisdiction should be followed unquestioningly, and are not subject to any new interpretation. To the modernists, Islam is a religion consistent with common sense, and its 'regulations and commandments are to be the objects of interpretation (*ijtihad*) which brings out the values and principles of which they are expressions'. Finally, fundamentalists 'understand Islam as a social order', and as the 'natural religion' laid down by God and therefore unchangeable. But whereas the traditionalist tends to ignore the blurring of boundaries between custom and religion, the fundamentalist resorts to rational arguments to demonstrate how the divine law of Islam has been tainted by alien customs (Hjarpe, 1983: 12–15). Clearly, these varied interpretations will have important implications for women's legal status with respect to inheritance, marriage, divorce and custody of children, to the relationship between men and women, as well as to the scope of women's activities outside the home (cf. Kusha, 1990). At the same time, the way in which the legal status of women in a given Muslim society is actually defined, and perhaps more importantly, the *de facto* application of their legal rights, cannot be isolated from a host of other variables, such as cultural specificity, social and political structures as well as the level of economic development.

Egypt presents an interesting example in this respect. Though family law remains subject to Shari'a injunctions, it is not the legal system alone which defines women's social status. Earl Sullivan's discussion of urban Egyptian women in public life (1986), and Soheir Morsy's analysis of rural Egyptian women (1990) demonstrate the many factors, such as education, class and employment, which, in conjunction with the patriarchal social system, affect women's status in Egyptian society. These accounts also highlight the truism that this status may vary from one situation to the next, and be subject to subtle or more far-reaching change over time.[11] Moreover, when the government repealed the 1979 reform law (no. 44) – which had given Egyptian Muslim women certain benefits with respect to divorce, alimony and custody of children – feminists were roused to take collective political action and succeeded in forcing the government in 1985 to restore some of the benefits (cf. Badran, 1991). In Pakistan also, women's groups organized demonstrations in protest against the government's Islamisation policies – for example, the 1979 Hudood Ordinance which abolished the differentiation between rape and adultery, as well as the *chadur aur chardiwari* (the veil and four walls) campaign to enforce female seclusion (Ahmad, 1991: 10–17).

The issue becomes even more complex when we include the status of women within Muslim minority groups, or within states where Shari'a law is superseded by secular law. In the case of the former, women's status may not only be affected as a result of being part of a minority in a non-Muslim society, but also by 'the application to them of the secondary characteristics of a minority', i.e. less economic control and political power (Wadud-Muhsin, 1989: 161). Barbara Pillsbury's description of Muslim women in China illustrates the effect which minority status, in conjunction with the accommodation between Islamic injunctions and cultural/social customs, may have on the social position of women (1978). The example of these Muslim Chinese is also a reminder that, whatever the commonality between women as members of a minority group, their social status will not be uniform.

In countries with secular legislation, its application may often be circumvented by Shari'a as well as customary law. Together with cultural, social, economic and political factors, this can perpetuate a patriarchal system in which, *de facto,* women hold disadvantaged legal and social status relative to men. Turkey is an interesting example of a secular state where the majority of the population is Muslim, and where definitions of women's status continue to be subject to patriarchal social structures inherent in Islam (cf. Kandiyoti, 1988). None the less, any generalisation about the social position of women needs to be guarded, particularly given that Turkish women may be active in defining their own status. For example, some women are involved with secular feminist groups in the conflict with the Islamic fundamentalist movement regarding definitions of female gender roles in society (Berik, 1990: 81), while others signal their social respectability by a stricter adherence to the Islamic female role model propagated by traditionalist elements in Turkish society (Moghadam, 1991: 271).

'Controlling' Women

The Ubiquitous Veil

In the general perception of the West, there is an association between the subordination of Muslim women and the physical as well as the symbolic segregation of the sexes. The former is reflected in separate space for men and women, which, at its most extreme, limits women's physical mobility to the home. For its part, symbolic segregation is reflected in a dress code – commonly referred to as 'the veil' – which shields the physical attributes or the identity of its female wearer from the eyes of non-kin males with whom social intercourse is limited or prohibited (cf. Papanek and Minault, 1982). Thus, this dress code functions as one of a number of possible forms of control of contacts between men and women in shared space (cf. Ardener, 1981a).

Both forms of segregation are inherent in a social system where concepts of honour and shame are central to an understanding of relations between men and women, and thus of the moral code operating in society. However, as Santi Rozario points out:

> While in theory codes of honour and shame refer to the behaviour of both men and women, honour is seen more as men's responsibility and shame as women's. This division of honour and shame is related to the fact that honour is seen as actively achieved while shame is seen as passively defended, resulting in different expectations of behaviour from men and women (1992: 86).

In effect, inherent in the notion of female shame is the concept of female sexuality which requires social control, a point which will be elaborated in a later context. What is of interest at this point is that the western eye tends particularly to focus on veiling, perhaps because it is a more visible manifestation of the separation between the sexes. Westerners generally tend to regard this dress code for women as part of Islam, and as more or less irrefutable evidence of the subordinate role of women in Muslim communities and societies.

Countering the notion of the veil as the *sine qua non* of Islam is particularly difficult given the fact that the historical origin of this dress code remains the subject of much controversy. Thus, while both Muslim traditionalists and fundamentalists will point to the Qur'anic verse which enjoins women 'to cover their ornaments', and 'draw their veils over their persons' as God's unequivocal command to conceal their physical attributes, modernists will tend to invoke the Qur'anic verse which specifically refers to veiling in relation only to the Prophet's wives, as an argument against the rigid adoption of this dress code in contemporary Muslim societies (Sherif, 1985: 130; cf. Kusha, 1990). Modernist Muslim feminists such as Frieda Hussein (1984a) and Azizah Al-Hibri (1982a) view the veil as one of a number of manifestations of the way in which patriarchy has circumvented the essential message of Islam regarding equality between the sexes. By contrast, a secular feminist such as Nawal El Saadawi relates the veil to pre-Islamic cultures (1982: 202), while Fatima Mernissi, another secular feminist, sees the veil as a means of male social control, with its roots in the patriarchal system, in order

to make women disappear, to eliminate them from communal life, to rele-
gate them to an easily controllable terrain, the home, to prevent them from
moving about, and to highlight their illegal position on male territory by
means of a mask (1982: 189).

Moreover, the term veil tends to be erroneously used in reference
to a range of female attire from the headscarf to the floor length garment covering the head, face and body. Equally erroneous is the tendency to associate the veiling of women with traditionalism, a practice presumed to be abandoned once Muslim societies signal their
social progress by becoming 'modernised'. This assumption ignores
the fact that modernisation does not necessarily equal westernisation, i.e. that development in terms of accepting new ideas and of
learning new skills regarded as being of 'western' origin, does not
inevitably imply the homogenisation of cultures. It also overlooks
the reality that the practice of veiling – a term used here in the complex sense described above – may reflect different cultural and social
contexts.

For example, the type of female attire generally referred to as the
veil, and which is compulsory for women of all social classes in Saudi
Arabia, will differ markedly in fabric and design from that worn in various Muslim areas in Africa, Indonesia, Malaysia or Senegal where it is
not mandatory (cf. von der Mehden, 1980; Bahry, 1982; Cederroth,
1983; Strobel, 1984; Creevy, 1991). Also, as with any other clothing,
subtle differences will signal the socio-economic status of the wearer,
and there will be variations from one generation to the next, as well as
differences between regions. Thus, despite the uniformity of dress
encouraged by the Islamic fundamentalist movement – with the aim of
diminishing the importance of cultural and class cleavages perceived to
be antithetical to the concept of the *umma* (community of Muslims) –
veiling in the contemporary Muslim world may exhibit quite a variety
of styles.[12]

In Egypt, up to the early decades of the twentieth century, veiling
was mainly an urban custom practised particularly by middle class and
elite women, who were also more likely to be secluded. This is believed
to have been related to the fact that women of these social strata were
more likely to receive their inheritance, which implied the necessity to
control their social contacts with male non-kin in order to safeguard the
patrimony (Keddie, 1991: 6). By the 1920s, elite women had begun to
publicly discard the veil in protest against their social and political marginalisation, though their demands were not set within a context which
would bridge the class barriers between them and women from the poor
sections in society (Badran, 1991: 207–15). In any event, this paved the

way for women from the urban middle class and, in time, from the lower middle class, to abandon this practice, and to adopt a western-inspired style of dress. By contrast, women from the low income and from the traditional strata in urban Egyptian society continued up to the early 1970s to observe a dress code which the westernised classes undifferentiatedly categorised as veiling. However, the type of modest female attire meant by veiling among these traditional social strata – generally referred to as *milaya laff* (literally enveloping sheet), which 'reveals the graceful bodily curves yet will "cover" what should not be revealed or what is shameful' (El-Messiri, 1978: 89) – differed marked-ly from the veil formerly worn by the more affluent urban Egyptian women in that it did not entail the covering of the face. By contrast, in Afghanistan, for example, the type of veil worn by women from the tra-ditional social stratum reflects a more rigid modesty code which demands the covering of the face and the concealment of any curves of the female body (cf. Majrooh, 1989).

The Islamic revivalism which began to make its mark at the beginning of the 1970s, and which has continued its spread up to the present decade, brought with it the bewildering phenomenon of urban educated women of mainly middle- and upper middle-class origin in various Muslim coun-tries of the Middle East who were donning variations of the veil discard-ed by the generations of their mothers and grandmothers. In Egypt, for example, this conservative dress code had by the early 1980s begun to be adopted also by lower middle and working-class women whose elders had been abandoning the *milaya laff* (Early, 1993: 118–22). The phenom-enon of what may be termed the 'Islamic' veil – denoting its association with the Islamic revival sweeping through much of the Muslim world – began to particularly impinge on the consciousness of the West with the appearance of *chador*-clad women (Iranian term for black cape-like gar-ment covering the head and body to the ankles) immortalised by the 1979 Iranian Revolution. These women's choice of donning the veil as a sym-bol of protest against the Shah's regime – and, by implication, against 'western cultural imperialism' – expressed a political activism which belied the widespread western image of the subservient Muslim female confined to the social margins of her society (Ramazani, 1983: 20). How-ever, this activism was soon undermined by the Islamic government's usurpation of this symbol as part of its ideology set on perpetuating asym-metrical gender roles. Not surprisingly, the reassertion of an ultra-conser-vative patriarchal system ended up by reconfirming the western view of the veil as a symbol of Muslim women's oppression.

Contemporary manifestations of veiling have led to a proliferation of debates on concepts of women's role and status within the Islamic movement in particular, and Muslim societies in general (cf. Ahmed, 1992). Westerners, puzzled over what they perceive to be the contradiction of young Muslim women pursuing their education and being economically active in the modern sectors in their societies while at the same time signalling their adherence to traditional concepts of gender roles by donning the veil, are often at a loss to explain this phenomenon, as may be secular oriented Muslims: 'Is it identity crisis, misguided leisure, a fad, youth protest, ideological vacuum, individual psychic disturbance, life-crisis, social dislocation?' (El-Guindi, 1981: 465). Can it be explained by piety or by protest? (cf. Ramazani, 1983). Most, or some, or different combinations, of these factors may be applicable, thereby signalling the commmonality and diversity of Muslim communities and societies, as well as the fact that the donning of the veil is motivated by a number of complex factors.

For some women, the veil may be a 'response to their vulnerability', encouraging them to 'retreat into the protective certainties of religious conservatism' (Kandiyoti, 1991a: 18). For others, veiling may be a collective means of asserting cultural authenticity in the face of a dominant cultural model seeking to extinguish Islamically inspired social mores, such as, for example, in the Muslim republics of the former Soviet Union (cf. Bennigsen, 1985). For others again, the veil may function as a symbol of national liberation, such as formerly in Algeria, where one of the aims of the French colonialist government was to 'civilise' Muslim society by bringing an end to veiling and thus to the oppression of women (cf. Shaaban, 1988). More recently, Muslim Palestinian women are being encouraged and often coerced into donning the veil as part of the *intifada* (uprising) against Israeli occupation (cf. Hammami, 1990). In effect, there remains the contradiction that the practice of veiling may be as much due to 'community norms and family pressures [which] continue to serve as a strong barrier to women's mobility, visibility and autonomy' (Afshar and Agarwal, 1989a: 5), as it may be a means of enabling women to assert their presence in male space by setting unavoidable contacts with non-kin males within a desexualised context. The veil may also be an expression of a feminist position 'supportive of female autonomy and equality articulated in terms totally different from the language of the West' (Ahmed, 1992: 226). Indeed, Farzaneh Milani argues that in recent years, veiled women in Iran are taking advantage of their access to the public arena to speak out and to reappraise the traditional spaces and boundaries, and to redefine their status (1992: 9).

The discourse on the veil is rendered more complex when one takes into consideration that it is largely if not exclusively an urban phenomenon in the Muslim countries in which it has been manifesting itself.

Thus rarely do conservative or fundamentalist Islamist writers make appeals to rural women to adopt the contemporary Islamic veil. Nor do they appear to address the reality that rural women's rights as prescribed by the Shari'a are more often than not neglected (Stowasser, 1987b: 279). Women's active (though largely unacknowledged) role in the rural economy in many parts of the Muslim world undermines the fundamentalist female role model demanding veiling or seclusion as a means of ensuring social morality. This ideology largely overlooks the economic reality that female dependence, perceived to be a cornerstone of patriarchy, is in many Muslim (as well as non-Muslim) communities in the Third World a luxury that can no longer be afforded. The reality, of course, is that the majority of Muslim women have never been entirely dependent beings, although the pretence that this was the case has often been maintained. As many authors have discovered in many circumstances, what people say they do is not always what they actually do.

While all these factors throw light on the complex phenomenon of the veil in contemporary Muslim societies, there is in addition a political factor to be taken into account. This is manifested in the financial aid which oil-rich Middle East countries offer to less affluent Muslim states. This support not only has an Islamisation string attached, i.e. it is used as an inducement to governments to repeal secular laws deemed inimical to Shari'a law, or as a means to subvert governments by financing Islamist opposition groups (Ahmed, 1992: 218). In addition, this aid flow reflects the rivalry between donors, most notably Iran and Saudi Arabia, both of whom are intent on exporting their own particular brand of Islam. Either way, the primary target of this political weapon are Muslim women, who may even be offered money to don the veil as a signal of appropriate Muslim behaviour (ibid). In some cases the financial inducements may be offered to Muslim men to pressure their female kin to conform.

Female Excision and Islam: A Mismatched Pair

A further misconception which the stereotypical image of Muslim women may conjure up is the association of the practice of female excision with Islam, thereby overlooking the diverse cultural contexts within which it is practised. In fact, nowhere in the Qur'an does this ritual find mention either for men or for women. Only one Hadith[13] refers to it: 'Circumcision is my way for men, but is merely ennobling for women' (quoted in Ammar, 1954: 120). Neither is female excision particular to all Muslim countries: for example, it is unknown in Algeria, Tunisia and Iran, but practised to various extents in Egypt, Oman, Yemen, Somalia, Indonesia and Malaysia. Nor is it confined to Muslim societies, but encountered in such predominantly Christian African countries as Ethiopia as well as in many parts of sub-Saharan Africa, both animist and Christian (Passmore-Anderson, 1981: 28).

Moreover, the severity of the practice may differ from one cultural area to another, as well as by social class. For example, the majority of northern Sudanese Muslim women of all social classes are excised, though the more educated strata will tend to opt for the milder form, i.e. circumcision rather than infibulation.[14] However, some Sudanese Muslim tribes have never practised this ritual, while in the southern part of the country some non-Muslim tribes have recently begun to adopt it (El Dareer, 1982: 8–12). By contrast, in Egypt, only the *sunna* form (circumcision) is practised. It is generally confined to the lower social strata in both urban and rural areas, where it is practised by both Muslims and Christians (Early, 1993: 105). Evidence also suggests that *sunna* excision is practised by the more traditional Muslim social strata in the Indian subcontinent, Indonesia, Malaysia and the Philippines (cf. UNICEF, 1992).

Whatever the form of female excision, the fact remains that in societies where this ritual is the norm, it is essentially viewed as a form of social control over women. In turn, this reflects the perception of active female sexuality as threatening the social order, and, equally important, the view of women as being inherently incapable of controlling their own sexual impulses (El Saadawi, 1980: 33–43; cf. Oldfield, 1975; Sabbah, 1984). Yet, just as this ritual is not encountered among all Muslim societies, the extent of social control inherent in its practice, as well as the implication for women's right to sexual gratification, may differ from one community/society to the next. For example, in Egypt, the traditional midwife 'who performs the operation is always cautioned against its [clitoris'] complete excision', confirming that 'women's right to sexual gratification within marriage is recognised' (Morsy, 1978: 611). This concurs with the view of Islam that sexual intercourse is a legitimate source of pleasure within marriage for both sexes (cf. Bouhdiba, 1975). None the less, it should be kept in mind that 'the sexual dimension of identity has been elaborated in the context of various expressions of Islamic belief and practice and a multiplicity of social structures' (Eickelman, 1981: 157). The practice of infibulation in some Muslim societies, which, through the mutilation of female genitalia, denies women's right to sexual gratification, aptly reflects this (cf. Dorkenoo and Elworthy, 1992).

Gender Relations and Islam

The diversity of contexts within which Muslim women live out their lives thus supports Deniz Kandiyoti's view that women's position in

Muslim societies 'can neither be read off solely from Islamic ideology and practice, nor be entirely derived from global processes of socio-economic transformation, nor from universalistic premises of feminist theory' (1991a: 2). While she rightly goes on to argue the need to focus on the role of the state, and 'the reproduction of gender inequalities through various dimensions of state policy' (ibid: 1), what is of particular interest in the context of our discussion on the diversity of Muslim women is the framework of male–female relations depicted in western-inspired feminist theory.

The often unconscious ethnocentric attitudes underlying this universalism which, up to the 1970s, tended more or less to dominate ethnographic descriptions of Third World women in general, and Muslim women in particular, has since become the focus of criticism (cf. Rohrlich-Leavitt, 1975; Leacock, 1981; Ahmed, 1992; Karim, forthcoming). Particular criticism has been directed at the tendency to depict gender relations in terms of a simplistic dichotomy, associating men with public space and therefore power and authority, and women with the private sphere and therefore relative powerlessness in society, and to assume that it can be applied worldwide (Nelson, 1974: 551, 552; Nelson and Oleson, 1977). By imposing western social categories onto the social experience of non-western societies, there has been a failure to recognise that the social construction of gender is subject to a complexity of factors affecting women's status in diverse cultural areas. Specifically with regard to gender relations, it should not be ignored that 'women as well as men [may] make decisions, either individually or in groups, for the activities for which they are responsible [as well as those] affecting the community as a whole' (Rohrlich-Leavitt, 1975: 624).

As Soraya Altorki illustrates, even in such a quintessentially sex-segregated society as Saudi Arabia, men's power may in specific situations be predicated on the support of women, however invisible this female role may be to outsiders (1986). This is reflected, for example, in the involvement of upper-class women as 'chief brokers' in marriage negotiations, which provides them with the opportunity of 'enlarging the domain of their own autonomy vis-à-vis their men'. In fact, men's attempt 'to convert marriages into political and economic alliances' may be hampered without the information which women provide (ibid: 145). Moreover, the segregation of women in Saudi Arabian society has not impeded their entry into the modern economy, however much this may be restricted to areas where minimal contact with non-kin males is guaranteed (Altorki and Cole, 1989: 188; cf. Bahry, 1982). This is not to minimise the influence of an ideology which propagates the image of the 'ideal Islamic woman', or to overlook the reality that 'women's mobility and independent access to the resources of the state' are very much controlled in Saudi Arabia (Doumato, 1992: 33). Rather, it is to remind us that even in rigidly sex-segregated societies, women's lives demonstrate much more flexibility than is generally assumed (cf. Rogers, 1975).

Another pertinent example from a different cultural area is that of Muslim women in Malaysia. While their lives are circumscribed by the interaction between customary law and interpretations of Islamic normative sources, factors such as class, education, age and rural versus urban residence also have an essential influence on gender relations. Though Malayan women have been incorporated into party politics, they have not been able significantly to influence decision-making processes which affect their roles and status within Malaysian society, and may even subscribe to generally held views of 'suitable' activities for women. None the less, they may wield considerable influence within their families and, however indirectly, in their communities (cf. Dancz, 1987). This has important implications for gender relations which are less asymmetrical than generally supposed, and which in rural areas, for example, 'reflect men's and women's different relationships to land and the different decisions that women take in the allocation of household resources' (Heyzer, 1986: 28).

The Saudi Arabian and Malaysian examples bring to the fore the inconsistent nature of relations between individual women and men, who may relate to one another 'now in a dependent, now in a dominant mode' (Ardener, 1992a: 3). They also point to variations in the basis upon which gender relations in Muslim communities and societies are predicated. In the contemporary Muslim world, these variations are reflected in a number of discourses. In turn, these may be placed along a continuum, which serves to depict both the distinguishing as well as the overlapping factors between them.

At one end are situated the Muslim modernists who, as explained earlier, wish to reinterpret the Qur'an in terms perceived to be more compatible with contemporary times. While modernists exhibit similar attitudes towards women in terms of according them more equality than Shari'a-based legislation and customary law has tended to, they are by no means a homogeneous group. There are those among them, for example, who would not unequivocally advocate equal personal status laws for both men and women, and who continue to see the function of the male role as 'the family's provider and protector' (Stowasser, 1987b: 268). Other modernists may subscribe to more egalitarian gender relations, while at the same time stressing women's important roles as wife and mother, in contradistinction to what is perceived to be a western female stress on individualism at the expense of family and community (cf. Arebi, 1991).

Further along this continuum are the Muslim traditionalists who defend the customary social and legal inequality separating men and women by advocating particular interpretations of the Qur'an and the Hadith which assert that women's subordinate status in Muslim society is 'God-willed'. As with the modernists, traditionalists too are a heterogeneous group. They include those who go beyond the normative religious sources, enumerating 'the physiological and psychological factors' pertaining to women's nature as additional proof of the 'God-willed order' which decrees men's superiority in every sphere (Stowasser, 1987b: 269). They also include those who, rather than setting gender relations within a framework of social asymmetry, stress 'the immutable and complete difference in the nature of the sexes, which is part of God's plan for the world', and which thus means that 'the sexes are mutually complementary' (ibid: 271). It is these perceptions of gender relations which underly traditionalists' belief in the moral imperative of confining women's role to the domestic sphere, and of defending male prerogatives such as polygamy as ordained by God. This more or less separates them from the modernists whose interpretation of Islam allows for women's public participation both in the economy and in politics (ibid: 272).

The third distinctive discourse is that propagated by the Muslim fundamentalists. Barbara Stowasser aptly refers to them as 'scripturalist activists', who 'translate the sacred texts directly into contemporary thought and action' (1987b: 275). In their quest for a just Muslim society, they believe that only a return to the Qur'an and the freeing of society from non-Islamic customs and practices can ensure the path to salvation. Their anti-westernism will tend to be particularly focused on the sphere of gender relations. As the traditionalists, they believe that Muslim women's essential roles are those of wife and mother, and that the 'so-called liberation of women' is a western deviation corrupting these God-given roles (ibid: 276).

Women's Views on their Role in Society

The factors which separate or unite the various contemporary discourses on women's 'proper' role in society, cannot be adequately understood without gauging to what extent Muslim women themselves participate in these discourses, and how they view their status within a Muslim social order. As Saddeka Arebi concludes, there are three reasons why Muslim women may generally find it difficult to adopt a western model of feminism predicated on premisses deemed universally applicable. Firstly, Muslim women do not necessarily perceive 'family ties and kinship ties [as] a hindrance to women's liberation'; secondly, there is a resentment of 'the West's identification of "the problem" of Muslim women as a religious problem'; and thirdly, wages have not necessarily functioned as a 'liberating force' in the sense advocated by western feminists (1991: 104).

The modernist Muslim feminist position is in this respect particularly revealing, since it attempts to reassess notions of male/female relations without subscribing to the female role models advocated by the traditionalists or the fundamentalists, while at the same time avoiding an identification with the western secular feminist framework. Thus, for some modernist Muslim feminists, it is 'feudalistic not Islamic thinking [which places] women under the control of men' (Hussein, 1984a: 2). To others, the fact that 'patriarchy itself was able to justify within its ideological bounds the existence of five different schools of thought' means that 'feminists can surely justify the addition of at least one more' (Al-Hibri, 1982a: ix).[15] Because modernist Muslim feminists hear 'the ethical, egalitarian voice of Islam', rather than the 'legalistic establishment version of Islam [which] largely bypasses the ethical elements in the Islamic message', they tend to perceive Islam as 'non-sexist' (Ahmed, 1992: 239). Common to all modernist Muslim feminists is the fact that they essentially refuse to see the status and roles of Muslim women judged solely in western cultural terms. While they are aware of the need to reject 'the androcentrism of whatever culture or tradition in which they find themselves', they do not see this in terms of adopting western aims and life-styles (ibid: 245).

It is worth digressing at this point and turning our attention to the volume mentioned earlier on the role of Christian women (Lees, 1991). While the Christian discourse on this topic not surprisingly exhibits varied interpretations of the Scripture with regard to women, it is interesting to note that rather than countering the notion of female submission, this term is reinterpreted in ways which appear to underline the complementarity of gender roles inherent in the patriarchal social system (Lees, 1991a: 203–10). In fact, reading the views of some of the more conservative participants in this discourse (for example, Field and Catherwood), one is struck by a number of parallels with conservative Muslim views of women's subordinate role *vis-à-vis* men in society.

The active participation of modernist Muslim feminists in contemporary Muslim discourses has probably been an important factor behind the secular feminist trend in parts of the Muslim world to analyse these discourses within their own framework. Thus, formerly, the 'women's question' generally tended to pit a secular, mainly western-inspired discourse against an Islamic one, a process which all too often became a dialogue of the deaf since the two camps based their arguments on different premisses. More recently, secular feminists have come to realise that, given the Islamic resurgence which has found fertile ground in economically depressed and politically disenfranchised Muslim communities and societies, they need to reinvestigate the normative religious texts.

This attempt to consider Islam from the perspective of a western ethos, while at the same time reinterpreting 'its fundamental teachings in such a way that it provides a sanctioning forum for the introduction of new ideas', aims to establish a framework for more egalitarian gender relations (Haddad, 1982: 8). Fatima Mernissi, for example, in launching an historical and theological enquiry into the condition of women at the dawn of Islam, is intent on proving that:

> We Muslim women can walk into the modern world with pride, knowing that the quest for dignity, democracy and human rights, for full participation in the political and social affairs of our country, stems from no imported Western values, but is a true part of the Muslim tradition' (1991: viii).

In effect, whereas Mernissi's earlier writings tended to focus on 'the Muslim social order [which] views the female as a potent aggressive individual whose power can, if not tamed and curbed, corrode the social order' (1975: 108), she now feels compelled to argue from within the framework in which Muslim discourses are taking place in order to find justification for her feminist beliefs through reinterpreted Islamic principles.

Similarly, Leila Ahmed set out to analyse how Muslim women's role and status have been perceived over the ages by investigating discourses on gender in 'the societies in which they are rooted, and in particular the way in which gender is articulated socially, institutionally and verbally' (1992: 2). She argues that although Islam, similar to Christianity and Judaism, was predicated on a hierarchical social structure, it also preached an ethical message regarding the equality of human beings. 'Arguably, therefore, even as it instituted a sexual hierarchy, it laid the ground, in its ethical voice, for the subversion of the hierarchy' (ibid: 238).

Another secularist approach, which has recently begun to surface in a number of Muslim countries, aims to set the issue of gender relations and the concomitant rights of women within the realm of human rights. By combining the social and political levels which affect women's status in society, this approach aims to avoid the marginalisation of the 'women's question' while at the same time addressing the factors which affect both their and men's rights in society (cf. Dwyer, 1991).

The reaction of conservative Muslims, both traditionalist and fundamentalist, to this trend is revealing. As Ann Elizabeth Mayer points out:

Accommodating the principle of equality in an Islamic human rights scheme involves dealing with two aspects in the Islamic tradition, one egalitarian and the other mandating sexual and religious discrimination, as well as the mixed reactions of contemporary Muslims to these two aspects (1991: 93).

Because the Islamic sources – the Qur'an and the different schools of religious jurisprudence – differentiate between men and women, and, for that matter, between Muslims and non-Muslims, the concept of human rights as laid down in the 1948 Universal Declaration of Human Rights is not easy to reconcile with interpretations of the Shari'a which emphasise the hierarchical aspects of the Islamic social order, in which the free male Muslim possesses the most rights (ibid). Indeed, conservatives today have attempted to expand Islamic rules to include aspects of modern life while at the same time restricting women's opportunities outside the home. This has resulted, for example, in '"Islamic" rationales for forbidding women to drive, banning women from participating in sports, and excluding them from working in television and radio programs' (ibid: 113).

Given such rulings by male interpreters intent on maintaining the patriarchal system with women in a subordinate role, modernist Muslim feminists and human rights activists are arguing that this is not the real voice of Islam. Thus, the struggle ahead is not whether Islam can survive the onslaught of change, but which voice will be heard the loudest: the ethical which stresses an indivisible equality, or the hierarchical which fits human beings into categories.

Muslim Women's Choices

It is these considerations regarding the complexities of women's way of life in diverse Muslim communities and societies, and the need to avoid the 'overemphasis of Islam as a cultural determinant' (Hale, 1989: 247), which have provided the impetus for putting together this volume.

The contributions, based on recent research in cultural and social settings, some of which have been hitherto little explored, focus on the way in which the accommodation between religious belief and social reality affects, and is affected by, the contexts within which women in diverse Muslim communities and societies live out their lives. In dealing with this general theme, each chapter provides us with insights into the complex ways in which Islam interacts with a host of other factors. By according us glimpses of the manner in which Muslim women negotiate their gender role, the contributers to this volume also throw light on the choices open to women in diverse Muslim social settings.

In some contexts, women's choices may be relatively limited, while in others they are more varied. Similarly, in some contexts, women may circumvent the constraints which limit their choices, while in others they appear to accept the limitations. Either way, the question of choice – a vein implicitly or explicitly running through this volume, and which contributed to its title – points to the reality that even in Muslim societies where the boundaries of their lives are rigidly prescribed, women may wield a modicum of power which enables them in various overt and subtle ways to 'influence factors related to their situation in order to serve clearly defined personal (or family, or community) interests' (Hijab, 1988: 140).

Thus, the Muslim women discussed in this volume represent different cultural areas each with its own particular historical, political and socioeconomic experience. In some cases, they are members of minority communities existing within a larger majority population from which they may differ in terms of race, ethnicity and/or religion. In others, they are part of the majority in their respective societies, where being Muslim is either almost taken for granted as a part of cultural identity, or where the parameters of this identity are being subjected to scrutiny. In any case, the impact which majority or minority status may have on religious consciousness, not to mention the political implications of this status, is rendered even more complex by a host of other variables, such as class origin, educational background, employment status, age group and geographical location (to focus on those deemed particularly relevant to the theme of this volume). Though the impact of Shari'a-based legislation and customary law on women's status is by no means minimised, the fact remains that the varied manner in which gender identity articulates with this complexity of variables points to the fallacy of attributing to Islam the sole influence in explaining the ways of life of Muslim women in different cultural settings, including the type of choices at their disposal.

A Diversity of Contexts

The Egyptian Muslim women described in Helen Watson's contribution to this volume are members of the religious majority in Egypt. This fact, in conjunction with Shari'a-based family law, has important implications for Muslim identity. But as Watson also illustrates, the women struggling to survive in the City of the Dead in Cairo – a graveyard dating back to Mameluk times which has become a sprawling squatter settlement – are an apt example of the way in which poverty, and its concomitant spatial marginalisation within the metropolis of Cairo, rather than Islamic injunctions per se, dictate the range of women's choices. This is reflected in the negotiation of marital disputes within this community, where economic and social expediency combine to undermine men's legally sanctioned prerogative of initiating divorce. Underlying this negotiation is the community's view of gender roles in terms of complementarity, an interdependence which both men and women recognise and uphold. However, while the decreased threat of divorce obviously enhances women's sense of security within the marriage institution, their general lack of education and marketable skills continue to narrow their economic options even more than is the case for men. Yet, the glimpses we are given of Muslim women in the City of the Dead is one of strength and endurance, rather than passivity in the face of adversity, no doubt fostered by the female networks which function as an important support system.

As in Egypt, the Muslim women discussed by Ziba Mir-Hosseini are members of the majority religion in their respective societies, more specifically Shi'a Muslims in the case of Iran, and Sunni Muslims in the case of Morocco. However, in contrast to the above discussed Egyptian women, who tend to avoid the law courts at almost any cost, the women presented by Mir-Hosseini feel compelled to take this step, albeit out of desperation in order to prove the existence of marital bonds with the fathers of their children in a culture where illegitimacy is tantamount to social death. In effect, it is the precariousness of their social position within their respective societies which dictates this choice. However important legal rulings may be for defining and regulating relations between the sexes, and though ambiguities in the interpretation of Shari'a-based personal law provide important loopholes, Mir-Hosseini's discussion also points to the importance of women's individual situation in defining these options.

In the case of the lower-middle-class Iranian woman who attempts to transform her status as a *sigheh* to the more socially desirable one of permanent wife,[16] her ability to manipulate to her advantage ambiguities in the interpretation of Shari'a law is in great part related to her educational level. Though her victory in court does not perceptibly improve her social status as a divorcée/non-virgin (which led her to accept a *sigheh* union in the first place), she does appear to enjoy some autonomy over her life through her paid employment, however meagre her salary.

By contrast, the case of the Moroccan woman portrayed by Mir-Hosseini, who petitions the law court to recognise her *fatiha* union,[17] reflects the extent to which women's lack of power is not only a function of a social order which legitimises male domination through legislation and custom, but also of the dynamics of social and economic marginalisation. Thus, her marriage options were as much affected by her poverty-stricken background, as they were by the shameful circumstances surrounding the loss of her virginity. Mir-Hosseini's contribution illustrates the social problems which Moroccan women with low

educational and skill levels face when men fail to honour the commitment implicit in a customary marriage which has not been registered in
court, and the effect of their relatively low social standing on the range
of choices at their disposal. Comparing the two case studies, one is also
struck by the extent to which the intangibles of personality appear to
have an impact on the way women manipulate factors impinging upon
their interests.

Muslims in Nigeria are believed to constitute around 40 per cent of
the total population, but are mainly situated in the North of the country.
Thus, in a geographical sense, the northern Nigerian Muslim women
discussed by Gloria Thomas-Emeagwali are part of the majority in
terms of religious (though not necessarily ethnic) affiliation and demographic concentration. As elsewhere in Muslim West Africa, contemporary Islam in Nigeria exhibits an accommodation between Shari'a
injunctions and pre-Islamic customs and mores. Thomas-Emeagwali's
attempt to draw up a 'balance sheet' illustrating the extent to which
Islam has been beneficial or detrimental to women, aptly reflects how
culturally specific this accommodation between religious belief and
social reality may be. By including an evaluation of the impact of the
on-going structural adjustment programme,[18] Thomas-Emeagwali also
sheds some light on the choices available to women. Thus, while religious ideology will tend to affect notions of women's appropriate roles
in present-day Nigerian Muslim society, economic imperatives, in conjunction with such variables as class background, urban or rural residence and type of economic activity outside the home, will have far-
reaching implications for the options open to women.

At the other end of the African continent are the Muslim women in
Cape Town, South Africa, discussed by Rosemary Ridd. The marginalisation of this mixed race Coloured community during the era of
apartheid, served to increase the importance of the home as a bastion
against the system. Women traditionally held sway within this social
space, and this served to strengthen their position, a development further encouraged by their role as custodians of the community's Muslim
faith. Women's importance as lynchpins of community cohesion
enabled them to encroach upon some prerogatives traditionally associated with the male gender role, a fact which Ridd perceives in terms of
them being in some instances even more influential than men whatever
the extent of separation between the sexes may be. However, while this
reality may have widened the scope of choices available for women,
their options have nevertheless also been circumscribed by limited education and marketable skills, as well as by their status as members of a
politically marginalised minority. Caught up in the unfolding power

struggle between White minority and Black majority, these Cape Town Muslims are torn between the temptation to assert their own separate culture, and the need for political expediency to ensure their survival in the new South Africa. Needless to add, these developments have important implications for gender relations.

The increasing consciousness of being Muslim, which seeps through Thomas-Emeagwali's and Ridd's contributions on Nigerian and South African women respectively, is even more apparent when we turn to the Bosnian Muslim community described by Cornelia Sorabji. Under the previous socialist federated Yugoslavia, women played a pivotal role as nurturers of Islamic inspired customs and traditions. Taking the *mevlud* as a focus of her study,[19] Sorabji aptly illustrates its function in women's lives and the effect of the Islamic revivalism on this ritual. At a time when Muslim national identity was being re-articulated in the face of tumultuous political changes, and community solidarity was at a premium, the *mevlud* was laying bare unwelcome schisms. Underlying these tensions were differences among the women participating in *mevluds*. These differences were not without implications for the manner in which female gender roles were being redefined away from secular notions of gender equality and more in line with complementary gender roles perceived to be more compatible with Islam. By implication, the choices open to women were also being subjected to scrutiny, a process, none the less, in which women were by no means passive participants. The disintegration of Bosnia-Herzegovina which, at the time of writing, continues unabated, can be presumed to be having drastic effects on the options available to Muslims, women as well as men, who are being subjected to the horrors of 'ethnic cleansing'.

In comparison, the minority/majority status of the Tajikistani community described by Gillian Tett has been more ambiguous. Under the former Soviet Union system, the mainly Sunni Muslim Tajikistanis were the majority within their republic, but very much a marginalised minority *vis-à-vis* the seat of political power in Moscow. Though officially suppressed, Islam in fact played an important role beneath the veneer imposed by the dominant Russian cultural model. As Tett illustrates, due to the authoritarian Soviet influence, Muslim men were inhibited from publicly practising their faith. While this may have increased the importance of the role of Tajik Muslim women as custodians of religious traditions, it also led to more pressure on them to conform to notions of 'Muslim' behaviour and 'Muslim' sexual honour. This fact served to constrain Tajik women's choices for adopting more liberal notions of their gender role and status as propagated by the then dominant Russian cultural role model. In contrast to men, such a choice would almost inevitably lead to social ostracism in their own community. The demise of communism and the birth of political independence have contributed to the surging and visible presence of Islam in the public domain. Though this has enabled men to publicly proclaim their Muslim identity, the emerging national identity continues to be in a state of flux, as are notions regarding women's 'proper' role in society.

The glimpses which Tamara Dragadze provides us of Azerbaijani Shi'a Muslim women provide an interesting contrast to Tett's case study on Tajikistan. Azerbaijan may be said to have experienced the same ambiguous minority/majority status *vis-à-vis* the seat of power in the former Soviet Union. Here too Islam was relegated to the private sphere, which in turn enhanced the importance of women's role in keeping the faith alive, but Azerbaijani women appear to have been less pressured into acquiescing to Islamically inspired female gender role models. This reality is reflected in the wider scope of choices available to them compared with their Tajik counterparts. Dragadze attributes this to a number of factors such as the importance accorded to women's education and the extent to which Azerbaijani society was secularised in comparison with other Muslim republics in the Caucasus, a development which predates Sovietisation.

Naila Kabeer's discussion of women workers in the Bangladeshi garment industry is a timely reminder of the fallacy of assuming that cultural constraints in Muslim communities and societies are immutable. In a country where the identity of the majority population is predicated on Islam, and where female seclusion was for centuries sanctioned by an accommodation between traditional customs and Islamic injunctions, female workers in garment factories have come to play an important role in the social transformation of Bangladeshi society. Kabeer illustrates how economic imperatives and cultural considerations combine to affect women's choices in breaking out of the confines of traditional female roles, while at the same time enabling the women to redefine these cultural models in terms considered more appropriate to 'keeping step with the rhythm of change'. By stretching the cultural boundaries defining female gender status and roles, these Bangladeshi women workers have been able to reduce their economic dependence on male guardians, while at the same time preserving the symbols which signal their status as honourable Muslim women worthy of respect.

As an ethno-religious minority group, the Muslim community in Mindanao in the southern Philippines discussed by Jacqueline Siapno has for centuries been relegated to subordinate political and socio-economic status within a predominantly Christian society. The central government's attempts to pacify the area have not brought about the desired peace, and the guerrilla war launched by the various liberation fronts for the independence of Mindanao continues to claim victims on both sides of the political divide. As Siapno shows, gender relations are inevitably caught up in the increasing importance of Islam in a community striving to assert its cultural distinctiveness. This chapter also presents another variation on an old theme, namely the problems and choices faced by women when national liberation and feminist priorities come into conflict. Thus, though the Muslim women of Mindanao have been drawn into spheres traditionally associated with male prerogatives, this has generally not led to greater equality with men, and women's gender role continues to be subject to 'conventional ideas of patriarchy'. Nevertheless, while this apparent subordination has some implication for women's options, it masks the reality that Filipino Muslim women are not necessarily passive spectators to the changes taking place in their community. The attitudes surrounding the donning of 'the Islamic veil' are in this context particularly revealing, exposing the difficulty of providing a clear-cut answer to the perennial question of whether the veil is indicative of piety or protest, or a combination of both.

Notes

1. Shari'a is the canonical law of Islam.

2. The question concerning the implications of the pluralism of Muslims for the unity of Islam, and vice versa, and whether one should in fact be speaking of 'Islams', continues to be the subject of much debate. It has been placed centre stage with the spread of Islamic fundamentalism and its belief in the totality of Islam and its applicability to all times and all places (cf. Bijlefeld, 1981; Roff, 1987a; Lee, 1988).

3. See, for example, 'Furore erupts in Paris over girls' Islamic scarves', in *The Times*, 31 October 1989. In this context, the contributions in Gerholm and Lithman (1988) provide interesting analyses of contemporary attitudes towards Muslim immigrants in western Europe, as well as pointing out the fact that there is an 'indigenous' Islam, i.e. western converts to the faith.

4. See, for example, 'When religion can draw a veil over the class-room', in *Observer*, 3 September 1989; 'Minefield of racist violence in the making', in *The Guardian*, 6 February 1991; and 'A Muslim Parliament', in *The Daily Telegraph*, 4 January 1992. See also various issues of *The Muslim News* (monthly newspaper published in London).

5. In this context, see, for example, 'The immigrants Europe wants to forget', in *The Sunday Correspondent*, 24 September 1989; and 'Intolerance on a European scale', in *The Middle East*, February 1991.

6. An, albeit extreme, example of such bigotry is an article relating the con-

sumption of pork to sexual immorality in western Christian societies. See *Al-Noor*, vol.1, no. 2, 1991 (monthly published in London).

7. See, for example, 'Islam resumes its march', in *The Economist*, 4 April 1992; and 'The West's role in Muslim Central Asia', in *Middle East International*, 24 January 1992.

8. See, for example, 'Balkan Muslims', in *The Middle East*, October 1992; and 'The Eagle's Curse', in *The Sunday Times*, 9 August 1992.

9. This is the focus of *Women Against Fundamentalism* (journal published in London). The recent controversy over the ordination of women priests in the Anglican Church in Britain, including the fact that opposition to ordination was not divided along gender lines, is in this context a particularly apt example. See, for example, 'Rent Asunder', in *The Sunday Times*, 15 November 1992.

10. See *Women Living Under Muslim Law*, an occasional publication published by the International Solidarity Network of Women Living Under Muslim Law, based in France.

11. Moreover, as Andrea Rugh illustrates (1985), this may apply equally to Coptic (Christian) women in Egypt. For other similarities between Coptic and Muslim Egyptian women, see Rugh (1986) and Early (1993).

12. In fact, this has spawned a whole fashion industry, such as the 'Islamic boutiques' which have, for example, sprung up in urban centres in Egypt. While the modesty code – the covering of the hair, arms and legs – is strictly adhered to, the female attire on sale, generally referred to as *al-ziyy al-islami* (Islamic dress), reflects not only a fashion consciousness subject to change. It is also indicative of class differences instanced by the quality and cut of the material.

13. Hadith refers to the oral sayings and actions of the Prophet. These traditions, as they are also called, were only written down after his death. There has been much dispute regarding their authenticity and reliability, and few Hadith have come to be attributed with the same undisputed authority as the Qur'an.

14. Circumcision implies the removal of the prepuce of the clitoris and is the mildest form of excision. It is often referred to as *sunna*, i.e. following the Prophet's tradition, in the belief that it is the type of excision advocated by Islam. Infibulation is the most drastic form, consisting of the removal of the clitoris, as well as part or all of the labia minora and majora respectively (El Dareer, 1982: 1–4).

15. The five schools of Muslim jurisprudence referred to here are the four Sunni schools – Shaf'ei, Hanbali, Hanafi and Maliki – and the Shi'a school. All four Sunni schools differ in subtle or overt ways from one another with respect to women's legal rights, though the factors they have in common in this respect largely outweigh their differences. Together they have many commonalities with the Shi'a school, but differ from the latter with respect to, for example, marriage and inheritance. Thus, Shi'a Islam distinguishes between permanent and temporary marriage. In Sunni Islam girls inherit only their legal share even if there are no sons in the family, the sons' share being divided among male kin on the father's side. By contrast, among Shi'a Muslims, where there are no sons, the patrimony remains within the nuclear family and is divided equally between daughters. On the other hand, both Sunni and Shi'a Muslim women receive the

same half-share if they have brothers (cf. Eickelman, 1981; Sherif, 1985).

16. *Sigheh* is the Iranian colloquial term for wife in a temporary marriage permitted by Shi'a Islam.

17. The term *fatiha* derives from the first verse of the Qur'an, used in Morocco to conclude a marriage accepted under customary but not modern law.

18. Structural adjustment programmes (SAP) have been introduced in a number of Third World countries to bring their economies in line with the capitalist market system. There has been increasing criticism of the way the social impacts of SAP on vulnerable population groups, in particular women, children and the elderly, have been neglected (cf. Hesse et. al., 1989).

19. *Mevlud*, which derives from the Arabic *mawlid*, refers to the celebration of the birth of the Prophet.

References

Afshar, H. and B. Agarwal, eds., 1989, *Women, Poverty and Ideology in Asia: Contradictory Pressures, Uneasy Solutions*, London: Macmillan.

Afshar, H. and B. Agarwal, 1989a, 'Introduction', in H. Afshar and B. Agarwaal, eds, *Women, Poverty and Ideology in Asia: Contradictory Pressures, Uneasy Solutions*, London: Macmillan.

Ahmad, R., 1991, *We Sinful Women: Contemporary Urdu Feminist Poetry*, London: The Women's Press.

Ahmed, L., 1992, *Women and Gender in Islam*, New Haven & London: Yale University Press.

Al-Hibri, A., ed., 1982, *Women and Islam*, Oxford: Pergamon Press.

Al-Hibri, A., 1982a, 'A Study of Islamic Herstory: Or How Did We Get Into This Mess?", in A. Al-Hibri, ed., *Women and Islam*, Oxford: Pergamon Press.

Altorki, S., 1986, *Women in Saudi Arabia: Ideology and Behaviour Among the Elite*, New York: Columbia University Press.

Altorki, S. and D. P. Cole, 1989, *Arabian Oasis City: The Transformation of 'Unayzah*, Austin: University of Texas Press.

Ammar, H., 1954, *Growing up in an Egyptian Village: Silwa, Province of Aswan*, London: Routledge & Kegan Paul.

Ardener, S., ed., 1981, *Women and Space: Ground Rules and Social Maps*, London: Croom Helm; 1993 revised edn, Providence & Oxford: Berg Publishers.

Ardener, S., 1981a, 'Ground Rules and Social Maps for Women: An Introduction', in S. Ardener, ed., *Women and Space: Ground Rules and Social Maps*, London: Croom Helm.

Ardener, S., ed., 1992, *Persons and Powers of Women in Diverse Cultures*, Providence & Oxford: Berg Publishers.

Ardener, S., 1992a, 'Persons and Powers of Women: An Introduction', in S. Ardener, ed., *Persons and Powers of Women in Diverse Cultures*, Providence & Oxford: Berg Publishers.

Arebi, S., 1991, 'Gender Anthropology in the Middle East: The Politics of Muslim Women's Misrepresentation', in *The American Journal of Islamic Social*

Sciences, vol. 8, no. 1.

Azari, F., ed., 1983, *Women of Iran: The Conflict with Fundamentalist Islam*, London: Ithaca Press.

Badran, M., 1991, 'Competing Agenda: Feminists, Islam and the State in 19th and 20th Century Egypt', in D. Kandiyoti, ed., *Women, Islam and the State*, London: Macmillan.

Bahry, L., 1982, 'The New Saudi Woman: Modernizing in an Islamic Framework', in *The Middle East Journal*, vol. 36, no. 4.

Beck, L. and N. Keddie, eds, 1978, *Women in the Muslim World*, Cambridge, Mass. & London: Harvard University Press.

Bennigsen, A., 1985, 'Islam in the Soviet Union', in *Journal of South Asian and Middle Eastern Studies*, vol. viii, no. 1.

Berik, G., 1990, 'State Policy in the 1980s and the Future of Women's Rights in Turkey', Review Article in *New Perspectives on Turkey*, no.4.

Bijlefeld,W., 1981, 'Observations on Contemporary Islam', in P. H. Stoddard et. al., eds, *Change and the Muslim World*, Syracuse: Syracuse University Press.

Bouhdiba, A., 1975, *La Sexualité en Islam*, Paris: Presses Universitaires de France.

Bovin, M., 1983, 'Muslim Women in the Periphery: The West African Sahel', in B. Utas, ed., *Islamic Societies: Social Attitudes and Historical Perspectives*, London: Curzon Press.

Catherwood, E., 'Woman in the Home', in S. Lees, ed., The Role of Women: When Christians Disagree, Leicester: Inter-Varsity Press.

Cederroth, S., 1983, 'Islam and Adat: Some Recent Changes in the Social Position of Women Among Sasak in Lombok', in B. Utas, ed., *Women in Islamic Societies: Social Attitudes and Historical Perspectives*, London: Curzon Press.

Creevy, L. E., 1991, 'The Impact of Islam on Women in Senegal', in *The Journal of Developing Areas*, vol. 25, April.

Dancz, V. H., 1987, *Women and Party Politics in Peninsular Malaysia*, Oxford: Oxford University Press.

Dorkenoo, E. and S. Elworthy, 1992, *Female Genital Mutilation: Proposals for Change*, London: Minority Rights Group International Report.

Doumato, E. A., 1992, 'Gender, Monarchy, and National Identity in Saudi Arabia', in *British Journal of Middle Eastern Studies*, vol. 19, no. 1.

Dwyer, K., 1991, *Arab Voices: The Human Rights Debate in the Middle East*, London & New York: Routledge.

Early, E. A., 1993, *Baladi Women of Cairo: Playing with an Egg and a Stone*, Boulder & London: Lynne Rienner Publishers.

Eickelman, D. F., 1981, *The Middle East: An Anthropological Approach*, Englewood Cliffs, New Jersey: Prentice-Hall.

Eickelman, D. F., 1987, 'Changing Interpretations of Islamic Movements', in W. R. Roff, ed., *Islam and the Political Economy of Meaning: Comparative Studies of Muslim Discourse*, London & Sydney: Croom Helm.

El Dareer, A., 1982, *Woman, Why Do You Weep? Circumcision and its Conse-*

quences, London: Zed Press.

El Guindi, F., 1981, 'Veiling Infitah with Muslim Ethic: Egypt's Contemporary Islamic Movement', in *Social Problems*, vol. 28, no. 4.

El-Messiri, S., 1978, *Ibn Al-Balad: A Concept of Egyptian Identity*, Leiden: E. J. Brill.

El Saadawi, N., 1980, *The Hidden Face of Eve: Women in the Arab World*, London: Zed Press.

El Saadawi, N., 1982, 'Woman and Islam', in A. Al-Hibri, ed., *Women and Islam*, Oxford: Pergamon Press.

Esposito, J. L., 1980, *Islam and Development: Religion and Sociopolitical Change*, Syracuse: Syracuse University Press.

Esposito, J. L. , 1982, *Women in Muslim Family Law*, Syracuse: Syracuse University Press.

Esposito, J. L., 1984, 'Law in Islam', in Y. Haddad et. al., eds, *The Islamic Impact*, Syracuse: Syracuse University Press.

Field, D., 1991, 'Headship in Marriage: The Husband's View', in S. Lees, ed., *The Role of Women: When Christians Disagree*, Leicester: Inter-Varsity Press.

Gerholm, T. and Y. G. Lithman, eds, 1988, *The New Islamic Presence in Europe*, London & New York: Mansell Publishing Limited.

Gerner-Adams, D. K., 1979, 'The Changing Status of Islamic Women in the Arab World', in *Arab Studies Quarterly*, vol.1, no.4.

Haddad, Y., 1982, *Contemporary Islam and the Challenge of History*, Albany: State University of New York Press.

Haddad, Y., et. al., eds, 1984, *The Islamic Impact*, Syracuse: Syracuse University Press.

Hale, S., 1989, 'The Politics of Gender in the Middle East', in S. Morgan, ed., *Gender and Anthropology: Critical Reviews for Research and Teaching*, Washington, D. C.: American Anthropological Association.

Hammami, R., 1990, 'Women, the Hijab and the Intifada', in *Middle East Report*, May–August.

Hay, M. J. and S. Stichter, eds, 1984, *African Women South of the Sahara*, London and New York: Longman.

Hesse, M. C., et. al., 1989, *Engendering Adjustment in the 1990s*, London: Commonwealth Secretariat.

Heyzer, N., 1986, *Working Women in South-East Asia: Development, Subordination and Emancipation*, Milton Keynes & Philadelphia: Open University Press.

Hijab, N., 1988, *Womanpower: The Arab Debate on Women at Work*, Cambridge: Cambridge University Press.

Hjarpe, J., 1983, 'The Attitude of Islamic Fundamentalism Towards the Question of Women in Islam', in B. Utas, ed., *Islamic Societies: Social Attitudes and Historical Perspectives*, London: Curzon Press.

Hourani, A., 1991, *Islam in European Thought*, Cambridge: Cambridge University Press.

Hussein, F., ed., 1984, *Muslim Women*, London & Sydney: Croom Helm.

Hussein, F., 1984a, 'Introduction: The Ideal and Contextual Realities of Muslim Women', in F. Hussain, ed., *Muslim Women*, London & Sydney: Croom Helm.

Kandiyoti, D., 1988, 'Bargaining with Patriarchy', in *Gender & Society*, vol. 2, no. 3.

Kandiyoti, D., ed., 1991, *Women, Islam and the State*, London: Macmillan.

Kandiyoti, D., 1991a, 'Introduction', in D. Kandiyoti, ed., *Women, Islam & the State*, London: Macmillan.

Kandiyoti, D., 1991b, 'Islam and Patriarchy', in N. R. Keddie and B. Baron, eds., *Women in Middle Eastern History: Shifting Boundaries in Sex and Gender*, New Haven & London: Yale University Press.

Karim, W. J., ed., forthcoming, *'Male' and 'Female' in Southeast Asia*, Providence & Oxford: Berg Publishers.

Keddie, N. R., 1991, 'Introduction', in N. R. Keddie and B. Baron, eds, *Women in Middle Eastern History: Shifting Boundaries in Sex and Gender*, New Haven & London: Yale University Press.

Keddie, N. R. and B. Baron, eds, 1991, *Women in Middle Eastern History: Shifting Boundaries in Sex and Gender*, New Haven & London: Yale University Press.

Keppel, G., 1990, *Les banlieues de l'Islam: naissance d'une religion en France*, Paris: Editions du Seuil.

Kusha, H. R., 1990, 'Minority Status of Women in Islam: A Debate Between Traditional and Modern Islam', in *Journal of the Institute of Muslim Minority Affairs*, vol. 11, no. 1.

Leacock, E. B., 1981, *Myths of Male Dominance: Collected Articles on Women Cross-Culturally*, New York and London: Monthly Review Press.

Lee, R. D., 1988, 'Islamic Revolution and Authenticity', in *Journal of South Asian and Middle Eastern Studies*, vol. xiii, no. 3.

❦Lees, S. , ed., 1991, *The Role of Women: When Christians Disagree*, Leicester: Inter-Varsity Press.

Lees, S., 1991a, 'Where Do We Go From Here?', in S. Lees, ed., *The Role of Women: When Christians Disagree*, Leicester: Inter-Varsity Press.

Mabro, J., 1991, *Veiled Half-Truths: Western Travellers' Perceptions of Middle Eastern Women*, London: I. B. Tauris.

Majrooh, P. A., 1989, 'Afghan Women Between Marxism and Islamic Fundamentalism', in *Central Asian Survey*, vol. 8, no. 3.

Marcus, J., 1992, *A World of Difference: Islam and Gender Hierarchy in Turkey*, London and New Jersey: Zed Books.

Matsui, J., 1991, *Women's Asia*, London and New Jersey: Zed Books.

Mayer. A. E., 1991, *Islam and Human Rights: Tradition and Politics*, Boulder & San Francisco: Westview Press.

❦Mernissi, F., 1975, *Beyond the Veil: Male-Female Dynamics in a Modern Muslim Society*, New York & London: Schenkman Publishing Company.

Mernissi, F., 1982, 'Virginity and Patriarchy', in A. Al-Hibri, ed., *Women and Islam*, Oxford: Pergamon Press.

Mernissi, F., 1991, *Women and Islam: An Historical and Theological Enquiry*,

Oxford: Basil Blackwell.

Milani, F., 1992, *Veils and Words: The Emerging Voices of Iranian Women Writers*, London and New York: I. B. Tauris.

Moghadam, V. M., 1990, *Gender, Development, and Policy: Toward Equity and Empowerment*, Helsinki: World Institute for Development Economics Research of the U.N. University.

Moghadam, V. M. , 1991, 'Islamist Movements and Women's Responses in the Middle East', in *Gender & History*, vol. 3, no. 3.

Morgan, S., ed., 1989, *Gender and Anthropology: Critical Reviews for Research and Teaching*, Washington D.C.: American Anthropological Association.

Morsy, S. A., 1978, 'Sex Differences and Folk Illness in an Egyptian Village', in L. Beck and N. Keddie, eds, *Women in the Muslim World*, Cambridge, Mass. & London: Harvard University Press.

Morsy, S. A., 1990, 'Rural Women, Work and Gender Ideology: A Study of Egyptian Political Economic Transformation', in S. Shami et. al., eds, *Women in Arab Society: Work Patterns and Gender Relations in Egypt, Jordan and Sudan*, New York & Oxford: Berg Publishers & UNESCO.

Nelson, C., 1974, 'Public and Private Politics: Women in the Middle Eastern World', in *American Ethnologist*, vol. 1, no. 3.

Nelson, C. and V. Oleson, 1977, 'Veil of Illusion: A Critique of the Concept of "Equality" in Western Feminist Studies', in *Catalyst*, 10–11.

O'Barr, J., 1984, 'African Women in Politics', in M.J. Hay and S. Stichter, eds, *African Women South of the Sahara*, London and New York: Longman.

Oldfield, R., 1975, 'Female Genital Mutilation, Fertility Control, Women's Roles, and Patrilineage in Modern Sudan', in *American Ethnologist*, vol. II, no. 4.

Papanek, H. and G. Minault, eds., 1982, *Separate Worlds: Studies of Purdah in South Asia*, Delhi: Chanakya Publications.

Passmore Anderson, L., 1981, *Against the Mutilation of Women: The Struggle to End Unnecessary Suffering*, London: Ithaca Press.

Pillsbury, B. L. K. , 1978, 'Being Female in a Muslim Minority in China', in L. Beck and N. Keddie, eds, *Women in the Muslim World*, Cambridge, Mass. & London: Harvard University Press.

Ramazani, N., 1983, 'The Veil – Piety or Protest?', in *Journal of South Asian and Middle Eastern Studies*, vol. vii, no. 2.

Roff, W. R., ed., 1987, *Islam and the Political Economy of Meaning: Comparative Studies of Muslim Discourse*, London & Sydney: Croom Helm.

Roff, W. R., 1987a, 'Islamic Movements: One or Many?', in W. R. Roff, ed., *Islam and the Political Economy of Meaning: Comparative Studies of Muslim Discourse*, London & Sydney: Croom Helm.

Rogers, S., 1975, 'Female Forms of Power and the Myth of Male Dominance: A Model of Female/Male Interaction in Peasant Society', in *American Ethnologist*, vol. 2, no. 4.

Rohrlich-Leavitt, R., 1975, *Women Cross Culturally: Change and Challenge*, The Hague & Paris: Mouton Publishers.

Rozario, S., 1992, *Purity and Communal Boundaries: Women and Social Change in a Bangladeshi Village*, London & New Jersey: Zed Books.

Rugh, A., 1985, *Family in Contemporary Egypt*, Cairo: The American University in Cairo Press.

Rugh, A., 1986, *Reveal and Conceal: Dress in Contemporary Egypt*, Cairo: The American University in Cairo Press.

Rushdie, S., 1988, *The Satanic Verses*, London: Penguin Group.

Ruthven, M., 1991, *A Satanic Affair: Salman Rushdie and the Wrath of Islam*, London: The Hogarth Press.

Sabbah, F. A., 1984, *Woman in the Muslim Unconscious*, New York and Oxford: Pergamon Press.

Shaaban, B., 1988, *Both Right and Left Handed*, London: The Women's Press.

Shami, S., et. al., eds, 1990, *Women in Arab Society: Work Patterns and Gender Relations in Egypt, Jordan and Sudan*, New York & Oxford: Berg Publishers & Unesco.

Sherif, F., 1985, *A Guide to the Contents of the Qur'an*, London: Ithaca Press.

Stoddard, P. H., et. al., eds, 1981, *Change and the Muslim World*, Syracuse: Syracuse University Press.

Stowasser, B. F., ed., 1987, *The Islamic Impulse*, London & Sydney: Croom Helm.

Stowasser, B. F., 1987a, 'Religious Ideology, Women, and the Family: The Islamic Paradigm', in B. F. Stowasser, ed., *The Islamic Impulse*, London & Sydney: Croom Helm.

Stowasser, B. F., 1987b, 'Liberated Equal or Protected Dependent? Contemporary Paradigms on Women's Status in Islam', in *Arab Studies Quarterly*, vol. 9.

Strobel, M., 1984, 'Women in Religion and Secular Ideology', in M. J. Hay and S. Stichter, eds, *African Women South of the Sahara*, London & New York: Longman.

Sullivan, E. L., 1986, *Women in Egyptian Public Life*, Cairo: The American University in Cairo Press.

UNICEF, 1992, *State of the World's Children Report*.

Utas, B., ed., 1983, *Islamic Societies: Social Attitudes and Historical Perspectives*, London: Curzon Press.

von der Mehden, F., 1980 'Islamic Resurgence in Malaysia', in J. L. Esposito, ed., *Islam and Development: Religion and Sociopolitical Change*, Syracuse: Syracuse University Press.

Wadud-Muhsin, A., 1989, 'Muslim Women as Minorities', in *Journal of the Institute of Muslim Minority Affairs*, vol. 10, no. 1.

Waugh, E. H. et. al., eds, 1991, *Muslim Families in North America*, Edmonton, Alberta: The University of Alberta Press.

1

Separation and Reconciliation: Marital Conflict among the Muslim Poor in Cairo

Helen Watson

'When a marriage is under stress the wife runs off. After the separation, she'll come back again and it all ends happily.' Faced with the question 'why?' the woman explained, 'Why not? She leaves him because he makes her feel useless, but then he realises just how precious she is and he wants her to come home. She will before too long of course, but not until she's received some sign and token of her worth as a wife.'

This woman's account of the process of separation and reconciliation provides an accurate description of what happens in cases of marital conflict in a poor area of Cairo, the City of the Dead. The City of the Dead is a graveyard on the outskirts of Cairo which dates from the Mameluk era, but its Anglicised title is something of a misnomer given that it is now inhabited by about half a million people. A high proportion of the graveyard's living occupants is made up of recent migrants from rural regions (as much as 90 per cent in some quarters), and increasingly the migrants are being joined by the urban homeless as Cairo's housing crisis is exacerbated by rapid population growth and urban decline.[1]

Many observers have described the impact of cityward migration in terms of the 'ruralisation' of Cairo rather than the urbanisation of its inhabitants (cf. Abu Lughod, 1969, Hopwood 1985). The ruralisation of the City of the Dead and the replication of rural life among migrant families is aided by the area's physical separation from other popular urban districts. The graveyard is bounded on two sides by a busy multi-lane motorway which runs to the airport and suburbs of Heliopolis in one direction, and to Old Cairo and the Citadel in the other. The migrant community is surprisingly self-contained and isolated from the rest of the metropolis given the graveyard's geographical location. People prefer to stay within the boundaries of the area and strive to maintain a distinct sense of identity.

The close-knit, separatist nature of the community is reflected in people's aversion to 'city people' and 'city ways', perceived as dangerous, immoral and corrupt. All members of the community stress that they are 'country people' who (unfortunately) live in the city. All families are Muslim and people describe themselves as pious and true to Islam, in contrast to the majority of city people who have been tainted by the decadent and modern, western mores and behaviour associated with the urban environment. Although few people are educated beyond the primary school level and there is no knowledge of the letter of Islamic law or fundamental theological issues, this has no impact on the shared view that the community is made up of 'model Muslims'. In local eyes being of rural descent and a true believer are two sides of the same coin; both characteristics are regarded as inextricably linked, if not synonymous.

In the City of the Dead there is a high level of marital stress, an obvious consequence of cityward migration for the rural poor, and the pressures which result from inadequate living conditions, employment problems and widespread material deprivation. These are the sources of conflict and everyday problems which women and men have overcome simply in order to co-exist, make ends meet and survive in a harsh environment. The main threats to marital stability stem from the lack of money and resources; particular concerns are work, health, personal and family welfare and the future itself. The transition to a new urban lifestyle is complicated for men with few skills suited to the urban labour market, but employment is even more problematic for women. Much importance is attached to the ideal of separate gender roles – the complementarity of women's domestic and men's public responsibilities. However the economic necessity of women's employment confounds the cultural ideal and challenges the complementary model of male breadwinners and female homemakers. This poses one of the most serious sources of social and personal conflict.

Tension in Marital Relations

One practical consequence of migration which affects relations within the family is that there is little chance of an escape from this poor quarter of the city. People cannot afford the cost of return migration, and in many cases there is no land left to return to. At the same time, the prospect of buying new farms, finding agricultural work or simply going back to one's natal village are often discussed with pipe-dream enthusiasm. Men are painfully aware of their economic and social failings. Two interrelated aspects of this sense of inadequacy are that men cannot earn sufficient money to provide for the family and are forced to rely on women's wages.

Studies of displaced populations facing similar problems have demonstrated how men seek to intensify their power over wives and female kin when other domains of power and influence have been curtailed or eliminated. This behaviour has been examined in the Palestinian refugee camps and migrant communities in Tehran (cf. Bauer, 1984; Pedersen, 1983). If the family remains the one sphere of everyday life where men's position is not openly threatened or undermined by external constraints, men increase their control over female kin as a kind of compensation for perceived inadequacies and loss of authority in other areas of social life. However this situation has not evolved in the City of the Dead, partly as a result of the high degree of mutual assistance and cooperation within the migrant community in general, and among women in particular. Women establish close networks of practical and emotional support with female friends and neighbours, which consolidates their position at the core of the family and mitigates against their isolation. The strength of female sociability and solidarity also serves to marginalise men, revealing their peripheral role in family affairs and reducing the nominal (male) head of the household's control of domestic life.

Many traditional sources of male authority have disappeared in the urban setting, such as control of female labour for agricultural production, whereas traditional female domains, centred on the household and kin group, have been reinforced under the pressures of poverty. At the same time, new urban occupational roles and relationships allow women to exploit alternative sources of influence. In general there are fewer structural constraints on women's self-determination after cityward migration. This is a consequence of indirect factors (such as the decline in the number of activities which men can and do control) and of an increase in the possible sources of direct authority for women which are outside male control: in addition to family affairs, these include income production, and intra-female ties through membership of savings clubs and ritual groups like the *zar*.[2] All the factors which strengthen women's position in relation to men have one common dimension: they centre on relationships with other women – ties of solidarity, mutual help, shared emotional experience and awareness of the everyday problems they have in common.

Although there are many sources of marital conflict, expressed in high levels of domestic violence, and numerous factors which exacerbate marital breakdown, divorces are uncommon. The low divorce rate in the community contrasts with a relatively high rate of divorce in

Egypt as a whole.[3] The typical pattern in cases of marital breakdown in the City of the Dead involves a period of separation followed by the couple's reconciliation and reunion.

The Local Solution to Marital Breakdown

When serious marital conflict occurs, a period of intensifying hostility within the relationship tends to lead to the wife's desertion. The act of desertion signals the couple's estrangement which calls for the intervention of the spouses' family and close friends. Negotiations between the estranged spouses and their supporters focus on resolving the conflict and bringing about the couple's eventual reunion. Given the usual outcome of negotiations, a wife's desertion and the subsequent action of the spouses' supporters can be seen as a way of setting problem-solving mechanisms in motion to preserve marital unions.

Four separate stages were apparent in all cases of the separation-reconciliation process. First, the wife leaves the marital home, usually after a serious quarrel which marks the climax of a stressful period of conflict. Secondly, close family members meet to discuss the affair and mediators are appointed to arrange formal negotiations. Thirdly, both spouses are called to meet in the presence of family and the mediators and give their account of the background to the conflict and the wife's desertion. Finally, after one or more family gatherings both spouses' positions are established, debated and evaluated. Compromises are suggested, concessions from the husband are negotiated and gifts may be offered to entice the wife back to the marital home. From a wife's point of view, any concessions or gifts her husband makes are seen as a 'token of her worth'.

Separation, as a way of resolving marital disputes, is ideally suited to local conditions for a number of different structural and practical reasons. Initially it requires little more than a rearrangement of sleeping quarters. This causes few problems in a close-knit community with a large number of friends and family close at hand. The runaway wife continues to live nearby in the same district which keeps costs to a minimum and causes no major disruption to childcare or work routines. There is also an implicit understanding that the woman will be a very short-term 'guest' who will pay her way through helping with domestic tasks. Other advantages stem from more general concerns about involving people outside the community in local matters. It is particularly important that the courts are not involved and no formal declaration of marital breakdown is necessary. A spouse's departure signals the need for immediate action to deal with the problems in the marriage, and perhaps most importantly, the separation gives the couple the necessary time and space to consider their position and negotiate a settlement. This is especially important for the woman, given her active role in initiating the separation. During the first few days of the separation she has to mobilise a support group and generate as much sympathy and positive understanding of her position as possible.

There are both material and moral explanations for preferring separation-reconciliation to divorce. At this level of explanation it is possible to identify two interrelated factors which explain why the couple's reunion is considered the best option: the economic costs imposed by legal dissolution of marriage and the high value attached to the security and stability of family life and conflict resolution.

Economic and Legal Factors

Some mention of the material and symbolic investment represented by marriage will put the economic and legal constraints on divorce into perspective. The economic transfers involved in marriage centre on gifts given to mark engagement and the wedding (*shabka* and *mahr*). The material exchanges comprise a mix of goods and cash which can be described as indirect dowry or a conjugal fund for the couple's use in the marriage (cf. Kurian 1979). The economic contribution of each party is interdependent, and notwithstanding its material significance in establishing a foundation for the marriage, marriage payments also have social and symbolic importance. In Wikan's description: 'The more the groom gives the more he can demand' and this is 'a public measure of the status of the bride's family and just as much, of the bridegroom's' (1980:85). Or, to put it another way, in the words of a recent bride: 'When people see your gifts, they see who you are, see who you're marrying and see the whole future of your marriage!'

The idea of investing in marriage was often advanced when people explained the high cost of marriage payments in relation to general material scarcity and insecurity about the future. Parents agreed that they should transfer all the goods and cash they could afford on their children's marriage since their sparse savings could be swallowed up at any time by some unforeseen emergency. In any case most families had few material resources and valuables for children to inherit on the death of the head of the household. The type of explanations given for preferring high-cost marriage payments can be summarised in the three general propositions:

– the higher the cost, the greater the parent's faith in their children's marriage;

– the higher the cost, the better the couple's economic security in married life;

– the higher the cost, the higher the public estimation of the marriage.

Within the scope of discussions of the disadvantages of divorce, explicit mention is made of the difficulty of returning expensive gifts if a marriage is dissolved. The overall tone of these arguments fit many familiar ideas from cross-cultural studies of the general relationship between high bride-price and low divorce rates (cf. Comaroff, 1980).

The legal position on marriage and divorce is drawn from the Shari'a and the legislative reforms in 1979 were intended to improve women's status and security in marriage.[4] This attempt to shift the male bias in divorce legislation built on the earlier dissolution of the *bayt al-ta'a* law which gave a husband the right to force a run-away wife to return to him against her will. With regard to repudiation and remarriage, the reforms stipulated that a man must inform his wife of his intention to divorce her, and of an impending remarriage if he plans to take a second wife. The new laws represented an incentive to marital stability by imposing economic constraints on men who repudiate a wife and intend to remarry after the divorce. The state also accepted responsibility for safeguarding the financial support of divorcées and their children by advancing maintenance payments and deducting the payments from the husband's wages (cf. Minces, 1980).

Under existing law a repudiated wife is entitled to maintenance payments and shelter. After divorce a woman has the right to remain in the family home with her children (custody of children is granted to the mother until the daughters marry and sons are 15 years old),[5] or alternative accommodation must be provided. Significant problems for the urban poor are posed by either arrangement, given Cairo's chronic housing shortage and inflationary accommodation costs. Other economic constraints incurred by men on divorce concern the cost of replacing household furnishings. After divorce a wife has the right to retain possession of all the goods listed on her *quaima* (a record of the goods which a bride brings to the marriage in her own name).[6] Another basic consideration for any man contemplating divorce is the cost of his next marriage (engagement gifts, marriage payments and the rest), since men will almost always remarry unless they have female relatives prepared to take on domestic responsibilities and the management of the home.

In short, divorce is an unpleasant and unsatisfactory solution to marital problems on these material grounds alone, notwithstanding the social, psychological and personal factors associated with divorce such as loss of face, gossip, loneliness, and a sense of failure. Such feelings and fears intensify the general sense of insecurity and inadequacy which pervades life in a poor migrant community, most especially among men. Although the economic constraints of divorce are obvious and recognised by people themselves, I would warn against a crude economic determinism and any overemphasis of material factors which diminish the influence of the social and moral context of decision-making. It is important to recognise the crucial role played by family and friends in promoting marital stability. Peters' qualification of the correlation between high marriage payments and marital stability sums up the argument: 'Material goods do not hold human beings together. Marital stability is rooted in the moral context created by a community, symbolically expressed through the (goods) which change hands . . . on the way to a union' (1980:151)

Marital Stability and Conflict Resolution

In many respects the family is the core of Egyptian society, being the primary social unit which provides all essential personal, emotional and material support (cf. Rugh, 1985). Arguably, family solidarity and stability are of most importance to those with least resources and other alternative sources of security. From the outset, a marriage is surrounded with two social rings of defence, an outer circle of friends and neighbours and an inner circle of family and close kin. In combination with material considerations, the intervention of concerned individuals has a strong influence on marital stability. Local marriages survive because people decide that they must, given the negative social and material consequences of divorce. One of the most valuable assets in everyday life is a secure family, and a poor migrant community composed of secure families has the greatest potential for mutual assistance and solidarity. This summation of the moral context of marriage can be represented by a simple statement: better an enduring (if scarred) marriage than a family divided and weakened by divorce.

It is essential to avoid permanent dislocation of community relations when a majority of families depend on each other for everyday assistance. An informal, spontaneous system of borrowing and lending of foodstuffs exists among neighbours and friends which can make the difference between feast and famine in times of hardship. The antagonism associated with divorce, as people take sides in the marital dispute, proves a serious threat to any reciprocal assistance of this kind.

One clear example of how the aim of maintaining community solidarity acts to inhibit formal dissolution of marriages concerns the necessary interdependence of women engaged in waged work. The dual burden of employment and household management borne by working mothers is accentuated by a fear that their job forces them to neglect child care and domestic responsibilities. Criticism of working women voiced by both men and women focuses on the time devoted to waged work which inevitably means time lost to a wife's 'primary duty' of caring for her husband and children. The fact that women explain or justify their employment in terms of their maternal role (wages are for children's welfare, household expenses, or simply to ensure the family's survival), does nothing to lessen the pressures they face in managing and allocating time and energy between the home and the job (cf. Ibrahim, 1985; El Messiri, 1980).

Most women work from home on a piece-work basis, which allows for maximum flexibility in time management while minimising the 'public' fact of their employment. However, pooling resources and sharing common tasks makes an important difference to women in their struggle to fulfil everyday responsibilities. For instance, if one woman has fallen behind in her allotted work load for an employer, other women will provide help with the domestic work by taking care of her children or preparing meals in advance of the husband's return. In the absence of child care services such favours play a crucial part in every working mother's daily routine. Working women have a lot to lose if such informal reciprocal arrangements are complicated by family feuds and in-fighting. This may be one reason for the active interest women take in the reconciliation process which follows marital breakdown. Of course, the obvious key factor in this respect is that a wife's employment is the most common source of marital tension in the disputes which lead to separation.[7]

The Advantages of Reconciliation

Local consensus on the advantages of informal, community-based reconciliation processes is a mirror image of the popular view of state law and courtroom settlements. People have a deep distrust of courtroom justice. They consider their access to the courts limited because of an incomprehensible bureaucracy. The legal system is said to be complicated, expensive and corrupt and in the control of well-off, educated elites. There is also the issue of family reputation to consider when the courts are involved, in particular, the shame associated with revealing private family affairs to complete strangers. Despite existing legislation which regulates divorce, child custody, maintenance payments and so on, people have only vague ideas about their content. In all these respects, the advantages of settling and resolving marital disputes within the community are obvious and the general opinion is that it is better to avoid involving the courts in any kind of family business.

In many respects the separation-reconciliation process, as it operates in the area, can be considered as an informal, do-it-yourself, legal system. The spouses' family and friends are considered to be the best representatives and 'judges' in cases of marital breakdown because they have direct knowledge of the people concerned and all the necessary information at hand to bring the dispute to an appropriate settlement. Once a separation occurs the necessary stages of the process are obvious. Basic principles of procedure are enshrined in common-sense knowledge, shared by all local people, men and women alike. The essential factors to establish the most just and favourable circumstances for a reconciliation can be reduced to four basic principles: (1) a hearing must take place as soon as possible; (2) both parties must be represented and given a fair say; (3) the welfare of those most directly affected, the children in particular, is a priority issue; (4) the affair must be resolved through negotiation until both sides reach an agreeable compromise.

When marital problems are discussed in religious or moral terms, the emphasis is on any process which increases the chances of reconciliation and the restoration of marital stability. The example of the Prophet is cited to support the aim of consensus through consultation and discussion to solve problems for the good of the entire family. In this respect, separation is viewed positively, because it provides the opportunity for an estranged couple to present their grievances to a familiar audience which will have the interests of the family at heart when reaching an agreement on how best to resolve the dispute.

People talk about the importance of marriage in relation to the continuity of the family line, the necessity of providing and caring for children, the complementary roles of parents in nurturing and educating offspring. Romantic love may or may not be present between spouses, but it is of little practical value when compared with the family-oriented aspects of the marriage bond (cf. Rugh, 1985). Within the community there is a sense of pride implicit in descriptions of marriages which have endured long-term problems and disputes, and people talk of divorce as the irresponsible, 'easy' solution to marital disputes preferred by irreligious, immoral urbanites who are heedless of religious duty, family responsibilities and children's welfare and happiness. In short, reconciliation has all the advantages of maintaining good relations and resolving conflict, whereas divorce is seen as a threat to family security and the stable functioning of society itself.

The Paradox Of Divorce Threats

Nevertheless, there is something of a contradiction between what people say about divorce and how they actually behave when a marriage is in crisis. Major interests in local discussions of divorce fall into two categories which concern what is permissible and what is possible. The distinction lies in the crucial difference between actually initiating divorce and threatening to initiate divorce. When divorce is discussed as an abstract or theoretical proposition, men advance numerous reasons for repudiating a wife. Some are culturally derived, others are from the Qur'an, but it is practically impossible to disentangle the two in people's statements. If a wife is to avoid divorce she must be obedient, fulfil her domestic duties, gratify her husband's sexual desires, safeguard her honour and be respectful. A wife must remain faithful to her husband both in herself and with regard to his property. In theory any breach of these requirements merits divorce.

Women agree with these theoretical grounds for divorce but maintain that a wife would have to be in mortal danger before she would consider initiating divorce proceedings against her husband. They stress that divorce is every wife's greatest fear and give particular emphasis to the view that divorce is more easily initiated by men than women. When women discuss the issue of actually initiating divorce in an intolerable marriage, one area of unanimous agreement is that it would be impossible for them to undertake divorce proceedings because of a lack of information about the law, and the absence of any practical example or knowledge of women who had initiated divorce.

In discussion of the threat of divorce there is another difference in male and female perspectives. Men have a long list of the advantages of threatening to divorce a wife which are described in terms such as: 'It keeps a wife conscious of the need for good behaviour' or 'It keeps her obedient and peaceful' or 'It makes her careful'. Men frequently make what are construed as threats of divorce, women rarely do. In fact, women perceive men's divorce threats in a quite different way which can be represented by one woman's comment: 'The threat of divorce only brings more tears and tempers. What's the point, if a man doesn't mean what he says?' This indicates that women distinguish between the threat and the reality of divorce, the former common, the latter rare. For women, this is the paradox of the threat of divorce. Since women appear unable or unwilling to initiate divorce themselves or to resort to the law, it is possible to argue that a process of marital separation and ultimate reconciliation is an alternative way for women to deal with problematic marriages. Such an argument raises questions about women's views of the likelihood or reality of divorce in their own lives, particularly in relation to the process of marital separation and reconciliation.

Strategic Elements of the Separation Process

It is possible to argue that the local process of marital separation and reconciliation gives women a practical way of coping with intolerable marital tensions. Certain strategic elements can be associated with women's recognition that men make empty threats of divorce, and separation can be seen as a female strategy for making the best of a bad marriage. Despite the public role of men as mediators and peacemakers in the separation-reconciliation process, women run things behind the scenes and manipulate events in their own interests. In fact, although everyone prefers separation to divorce as a means of dealing with marital breakdown, women play an active mutually-supportive part in the process.

One crucial point is that separation provides women with a chance to redress marital grievances and shift the balance of power in their own favour. Since men are reluctant to carry out the threat of divorce they must take less drastic action. An angry husband must avoid an empty threat of divorce becoming public knowledge since he risks the scorn of others if he openly proclaims the desire to divorce his wife but fails to do so. Women's awareness of this has important consequences for the subsequent course of events in marital disputes. Women know that husbands make empty threats of divorce, often over trifles, and in a typical case of marital breakdown the acceleration of conflict follows a particular pattern.

When tensions surface in a problem marriage, a husband tends to resort to a complicated type of emotional blackmail within the relationship. He may imply or even state that he would like to abandon or repudiate her and take another wife, but he has to stop short of declaring an explicit intention to initiate divorce proceedings. In a situation of increasing marital stress common male tactics are to ignore a wife, spend longer than usual in the coffee house and leave home in ostentatious delight. A man may praise other women's beauty, house-keeping skills, efficiency, cheerfulness and good character. He may stress that he is not jealous and encourage her to go wherever she pleases, as if her behaviour is of little consequence to him. This demonstrates that he does not care for her, since a wife expects a loving husband to be a jealous, demanding one.

But the greater the use of such tactics, the greater the desire to bring hostilities to an end. There is a growing compulsion to break out of this cycle of tension which makes daily life unpleasant for both spouses. As marital tensions intensify, a wife has two basic options. She can overtly ignore her husband's behaviour and behave as if trying to show him the error of his ways, or she can embark upon the more dangerous path towards open conflict. In the latter situation, a wife may withdraw domestic services and refuse to do more housework than the bare essentials of cooking and laundry. Refusing sex is another option. This is a useful protest strategy for women because it can be seen as an inevitable result of deteriorating marital relations when a couple are avoiding or ignoring each other in public and in private. But more importantly, men are in a no-win situation and only likely to tolerate withdrawal of sex for a limited period of time since celibacy always reflects badly on a husband's virility and authority, and men are unlikely to risk their manly reputation by discussing a wife's refusal of sex. In this situation the inevitable outcome prompted by the wife's action is an acceleration of conflict and an eventual confrontation of the problems in the marriage following the wife's desertion.

At this stage of marital conflict, women are in a superior tactical position. This becomes apparent when the role other women play in the matter is taken into account. While a man would risk losing public face by admitting marital problems to other men, problem husbands and marital conflicts are a common topic of conversation among women. A woman's close friends and kin will know many intimate details of her marriage and the extent of any problems which exist between husband and wife. For instance a woman will readily discuss plans to refuse sex with her husband and report on his subsequent reactions. The wife in a problem marriage has a ready-made network of support from female friends and kin throughout phases of accelerating conflict. If a wife abandons the marital home when the level of conflict is perceived as intolerable, she has some sense of security in the knowledge that her friends are aware of the background to her desertion and will support her.

After a wife's desertion, men have to play the situation in a way which entails no loss of face. On the one hand they must secure their own authority and status, assert control over a troublesome wife and restore domestic order. On the other, they have to respond to a wife's grievances and demands while not appearing to give way under female-initiated pressure. The double dilemma for every husband faced with a runaway wife is how to reconcile her desertion and alleged misdemeanours with his desire for an agreeable reconciliation.

Women appear to have more control over their position within a problem marriage than do men, or at least men act as if this is so. What may have altered the balance in marital relations is the paradox of divorce threats – the fact that women know men are unwilling or unable to carry out their threat of divorce. In a problematic relationship which has progressed through various stages of criticism, recrimination and counter-attack from both sides, a wife does not find herself in a personal cul-de-sac where she has to accept her husband's word as final. The knowledge that reconciliation is more likely than repudiation means that a wife can dare to take matters into her own hands and force a settlement through leaving the marital home.

This development represents a significant change from the experience of women of previous generations. In the past desertion was a dangerous action from a strategic viewpoint. A woman who deserted her husband in the hope of forcing a peaceful reconciliation faced being repudiated or being brought back to him and an even more unhappy marriage under the *bayt al-ta'a* law. However there are also stories of the past which circulate in the community about husbands who made the most of a wife's desertion and ignored their rights under *bayt al-ta'a*. There are accounts of one angry husband who sold his wife's furniture the evening of her departure, another who repudiated his wife before she had turned the street corner, yet another who loaded all his wife's belongings on to a cart and had them delivered to her parents' house several hours before she arrived there herself.

But despite local evidence to the contrary, the existence of the law means that desertion is a high-risk strategy for wives. Since legal reform has removed this strategic element of risk, a wife's desertion can now be seen as a typical, if last-straw, solution to marital problems. Insofar as a wife's departure cannot be ignored by the husband in question, it forces marital problems into the open where a solution can be sought. Since divorce is an unacceptable, if obvious solution, the outcome is invariably negotiations in an attempt to end the separation and reconcile the couple. As such, separation provides women with a way of redressing grievances in marriage, of airing their opinions about the conflict, drawing attention to their husband's faults, and of seeking compensation for emotional or material suffering.

Women's Role in the Separation Process

To explore the social and personal dimensions of separation and reconciliation, it is necessary to re-examine the different stages involved giving special emphasis to the part women play. While men assume the most public roles in negotiating a settlement, I would argue and this is also generally a wife's viewpoint, that men's speech-making and posturing is largely irrelevant to the successful outcome of negotiations.

In the public role of mediator in negotiations, men tend to base their speeches on the information women have given them, since they rarely discuss marital problems among themselves and so have little access to gossip about such matters. Men depend on women for information about the background to the conflict, for accounts of past quarrels and settlements, details of the couple's domestic affairs, the marriage arrangements and contractual agreements. While men are aware that much of this information may be false or biased in favour of the wife, they have to rely on it in the absence of other equally well-informed sources of information. In short, women are experts on the background to marital conflicts and men must rely on their accounts.

There is a strong commitment to ensuring that negotiations are conducted without bias and are seen to be fair, hence the attention to details and what Wikan calls 'objectivity' (1980:52). For instance, women who have no close male kin to argue their case in a hearing will be represented by a 'neutral' male party. One man who offered his public services as mediator *in loco parentis* said that his most important duty was 'to be sure of all the facts'. However, this man was married to the closest friend of the estranged wife he was representing, and inevitably his wife had supplied 'all the facts' heavily weighted in her friend's favour.

Women's control of information is also crucial during the 'public posturing' stage of negotiations (by this I mean the mediators' continual to-ing and fro-ing between the estranged spouses' homes). Women gather many important types of information which men can use in managing the negotiations. While men may regard this as just gossip, *kalam al-sittat* (women's talk), women are presenting barely masked instructions about what steps should be taken next for maximum impact on the other camp. Women relay the latest news of the separated couple which is vital to the tactical timing of subsequent mediation. As doorstep observers and eavesdroppers, they know when a kinsman arrives at the husband's house, how long the visit lasted, his apparent mood when he left and whether he arranged to return. From such seemingly random facts female observers construct a story and sub-plot to the separation which can be used to guide the course of subsequent negotiations and influence the couple's reunion. Since a mediator's initial approach and reception is important, information about current developments in the other party's home is an essential guide to the optimum time to arrange a meeting. A variety of other useful facts can be gleaned from women's doorstep research – such as the degree of support a husband is getting from his neighbours, or the size and social spread of his group of allies.

When such strategic aspects of the separation process are considered, an impression emerges which is quite different from Wikan's description of male and female roles in the resolution of marital disputes: 'In marital conflicts it is the men who by virtue of their authority assume the role of mediators. Although they represent family units and interested parties, they try to keep the rules of relevance and objectivity which contrasts sharply with women's style which has few rules of relevance. In that way they can reach a solution which is acceptable to all and settle the conflict' (1980:52).

While men play the prominent public role in negotiations, I would argue that this is largely irrelevant to the success of a negotiated settlement, because women exercise the 'real' power which determines the content and outcome of discussions through their control of information and events behind closed doors. There are also problems implicit in Wikan's rather negative view of the female 'style' of conflict (disorganised, subjective, emotional), because of the assumption that male 'rules of relevance and objectivity' are the essential determinants of successful mediation of conflict (ibid). Moreover, considering the description of the difference between male and female approaches to conflict resolution in the City of the Dead, there are grounds for reversing the bias in Wikan's formulation. I would suggest that it is women's hidden role in negotiations (and their *ad hoc*, spontaneous and subjective contribution to the hearings) which is most useful in fostering compromises conducive to a reconciliation settlement agreeable to all. An emphasis on men's public role in negotiations ignores the strategic importance of separation from a wife's perspective, as well as the essential part women play in informing the process itself.

A brief description of two cases of separation and reconciliation will illustrate the range and style of the processes at work.

Case A

Wife A had been married for less than two years and the relationship with her husband was deteriorating under his constant criticism of her neglect of the home and her child. She worked from home cutting fabric for a textile merchant, but the couple still found it very hard to make ends meet. She had been beaten several times before she ran away from her husband to the home of a paternal cousin. After earlier beatings she had mentioned the problem to her in-laws and appealed to her sister-in law to intervene, but she had been advised to wait until the husband's economic problems lessened. His violence was accepted as a result of his worries about the future and failure to secure a steady job.

After his wife's desertion Mr A asked his sister to visit the house where his wife had taken refuge. Mrs A told her sister-in-law that she loved her husband and simply wanted him to stop beating her. She said that she had not planned to run away, it had been an instinctive action when she felt in danger of her life and the need to protect the baby. The sister-in-law brought her mother to see Mrs A and they went over the details of the background to the conflict. The women agreed that the lack of money was at the root of the violence. Mrs A's mother-in-law remarked: 'Money problems lie behind all women's bruises and broken hearts'. The men of Mrs A's family agreed that the dispute should be discussed at their house, and Mr A's sister's husband, briefed by his wife and Mr A himself, agreed to mediate on his behalf. At the hearing both parties discussed their problems and several basic positions emerged.

Mr A was under extreme pressure which made him violent and he resented his wife having to work. Mrs A had not deserved the beatings but she had not given her husband enough care and attention because of her job. She may have intensified her husband's worries by talking openly about how much she earned (her wages formed more than half the family income). A stable marriage was built on more than a firm economic foundation. The present lack of money was a major problem but things were bound to improve. The couple had not discussed their worries together which would have diffused the growing tension.

Mrs A's cousin agreed to help Mr A to find a better job and stressed that a good marriage should be able to endure hard times. Mr A's brother-in-law suggested that Mrs A should concentrate on her duties as a wife and not spend so much time earning money. If the couple were in financial need they should rely on their kin and emotional support and not grow further apart by neglecting each other. Mr A was ready to accept his wife's return and apologise for his unnecessary violence if she was prepared to devote herself to her proper domestic responsibilities. He agreed to give her a greater share of the wages from his new job to enable her to work less hours for the textile dealer. Mrs A was happy to do this and the couple committed themselves to discussing all problems in future.

Case B

Mrs B spent most days alone from dawn to dusk as her husband of eight years, a recent migrant, went in search of casual work. They had four children and very little money. Mrs B had started to work from home for a leather workshop, stitching strips of leather and cotton, but her husband was jealous of his attractive wife and suspicious of the dealer's assistant who delivered the leather to the house when he was out. Mrs B denied his initially veiled accusations, but became increasingly worried when she heard from a neighbour that her husband had started to spy on her and ask about her movements during the day. During a jealous quarrel she told Mr B that she would give up her job, but instead she sent a message to the dealer to have the work sent to a neighbour's house in future. She decided to continue working in order to save money for her sons' school expenses and confided this plan to her neighbour. The two women agreed that this should not cause any problems since Mrs B could stop working as soon as she had saved another few pounds and her husband would never find out about her (justifiable) deception.

The couple's quarrels grew more violent in subsequent months and the fight which prompted her desertion followed Mr B's discovery of the hidden leather work. He had searched the house after he found his wife in a new dress on an unexpected visit home one afternoon. Mrs B had borrowed the dress from her neighbour to attend a friend's engagement party, but her husband refused to listen to her account of the origin of the dress, and accused her of taking gifts from her employer during their secret liasons. He smashed the photograph taken on their wedding day then continued to beat Mrs B until she passed out. Mr B had gone when his wife regained consciousness. He did not return that night and Mrs B visited her friend (the fiancée of her husband's brother) with news of the crisis. The friend advised her to return and wait for her husband as if nothing had happened and told her fiancé of the problems in his brother's marriage.

On Mr B's return there was another violent quarrel. After a second vicious beating and her husband's departure, Mrs B took the children to her friend's house, where she left them in the care of her friend's mother while she went to see Mr B's brother. When Mr B returned to find the empty house he rushed to his brother's home and on finding his wife there, he attacked her again and accused her of adultery. The brother tried to calm Mr B and took him outside to hear details of the affair. When the men returned some hours later Mr B's brother called for a meeting of both spouses to be held immediately after morning prayers to discuss the breakdown of relations.

Three meetings were held during the following days. Mr B's brother and his prospective wife's brother acted as mediators for the estranged couple. Mr B had to be restrained from attacking his wife during the first meeting. By the second meeting discussions had become more orderly and rational. Mrs B was chastised for keeping her work hidden from her husband. Then Mrs B's representative stressed the value of education for migrants' children and the husbands of Mrs B's neighbours (who had been told about the innocent reasons for hiding her continued employment) added their testimony which detailed the arrangement with the dealer's assistant and cleared Mrs B of any suspicion of adultery. The husbands of various friends supplied information about the borrowed dress in support of Mrs B's story.

In the course of the ensuing debate Mr B was advised to join a *gam'iyya* (saving club) to cover the children's school costs. When Mrs B's representative announced that Mrs B was to give up working for the leather dealer, Mr B's brother suggested that alternative and 'safe' employment could be found in a shop where his fiancée worked which was owned by an old, respected family friend. In short the outcome of negotiations established several key points in the process of reconciliation: Mr B was wrong to attack his wife but his actions were understandable, if not wholly excusable. Mrs B had acted wrongly against her husband's authority but was fundamentally innocent of the much more serious charge of infidelity. The couple should forget the past and reunite for the sake of the children as soon as possible.

Mrs B said she was too ashamed to meet her husband face-to-face and was scared that he was not wholly convinced of her innocence. Her friend and the senior women of the house advised her not to return until her husband had sent a formal invitation and unambiguous sign of his good faith. The prospective brother-in-law told his fiancée that Mr B was embarrassed by the false accusations he had made and feared that his wife no longer loved him. Mrs B received this news shortly before a sealed parcel arrived from Mr B which contained their wedding picture in a new frame. The women of the house of refuge and Mrs B discussed how the reunion should take place and settled on a plan to reduce the emotional impact of the initial meeting for both spouses. Mr B received word from his brother that Mrs B would return the following morning when he had left for work. Both spouses agreed to act as if the separation and its prologue of suspicion and hostility had not taken place. When Mr B returned the following evening it was said that the children were asleep, the house had been thoroughly cleaned and his wife had prepared his favourite food for dinner. Subsequent visitors noticed that the wedding picture was placed in a prominent position on the wall opposite the door.

Concluding Remarks

In general terms, all separations involved phases of negotiation and reconciliation which can be described as follows. The estranged spouse, always the wife, returns to her natal home. Her male kin or a close family friend arrange to mediate with her husband. The husband is given an opportunity to state his case, which involves the woman being chastised for alleged misdemeanours which accelerated the conflict and brought about the desertion itself. The wife's claims of neglect or cruelty are discussed and rarely challenged. Finally, there is a proposal of a reconciliation which usually involves some gift or token from the husband and his family which marks an end to the couple's estrangement. Once an agreement is reached, with compromises on both sides, the run-away wife will return to her husband. From a woman's perspective, the money or gift received is seen as a token of her worth, evidence of her husband's commitment to the marriage and recognition of her personal and practical value to him.

It is clear that the overall preference for separation and reconciliation over divorce attests to the high value placed on marriage, on constant family structures, and on the resolution of conflicts which might endanger community solidarity and interdependence in a poor neighbourhood. Key aspects of the advantages of separation and reconciliation can be summarised as follows. Separation is a preferred means of dealing with a breakdown of marital relations because of the economic constraints of divorce, and local aversion to the law and courtroom justice in the resolution of marital conflict. It is important to locate these factors within the broader context of cultural values which emphasise social cohesion and stability in terms of the pre-eminence of the family unit. In cases of separation it is also vital that neither party is seen to lose face or be disadvantaged during the separation process. However when both sides meet to discuss the causes of the separation and get a chance to air their grievances, the actual facts of the dispute become less of an issue than the material means of reconciliation. Quite simply, a reunion serves the best interests of both spouses and both families.

I would further argue that despite evidence of a general abstract fear of being divorced, women can exploit men's economic inability to carry out their threat of divorce proceedings. It is evident that separation is a way of tackling marital problems with the knowledge that men cannot afford the compensatory maintenance payments required after divorce. Men and women both admit that reconciliation is less expensive and more socially valuable in the long term than divorce. After any resolution of marital breakdown and the runaway wife's return, men's responses, at least in public, suggest that the incident as a whole is not thought of as a victory over their wife.

There are numerous approaches to reconciliation which allow men to save face, although they tend to sound rather unconvincing. For instance, men identify the advantages of reconciliation in largely negative terms. They may stress the inconvenience of a missing wife, the bad feeling which has been avoided with neighbours and their wife's kin, or the restoration of good relations within the community after a dispute has been resolved. In general men offer a series of explanations for end-ing the separation which sound a bit like excuses for the token they have given their runaway wife. Men show no sign of personal triumph after a wife's return. For them, it seems, it is not a victory over the woman, merely a good settlement to a marital dispute. Moreover in structural terms a husband merely gets back what is his by right – his wife.

In the process of separation and reconciliation women have gained all this and more, there is a cessation of hostilities and the restoration of peaceful marital relations. From the woman's perspective there are two ways of looking at the final solution. At the very least, a husband has come to realise and been forced to acknowledge a wife's value in the process of reconciliation. At best, there is a new spirit of mutual affection in the marriage once the family is reunited under the same roof. Women also return in possession of a token of their worth, a tangible item of material or prestige value which is a symbol of their importance to the man, and the relative security of their marital status.

The final word must go to the woman whose opening remark established the context for this contribution to an understanding of the social reality of marital conflict in the City of the Dead: 'Marriage is likely to be a disaster from time to time but however much your husband makes you weep and worry, there are ways to look after yourself and the family. The important thing is to make sure that he still wants you and is prepared to sacrifice something to get you back . . . He has to be shown that he needs you after all.'

Notes

1. The population of Cairo was estimated to be between 12 and 14 million in 1985. Hopwood states that the optimum population for existing facilities is 1.5 million, and comments: 'Cairo by a process of osmosis seems to absorb its new citizens by continuously lowering its standards . . . to keep up with the growth some 62,000 housing units are needed per year. This figure is more than double the annual rate of 30,000 units for the whole of Egypt during 1960–70' (1985:176).

2. Constantinides' study of women's membership of *zar* groups in northern Sudan concludes that: 'Membership . . . helps to counteract the initial shrinkage of the women's sphere of social activity when they move to towns. [Members] have a peer group among whom they can seek support in personal crises and compete for goods, service and status . . . The cult provides one of the few bases that exist for female solidarity in the towns' (1978:201).

3. Less than 3 per cent of local marriages (3 out of 125) ended in divorce compared with the divorce rate of 1 in 4.5 quoted by Hopwood in 1985 for Egypt as a whole (1985:170).

4. In theory, the reforms of personal status and family law made a significant difference to women's security in marriage. But in practice as Juliette Minces

and others have shown, 'the laws are often ignored and are far in advance of people's attitudes' (1980:97). The legal requirements of divorce are often ignored in practice. Many people remain ignorant of their rights under the law, and women are especially disadvantaged when it comes to adequate information about existing legislation and legal procedures.

5. The previous age limits for children remaining in maternal custody were 10 years for girls and 7 years for boys.

6. Typical items will include most of the furniture, cooking utensils, crockery, bedclothes and other essential household goods which will have to be replaced when the man sets up a separate home.

7. All the cases of separation in my study involved a long-running dispute about the wife's neglect of domestic duties as a direct result of her employment.

References

Abu Lughod, J., 1969, 'Varieties of Urban Experience: Contrast, Coexistence and Coalescence in Cairo' in I. Lapidus ed., *Middle Eastern Cities*, Berkeley & Los Angeles: University of California Press.

Bauer, J., 1984, 'New Models and Traditional Networks: Migrant Women in Tehran' in J.T. Fawcett et al, *Women in the Cities of Asia: Migration and Urban Adaptation*, Boulder: Westview Press.

Beck, L. and N. Keddie, eds, 1978, *Women in the Muslim World*, Cambridge: Harvard University Press.

Caplan, P. and J.M. Bujra, eds, 1978, *Women United, Women Divided*, London: Tavistock Publications.

Constantinides, P., 1978, 'Women's Spirit Possession and Urban Adaptation' in P. Caplan & J.M. Bujra, *Women United , Women Divided*, London: Tavistock Publications.

El Messiri, S., 1978, 'Self Images of Traditional Urban Women in Cairo' in L. Beck & N. Keddie, eds, *Women in the Muslim World*, Cambridge: Harvard University Press.

Fawcett, J.T. et al, 1984, *Women in the Cities of Asia: Migration and Urban Adaptation*, Boulder: Westview Press.

Hopwood, D., 1985, *Egypt: Politics and Society, 1945–1984*, London: Allen & Unwin.

Ibrahim, B., 1985, 'Cairo's Factory Women', in E. Fernea, *Women and the Family in the Middle East: New Voices of Change*, Austin: University of Texas Press.

Kurian, G., ed., 1979, *Cross Cultural Perspectives on Mate Selection and Marriage*, Westport: Greenwood Press.

Lapidus, I., ed., 1969, *Middle Eastern Cities*, Berkeley & Los Angeles: University of California Press.

Mernissi, F., 1984, *Doing Daily Battle*, London: Women's Press.

Minces, J., 1980, *The House of Obedience: Women in Arab Society*, London: Zed Press.

Pedersen, I., 1983, 'Oppressive and Liberating Elements in the Situation of

Palestinian Women' in B. Utas, ed., *Women in Islamic Societies: Social Attitudes and Historical Perspectives*, London: Curzon Press.

Peters, E., 1980, 'Aspects of Bedouin Bridewealth in Cyrenaica' in J.L. Comaroff, ed., *The Meaning of Marriage Payments*, London: Academic Press.

Rugh, A., 1985, *Family in Contemporary Egypt*, Cairo: American University in Cairo Press.

Utas, B., ed., 1983, *Women in Islamic Societies: Social Attitudes and Historical Perspectives*, London: Curzon Press.

Wikan, U., 1980, *Life Among the Poor in Cairo*, London: Tavistock Publications.

2

Strategies of Selection: Differing Notions of Marriage in Iran and Morocco

Ziba Mir-Hosseini

In Muslim countries marriage, though not a 'sacrament', occurs in a religio/legal framework, and is regulated by a code of law rooted in religious precepts. The relations between the precepts and the law are complex, and are further complicated by the distance between each of them and actual practice. This paper explores one aspect of these complex relations, as reflected in the existence of three different but interrelated notions of marriage validity. The first derives its legitimacy from the Shari'a, a body of sacred law in Muslim belief, the second from the modern legal system and the third from society at large, grounded in popular beliefs and social practices. In other words, there are three distinct constructions of what constitutes a legitimate marital relation. When they concur, the validity of marriage is beyond dispute, which is the case for the majority of marriages. But there are other instances in which the marriage meets the requirements of only one or two of these realms. These cases are the ones that make their way to the courts.

Through a detailed analysis of two court cases, I shall demonstrate the ways in which social constructions of marriage are at times at odds with those of the Shari'a and the modern legal system. The material for this analysis comes from fieldwork in the family courts of Iran and Morocco.[1] My main focus is on a special type of dispute that comes under the general title of 'Proof of Marital Bonds'. Although these disputes comprise a small proportion of all marital disputes (approximately 5 per cent) in both countries, they are significant as they lay bare some of the main assumptions behind the religio/legal conception of marriage. Their analysis illustrates the contrast between the ideal model of marriage and family embodied in the Shari'a and actual prevailing patterns of social behaviour. Before discussing these disputes, it is essential to place them in context by presenting an overview of the ways in which religious precepts and positive law interact in modern Muslim countries.

The Problem: The Shari'a and Modern Legal Systems

What distinguishes Islamic law (the Shari'a) from modern systems of law is its sacred and transcendental dimension. In Muslim belief its source is divine revelation, from which ensue two assumptions underlying the ideal of the Shari'a: first, that there are divinely revealed norms and rules to which Muslims are under constant duty to conform; secondly, that these are immutable and all-encompassing, regulating every aspect of life. The literature on Islamic law and Muslim societies shows that there has always existed a gap between Shari'a ideals and practice. The Shari'a has not only accommodated prevailing customs, but it has never been applied in its totality (cf. Anderson, 1959; Coulson, 1964; Schacht, 1964). Yet, the ideal of the Shari'a as the perfect law of the 'Golden Age of Islam' has endured, particularly in the area of family law, which has always represented the core of the Shari'a. The provisions of the Qur'an were most abundant and explicit in the area of personal relationships (Anderson, 1959: 15).

The tension inherent in the relations between Shari'a and practice has acquired a new dimension with the rise of Muslim nation-states in the present century. The enactment of modernist legislations by the governments of these states has considerably reduced the legal scope of the Shari'a. In almost every branch of law, western-inspired legal codes have replaced traditional Islamic law. Its only surviving branches are those of family law, inheritance and endowments. Even here the Shari'a was not retained intact. Rather, it was reformed and grafted onto a modern legal system through a process of codification.[2] An indirect repercussion of all these changes has been that family law has become the last bastion of the Shari'a. Today, the debate over family law is a sore spot in Muslim consciousness, revealing something of the on-going struggle between the forces of traditionalism and modernism in the Muslim world (cf. Hijab, 1988). For Muslim traditionalists, the Shari'a, now reduced to family law, is a sacred law upon which the most important social institution, the family, is founded. For secular modernists, the Shari'a as it stands is incompatible with modern life. They argue that Islam foresees and allows changes in family structure and relations, and that laws regulating them are not immutable. For feminists, the Shari'a is overtly discriminatory and unjust.

It is not my intention here to enter this debate, which I believe overlooks one major issue: family law as applied in today's Muslim countries is not the same as the Shari'a, although it is derived from it. Both codification and the concept of a unified legal system, with the state as an enforcing authority, are alien to the Shari'a.[3] The principal question that I am concerned with is the nature of the relations between the concept of marriage in the Shari'a and its legal and social constructions. In other words, how and to what extent is this last bastion of Islamic ideals of social relations relevant to contemporary Muslim societies? How do men and women relate to it, use it and abuse it for their personal interests in the course of a marital dispute? I believe that it is essential to address these questions, which touch upon a more immediate aspect of the tension between the ideal of the Shari'a and its practice, created by its grafting onto a modern legal system. Through a detailed analysis of two court cases from Iran and Morocco, I shall explore the relationship between the Shari'a and the modern legal system on the one hand, and social practices on the other. In both countries, family law has been codified and is implemented by a modern legal apparatus. Iran, the only Muslim country in which Shi'ism is the state religion, follows the *ithna 'ashari* (Twelver) rite to which the majority of the Shi'a belong.[4] Morocco adheres to the Maliki rite, one of the four schools of mainstream Sunni Islam.[5] The legal codes in both countries are translations and simplifications of the Shi'ite and Malikite rites respectively. Iranian family law, codified between 1928 and 1935, was substantially reformed in the Family Protection Law of 1967 under the Shah. These reforms were partially abandoned after the creation of the Islamic Republic in 1979.[6] In contrast, Moroccan family law has remained more or less unchanged since its codification in 1957.[7]

Shari'a Versus Legal Validity: An Iranian Case

Disputes in which the Shari'a notion of marriage is contested by the legal system arise from the co-existence of two equally valid kinds of marriage contract: a legal contract whose validity is established only through registration; and a Shari'a contract whose validity rests upon conformity with Shari'a provisions. The types of tension and conflict stemming from this duality vary with the legal machinery and the social context. In Iran, tension manifests itself in disputes involving *mut'a* (temporary) marriages, which are correct according to the Shari'a, but have been ignored by the modern legal system. In some cases they also lack social validity. The issues and processes involved can best be explored through analysis of an actual case which appeared in a Tehran court in 1986.

The dispute is initiated by Pari, an articulate woman who comes from a family of modest means. Pari, born in 1957, is a high school teacher who is also studying for a Master's degree in management at the Open University in Tehran. She was a divorcée (non-virgin) at the time she contracted her temporary union. Mehran, her temporary husband, is five years her junior and without any previous marital history. He comes from a prosperous merchant family, left high school at the age of fifteen and has since then worked with his father who is a trader in the bazaar. The petition is written by Pari herself. Her style is emotive and rhetorical, and in the translation, I have attempted to retain her wording if not the style:

> Two years ago I contracted a temporary marriage ('aqd monqata') with Mehran for a period of five years with defined conditions. Our agreement was that, in the event that I bore a child, firstly, he would make me his permanent wife, and secondly, he would pay our expenses. He swore several times that he would not break his promise. Now that I have given birth to a child through caesarian, involving great expense, he not only refuses to do the permanent contract ('aqd da'em), but also declines to pay the hospital costs. This has brought a great deal of shame and degradation for me among my family, relatives and acquaintances, as what I had told them (that my marriage was a proper one) proved to be untrue. Hence, with a bed-ridden mother and a meagre salary as a teacher, I am now condemned to a life full of hardship, misery and shame.

In support of her claim, she provides the certificates of her daughter's birth and her temporary marriage, hospital bills and a bank statement attesting to her indebtedness. During the first session, held five months after her petition, Pari elaborates on what she declared in her petition and repeats her demand for her union to be changed to a permanent one. Mehran, her temporary husband, states that he is prepared to pay for child support but will not, under any circumstances, agree to a permanent marriage. Their marriage was a temporary one, they never established a conjugal home together and he still lives with his parents. At this point, Pari bursts into tears, saying that the child support is not the main issue, it is because of her *aberu* (reputation) that she wants him to fulfil his promise and contract a proper marriage. But Mehran remains adamant and she retaliates by demanding 25,000 tomans for the hospital expenses and past maintenance of the child. The session ends with no definite conclusion. The judge attempts reconciliation, advises them to think the matter over and reach a mutually accepted position. The court fixes another date to hear the case.

To understand this case and the reasons for Pari's petition, we need to examine further the Shari'a notion of temporary marriage and its adaptation by the modern legal system in Iran. Only Shi'a Islam recognises a temporary marriage as valid.[8] Although this type of marriage existed at the time of the Prophet, it was banned by the second Caliph, and was later abandoned by other schools of Muslim law apart from the Twelvers. In Islamic jurisprudence (*fiqh*) this type of marriage is referred to as 'marriage of pleasure': *mut'a* in Arabic denotes pleasure; while in Iran it is known as *sigheh*. It is a marriage contract with a defined duration which can be from some minutes to ninety-nine years. It legitimates the sexual union as well as the children born into it.[9]

In discussing its legal structure, Shi'a jurists employ the analogy of rent as opposed to the analogy of sale which they use for permanent marriage. Through this contract a man acquires exclusive access to a woman's sexual faculties for a specified period in exchange for a clear and definite payment of *mahr* (dower) (Haeri, 1989: 51–4). Although children born into the marriage are legitimate, procreation is not the aim; it is strongly discouraged, if not explicitly prohibited.

A *mut'a* contract differs from a regular marriage in two major aspects: the rules related to its validity, and the sphere of rights and duties which it establishes between the couple. For a *mut'a* contract to be valid, its duration and the amount of *mahr* must be specified in definite terms. Any ambiguity in these areas could render the contract void.[10] A temporary wife, unlike a permanent one, has no claim to maintenance or sexual intercourse unless these are stipulated at the time of the contract. Even in the event of pregnancy, she is not entitled to *nafaqat al-haml* (maintenance of pregnancy), to which even a divorced woman is entitled. On the other hand, the husband has narrower control over her and she has wider autonomy: she does not require his permission to leave the house or to take up a job, provided that these actions do not interfere with his right to *istimta'* (sexual enjoyment).

There is no divorce in *mut'a*: the contract expires with the lapse of its duration. To continue the relationship, a new contract must be made. The contract can also be terminated by *bazl muddat*, which can be translated as 'making the gift of the remaining time'. It can be done only by the man. A woman does not have this option, but she can induce his consent through offering him compensations. Consistent with the logic of rent, a man can contract as many *mut'a* marriages as he wishes (more precisely, can afford), but a woman only one at a time. At the end of it she is required to keep an *'idda* (waiting period) for two months prior to contracting a new one.

The Iranian Civil Code recognises *mut'a* as a legally valid marriage and has retained its Shi'a conceptions and rules. In total, the Code devotes six articles to *mut'a*. Two articles (1075 and 1076) deal with the duration, and the rest with the *mahr* payment, mirroring the importance which is attached to these two elements of the *mut'a* union in the Shi'a rite. Apart from these few articles, the Civil Code remains silent on the formalities and legal aspects of this type of marriage. This silence is echoed in subsequent legislations. There is no reference to *mut'a* in the

Marriage Law of 1931, which confers legal validity only on registered marriages. Likewise, the Family Protection Act of 1967, by both omission and commission, excludes disputes involving *mut'a* from being adjudicated on the basis that they were not registered, and were thus devoid of legal validity, while registration was made impossible by the procedural rules set by the same act. Thus, prior to September 1979, i.e. the Islamic Revolution, although the Shari'a validity of *mut'a* marriage was not directly challenged, its legal validity was seriously curtailed. The aim was to discourage and even ban this type of marriage without offending the clergy and challenging the Shari'a directly. The end-result was that *mut'a* became a mutilated form of marriage with no legal consequences.

This situation changed after the 1979 Revolution when the Family Protection Act was dismantled and its courts were replaced by Special Civil Courts. The new courts, presided over by Islamic judges, see their main function as the administration of Shari'a rules, including conferring legal validity on *mut'a*. However, as the procedural rules for registering marriages have remained intact, a *mut'a* marriage still cannot be registered. The way out of this impasse is also foreseen: these marriages can acquire legal status and be registered if the new courts issue an order authorising their registration. The procedure is simple if the two parties are already in agreement and willing to make their union legal; otherwise the existence of a permanent marriage must be proven to the court.

Despite this new legal orientation, *mut'a* has remained a socially defective union: its transient nature violates the social construction of marriage. It is seen as a temporary union whose objective is gratification of sexual needs, and which rarely results in the establishment of a marital home. A *mut'a* wife is referred to as *sigheh*, a term which has derogatory implications. This is why Pari came to the court: to transform her temporary union to a permanent one which enjoys both social and legal validity. But her partner was unwilling to co-operate and she had no justification for her demand to register her union as a permanent one. However, during the second court session, Pari appears to have found a Shari'a argument for her demand and presents her case in a very different light. These are her words:

> The intention (*niyyat*) in our marriage was for a permanent contract. We made the temporary contract out of necessity (*zarurat*). At the time we could not register our marriage due to the fact that Mehran did not have his identity card: he was evading military service.[11] Our real marriage was permanent, and took place eight months prior to arranging for the temporary contract. I myself recited the marriage formula (*sigheh 'aqd*) from the Imam's book

(Ayatollah Khomeini's treatise, 1987), and Mehran accepted it. I can bring witnesses if necessary. It is not a question of money (referring to her demand for childbirth expenses); it is my reputation which is at stake. To be on the safe side I even repeated the marriage formula after we went to a mullah to draw up our temporary contract. This was done only because of necessity, since without it we risked harassment from the *komiteh* (revolutionary organisation responsible for observance of morals).

At this stage, the judge asks the defendant, Mehran, whether he admits her claim that they had recited the formula. He admits that eight months prior to arranging for the *mut'a* contract, she recited a formula from the Imam's treatise, but stresses that it was only to make them *mahram* (lawful) to one another, and there was no reference to duration.[12] He repeats his position that he is not willing to make the marriage a permanent one, and declares that he has decided to terminate the union. The judge once again attempts reconciliation. But Mehran remains adamant and only agrees to pay for the maintenance of the child according to his means. The judge gives them another chance to settle the matter peacefully, and advises them to put the future of the child ahead of their own individual interests. The court clerk sets another date for them to appear, and under the instruction of the judge summarises the proceedings of this session as follows:

> The woman's claim is for a permanent marriage (*zawjiyyat da'em*). The man's claim is for a temporary marriage (*zawjiyyat muvaqat*), but the man appears doubtful about this. Since the presumption (*asl*) in marriage is for permanency, it is the man who must provide evidence to its contrary.

Mehran's admission of Pari's claim as regards the recitation of a prior marriage formula reversed their roles in the dispute. It freed her from providing any further proof, as his admission proved her claim. He was now required to prove that the formula recited was for a temporary marriage.[13]

To understand Pari's new assertion, it is necessary to look at the formalities involved in contracting a marriage in Islam. In Islamic law, marriage is a civil contract and, in principle, it requires no religious ceremony. It is formed through offer and acceptance in the presence of two witnesses. Offer is made by the woman or her legal guardian and acceptance by the man. In Shi'a law the procedure is much simpler, there is no need for witnesses and a woman (provided she is a non-virgin, i.e. has already consummated a union) can contract her own marriage. This is done through the recitation of the marriage formula known as *sigheh 'aqd*, preferably in Arabic, though it can be done also in Persian. The formula is found in every Shi'a treatise. In Ayatollah Khomeini's (1987: 355–6), the one used by Pari, the whole procedure is explained in a number of legal points.[14] There are two formulae: one for permanent marriage and the other for temporary marriage. The only difference between them is that the phrase *fi al-mudat al-ma'lum* (for a definite period) is added in case of a temporary marriage. The absence of this phrase in the formula results in creating a permanent marriage bond.

During the last session, held a week later, Pari shows a greater awareness of these precepts. Her temporary husband's unfamiliarity with the Shari'a subtleties, on the other hand, results in his testifying to his detriment:

> It is so obvious that it was not a proper marriage: there was no wedding, no registration, no trousseau, no marital home, even my family did not know about it. What other proof do you want? Do you call this a marriage? It was a *sigheh* for five years.

The session ends in a bitter quarrel between the couple. The court renders its judgement after a week, accepting Pari's claim and recognising the union as a permanent marriage. The judgement also authorises the registration of the union and requires the husband to pay child maintenance and hospital expenses due for the delivery.

In reaching the judgement, the judge drew upon three Shari'a principles: the permanency of marriage, the intention (*niyyat*) and the necessity (*zarurat*). The first principle holds that a marriage is permanent unless its duration is clearly specified. This principle, peculiar to Shi'a law, applies to cases in which there is doubt over the question of duration in a marriage contract, i.e. the duration is either not specified or not clear. As regards the validity of such marriages, the Shi'a jurists are divided. The dominant opinion, to which Ayatollah Khomeini adheres, considers such a marriage correct but permanent. The other opinion considers such a marriage void, since it is defective in one of its structural elements, namely that of definiteness of duration (Muhaqqeq-Damad, 1986: 216). The court acted in accord with the dominant opinion. The second and the third principles are interrelated. Intent is an important criterion in evaluating the outcome of an act. Sometimes necessity compels an individual to act contrary to the real intent. In this case, the court accepted Pari's assertion that the real intent was for a permanent marriage, but that a temporary contract was the only possibility in the circumstances.

This case illustrates the existence of two overlapping areas of ambiguity: between the Shari'a and the modern legal system on the one hand, and between Shari'a and social reality on the other. All these are manifest in the institution of temporary marriage in Iran. In today's Iran, for a marriage to be valid it must meet certain conditions. On the legal

level, this means registration. By requiring the registration of all marriages, the 1931 Iranian Marriage Law created the notion of *rasmi*
(legal) marriage.[15] It also conferred the status of *shar'i* marriage on
unregistered ones: they are correct according to the Shari'a but without
any legal consequences. To discourage these unions, the same law prescribed the penalty for the parties involved as one to six months of
imprisonment, thus adding social stigma to legal ineffectiveness.[16]

In time, at least in urban Iran, legal validity has become an important
component of the social construction of marriage. This process has been
eased by the way in which *mahr* is practised in urban Iran. *Mahr* (or
sadaq) is an integral part of every Muslim marriage contract. It consists
of a sum of money or valuables that the husband pays or pledges to pay
to the bride upon marriage.[17] Marriage in Iran involves a substantial
mahr, an amount which is often beyond the immediate financial capacity of the groom. No transaction takes place at the time of marriage, but
the amount is written in the marriage contract and the bridegroom
pledges to pay it upon the bride's request. The stipulation of *mahr* in a
registered marriage, which becomes a legal document, grants a legal
dimension to request. *Mahr* plays an important role in the dynamics of
marital relations, giving a woman a high degree of security and a say in
deterring or inducing a divorce. At the same time, a substantial amount
of *mahr*, which is legally enforceable, reflects not only the social importance of the union, but also that of the bride and the two families
involved (cf. Mir-Hosseini, 1992).

Mut'a is resorted to by men and women for a variety of reasons and
considerations. If their motives converge in the course of the union, then
either the union ends by the lapse of its time or it is transformed into a
permanent one by obtaining court permission to register it. A dispute
arises when the partners' motives fail to converge. Court cases involving this type of dispute suggest that there is a wide disparity between
men's and women's perceptions and objectives in entering this type of
union. In all cases the men involved did not consider the union worthy
of a proper marriage, mainly because of the personal and social attributes of their partners; while the women agreed to a *mut'a* union in the
hope that in due time they could transform it into a permanent marriage.
The right time is usually perceived as coinciding with the birth of a
child. This explains why Pari was so shamed by her marriage and why
her reputation was tarnished. But to achieve her goal, she needed a
Shari'a justification.

She found this justification in another area of ambiguity, namely that
involving Shari'a concepts and their popular construction. Terms such
as *sigheh* and *sigheh 'aqd* have different connotations in colloquial Per-

sian from their Shari'a legal usage. *Sigheh* can have several meanings and functions according to the context in which it is employed. It literally means the special formula employed at the time any contract is made. Colloquially, *sigheh* means temporary marriage or a temporary wife. It is used both as a verb and a noun. In Shari'a legal terminology, *sigheh 'aqd* denotes the recitation of a certain formula which results in the creation of a contract. Colloquially, *sigheh 'aqd* is limited to the contract of permanent marriage, which is almost always done by religious functionaries in a marriage registry office. A temporary marriage, which is done by the couple themselves or by a mullah, is known as *sigheh*. The court's definition of these terms naturally reflects that of the Shari'a which is obscure and unknown to many.

It was through manipulation of these ambiguities that Pari was able to win her case. It is evident that when she contracted her marriage by reciting the formula, her understanding was the same as that of her husband-to-be, and that shared by the populace. Otherwise she would have used it in support of her claim in the first court session. All the facts about their union attest to its temporary nature: they all deviated from the norms and rules constituting a permanent marriage. He was a bachelor and she was both older than him and a divorced woman, two major disadvantages which rule out the eligibility of a woman from her social class. In addition, it was never intended to establish a marital home, an important element of a proper marriage. He continued to live with his parents and kept the union secret, whereas marriage involves publicity, celebration and announcement.

Legal versus Social Validity: A Moroccan Case

In Morocco, the tension created by the existence of parallel notions of marriage validity are manifested in a type of dispute involving unregistered marriages known as *fatiha*, so named because they are solemnised by recitation of the first *sura* (chapter) of the Qur'an. Theoretically, this marriage meets all the formal requirements of Maliki law. The woman is given away by her father, or in his absence by his nearest male relative, the amount of *sadaq* and the manner of its payment are defined, and the relevant marriage formula is uttered. Yet a *fatiha* marriage does not enjoy legal recognition, as it does not fulfil the modern criteria of a valid marriage, set by Article 5 of the Moroccan Code of Personal Status (the *moudawana*).

Unlike the Shi'a, Maliki law requires a marriage to take place in the presence of two reliable witnesses, known as *'adul* (the just). This requirement, in time, has produced a class of professional witnesses who now function under the supervision of the Ministry of Justice, located in the Court of Notaries.[18] They are specialists in the Shari'a, they act as witnesses and also draw up marriage, divorce and other contracts. A marriage is recognised as valid only when it is conducted by the *'adul*, who not only ensure the observance of Shari'a rules, but give it legality by drawing up the contract, referred to as *'aqd*.

Yet the possibility of rendering a *fatiha* marriage valid is not ruled out, as the Code includes a procedure for its registration. Section 3 of Article 5 empowers the Court of Notaries and its judge to legalise unregistered unions. The procedure is simple if the two parties acknowledge the existence of marital relations; for then they need only produce twelve witnesses to support their claim. This is done in a document (*lafif*) drawn up by two notaries, which is, in effect, the written testimony of twelve witnesses (all male, or two females in place of any male). This *lafif* is known as *thubut al-zawjiyya* (proof of marriage), and is analogous to a marriage contract.

The need to register a *fatiha* marriage usually coincides with the birth of the first child, who in order to become legitimate must be entered in his/her father's Civil Status Booklet. As already mentioned, when there is agreement between the parties, the procedure is simple, which is the case for a large majority, registered without further ado in the Court of Notaries. The problem arises when one of the partners, always the man, disavows the union, and it thus becomes incumbent upon the other to prove the existence of a marital relationship. These cases appear in the Court of First Instance and all of them are initiated by women, usually after the birth of a child and thus involving claims of paternity. They stand very little chance of success. A large majority of them are dismissed by the court on the grounds of insufficient documentation, as they lack a marriage contract, and the court entertains only legally valid marriages. This creates a vicious circle for women, who need a court order to register their *fatiha* union and give a legitimate status to their children.

Fatiha marriages, although decreasing, are still practised, especially in rural areas and among the urban poor.[19] They are concluded for many different reasons. Sometimes the girl has not attained the minimum age of 15 required by the law; the marriage payment may not be ready; the man may not be in a position to register the marriage; or he may be avoiding commitment by evading the legal consequences of a registered union. Whatever the motive behind such a marriage, a woman's fate and that of her children depend on the good will of the man. The following case illustrates some of the processes involved in dispute cases of this kind, and why women at times have little choice but to concede to them.

Fatima, now 38 years old, comes from a poor background. She was born in a small village near Sale, where her father, a small peasant, died when she was 13 years old. Shortly afterwards, to reduce the family's burden, she was given as a maid to a family in Sale. When she was 18, she entered her first *fatiha* marriage. The union had been arranged by her master and the father of the groom. The ceremony took place in her master's house and the *'aqd* was deferred until the accumulation of the *sadaq*.[20] Later, the father of her *fatiha* husband asked for her to move in with them, promising that he would arrange for the *'aqd* in a short time. She lived with his family for two years, but the promised *'aqd* was gradually forgotten. She became pregnant, but after a series of bitter fights with her mother-in-law, Fatima left her husband and returned to her mother's house, hoping that her in-laws would soon come after her. But no one came to take her back, and she gave birth to a son in her mother's home in 1972.

Meanwhile the husband contracted a proper marriage with another woman, with an *'aqd* and a paid *sadaq*. He no longer wished to continue his union with Fatima, denied paternity and refused to register the child. Fatima threatened to take him to court, but after the intervention of the family Fatima had lived with and worked for prior to her *fatiha* union, he gave in and agreed to register the child. The 'proof of marriage document' was made in October 1974, in which it was noted that they had been living as husband and wife for two years and a child was born into the union. The following day, they registered a *khul'a* (divorce), ostensibly requested by Fatima, in which she renounced all her rights.[21] In this way she realised her goal and gained legitimate status for her son. The divorce was part of their agreement for giving legality to the union.

Four years later, she entered another *fatiha* union, again without a contract. At the time she was living with her sister, and her new husband was her sister's husband's brother, who had just finished his baccalauréat and was joining the army. He promised marriage but said that he could not do the *'aqd*, since he was a trainee army officer and was not allowed to marry during the first four years of his service.[22] The *fatiha* was recited in a small ceremony. He rented a room for her in Sale and came to visit her while on leave. After a year she moved with him to his rooms in the military base in another town. The union lasted for four years, and she became pregnant in the final year. He wanted her to abort, but Fatima said 'I fear God and will never commit such a crime'. She gave birth to another son in 1982. In the same year, he contracted a proper marriage with a woman from Marrakech, where he was temporarily stationed, and asked Fatima to leave. At first she refused, but finally she gave in after he promised her that he would rent a room for her in Sale and would register the child. But he has never fulfilled his promises, mainly (according to Fatima) because of his legal wife's objection. In 1989 the boy was seven years old and without a legal identity, which was causing problems in registering him at school. So far all her attempts to resolve the problem, i.e. her brother-in-law's intervention and her threats to go to the court, have failed. She filed a petition in the Court of First Instance in Sale, in which she requested the registration of her child. She was asked to provide a marriage contract to prove that her child was born into a legal marriage; obviously she failed and then had to abandon the case. Having made more inquiries and having talked to the judge, she realised that she had no case. She needs to prove the prior existence of her marital union in order to demand registration of her son in his father's name. She has no other recourse than registering the child under her paternal name. To do so she first needs to apply for a separate booklet for herself, which is a lengthy process (woman normally do not possess one, being registered in their father's and later in their husband's name).[23]

> An element in Fatima's case which I came to learn of later, and which might explain her choices, is that she was not a virgin at the time of her first union. She was pregnant when she was taken as a maid by the family in Sale, who later became her patrons. They arranged for the adoption of her child by a barren woman, as well as for her *fatiha* marriage. She has not traced her first child and never refers to the incident while talking of her misfortunes.

Fatima's case shows something of the dynamics of these unions and the reasons behind women's acceptance of them.[24] A *fatiha* wife in Morocco is in the same precarious situation as a temporary wife in Iran, at the mercy of her partner's good will. To gain some degree of security in these precarious unions, a common strategy adopted by women is to get pregnant, a ruse resorted to by almost every woman who came to the court. In their petitions, they justify and argue their case on the basis of the welfare of the child. But it is difficult to avoid the impression that they purposely manipulate this fact to enhance their chances of winning the case. A child gives a woman the status of a mother; therefore, it gives a procreative dimension to the union, bringing her closer to the position of a proper wife. It can be an effective way of manipulating a reluctant man into a more committed union. If this stratagem works and the union is then transformed into a legal one, the case never reaches the courts. But if the man is not persuaded, the legal recourse otherwise available to women in these unions is very limited, as illustrated by the above case.

Concluding Remarks

Both *fatiha* and *mut'a* marriages, although theoretically correct from the Shari'a perspective, are defective. They satisfy only one of the two major criteria for a socially proper marriage. In social practice there are two phases to a marriage, both intertwined with the Shari'a rules. The first phase is known, both in Iran and in Morocco, as *'aqd* (contract); it consists of a small ceremony during which the marriage contract is drawn up. The second phase is the wedding celebration, known as *'urs* in Morocco and as *'arusi* in Iran. It marks the social recognition of the contract made during the first stage, allowing the consummation of the marriage and the establishment of a marital home. There is usually a time lapse between these two stages. In Morocco, *'urs* is delayed until all the conditions specified in the marriage contract regarding the payment of the *sadaq* are fulfilled; and in Iran *'arusi* is delayed until the bride's trousseau is ready.

The traditional distinction between these two stages, especially the time interval, was clear-cut until recently. Now they seem to be in the process of amalgamation, especially among the middle classes. The *'aqd* is often conducted in the afternoon, in the presence of the notaries; and the wedding celebration takes place in the evening. This is more evident in Iran, where the *'aqd* is acquiring more importance at the expense of the *'arusi* stage, whereas in Morocco, the *'urs* stage is still associated with the public announcement of the union, giving it social legitimacy. In a socially complete marriage the *'aqd* phase always precedes the consummation. It renders the couple *halal* (licit) to each other, but does not establish the conjugal unit. After *'aqd* a girl is expected to save her virginity until the wedding ceremony which marks her transfer to her new home. I know of a case in Morocco where the *'aqd* phase was done four years ago without any accompanying celebration, because of financial problems. The couple live together in the same house, again through necessity, but she is still a virgin and is determined to keep her virginity until the *'urs*. She told me: 'I am not a street girl who sleeps with a man without a real marriage.' For her, the *'urs* celebration is the true marker of a marriage, not the contract which is only the legal marker.

By way of analysis of two types of disputes from Iran and Morocco involving the validity of marriage, I have attempted to examine the areas of tension between the Shari'a, the modern legal system and practice. The grafting of the Shari'a onto a modern legal system has given rise to the existence of two parallel but distinct notions of legitimacy. The resultant ambiguity is at times successfully manipulated by the petitioners in order to negotiate the terms of their relationships, using the court as an arena. The selectivity that both men and women exercise in conforming to the Shari'a suggests that the main motivation stems not from a desire to conform to religious precepts, but rather from a need to circumvent the law in order to achieve a different purpose. If this is so, it places the Shari'a on the same level as other systems of law and challenges general assumptions regarding the popular belief in its sanctity. It is significant that women are more likely to suffer the adverse consequences of the blurred boundaries between Shari'a and legal legitimacy, reflected in the fact that they constitute the bulk of court customers. This is not surprising as, whenever there is tension in a system, its repercussions are most severe on the weakest, here the women of lower classes. These women in their relationships have to grapple with disadvantages that stem from the dynamics of class and male domination. In taking their cases to court, their main aim is to gain legal identity and status for their children, an indication that the legal definition of marriage is gradually but steadily gaining ground at the expense of the other two. A valid marriage according to the Shari'a or social practice needs legal registration in order to become a fully effective marriage. This imparts something of the importance of legal rules in defining and regulating relations between the sexes, as well as of their capacity to protect the weak.

Notes

1. I conducted fieldwork in Iran between 1985 and 1988; and in Morocco between 1988 and 1989. The latter was funded by grants from the British Academy, the Nuffield Foundation, the Wenner-Gren Foundation for Anthropological Research and the Institute for Intercultural Studies. I would like to thank these bodies for their generous help which made it possible to add a comparative dimension to my research. I am grateful to Richard Tapper for his comments on an earlier draft of this paper.

2. For an account of reforms and the application of Shari'a-based law see Anderson, 1976; for the present scope of family law in the Muslim world, see Mahmood, 1972 and Nasir, 1986; and for women's status in Muslim family law see Esposito, 1982.

3. These issues are dealt with in Mir-Hosseini, 1993.

4. The Shi'a believe in a line of divine-elected successors to the Prophet, starting with Ali, his cousin and son-in-law; they are in turn divided into sub-sects of which the *ithna 'ashari* (Twelver) branch is the majority. The Shi'a legal school owes its development to the fifth and sixth Shi'a Imams, who were among the leading jurists of their time. Its orthodoxy is recognised, and it is often referred to as the fifth school of Islamic law (Coulson, 1964: 57; Schacht 1964: 224).

5. The Maliki School takes its name from Malik ibn Anas, a prominent Medina jurist of the eight century. It has always been the dominant school among North African Muslims. See Borrmans, 1977 and Ruxton, 1916. The other three Sunni schools of jurisprudence are Hanafi (founded by Abu Hanifa in the eight century), Hanbali (founded by Ahmad ibn Hanbal in the ninth century), and Shafi'i (founded by Muhammad ibn Idris al-Shafi'i, also in the ninth century).

6. For the Family Protection Law, see Hinchcliffe, 1968; and for post-revolutionary changes, see Mir-Hosseini, 1986 and 1992.

7. For the codification and reform of family law in Morocco, see Borrmans, 1977 and Anderson, 1958; for an appraisal of attempts at reform see My Rachid 1985a and 1985b.

8. For an exhaustive study of the theory and practice of this type of marriage in Iran, see Haeri, 1989.

9. This is seen by the jurists as the main purpose of this marriage. The separation between the sexual and procreative sides is very distinct. Haeri (1989) brings this to light in her book. However I take issue with her contention that woman play an active role here and that *mut'a* becomes an arena for the expression of their sexuality. On the basis of my data, I suggest that *mut'a* is what a woman has to accept because of her disabilities, for example her age, not being virgin, and her lower social class. Women always strive to change the terms of their contract to attain the esteemed and socially accepted status of a permanent wife.

10. Article 1095 of the Iranian Civil Code.

11. This was at the height of the Iran–Iraq war when young men were evading their military service. One common trick was to disappear from the records through declaring their identity cards lost or faulty and demanding a new one with the aim of changing certain details including their date of birth, which could exempt them from the service. Thus, these men could not contract a permanent marriage as their identity cards were required for its registration.

12. This is known as *sigheh mahramiat*, which renders the parties lawful (*mahram*) and allows social intercourse between them and their immediate relatives. Haeri (1989: 89) calls it a non-sexual *sigheh* and sees it as a means of circumventing the rigid rules of sexual segregation imposed by the Shari'a. Its purpose is not the same as a *mut'a* marriage, although it can lead to a sexual relation if the woman gives her free consent. Evidently, Mehran's understanding of it was to permit sexual relations.

13. In cases like this in which the evidence is lacking, the most important thing is to determine which of the two parties carries the burden of the proof. The positions of claimant and defendant can be interchangeable. A defendant can become a claimant if he/she admits to a claim made (Russell and Al Suhrawardy, 1906: 89–103).

14. *Masaleh* (point) 2368 gives the instruction for contracting a permanent marriage, *masaleh* 2369 for a temporary marriage and *masaleh* 2370 to 2372 set exact conditions for the validity of these formulas. These are: (1) the formula must be read in correct Arabic; if the couple are unable to do so they can recite the formula in Persian; there is no need for a proxy. (2) The couple must have the intention. (3) The contracting parties must be sane and preferably have reached puberty. (4) The woman needs her legal guardian's permission if she is a virgin. (5) Both parties must give their free consent (Khomeini, 1987: 356–7).

15. Article 2 of Marriage Law of 1931.

16. Article 1 of Marriage Law of 1931.

17. Despite its uniform legal structure in all schools of Islamic law, the prac-

tice of *mahr* varies considerably in Muslim countries. For accounts of Iranian practices, see Mir-Hosseini, 1992; and for Moroccan practices, see Geertz, 1979 and Maher, 1974.

18. On the emergence of this class of professional witnesses, see Coulson, 1964: 146.

19. Baron (1953: 424–5) in her study of marriage and divorce in Casablanca, reports that around 52 per cent of all marriages registered in 1953 were of the *fatiha* type, where the marriage was later registered. This percentage rises to some 80 per cent among the inhabitants of shanty towns, i.e. recent rural migrants. Ten per cent and 11 per cent of all marriages registered in Rabat in 1987 and 1988 respectively were of this kind.

20. In Morocco, unlike Iran, a large portion of the *sadaq* must be paid prior to marriage. This money is used by the woman's father to provide her dowry. See Geertz, 1979 and Mir-Hosseini, 1992.

21. *Khul'a* is a type of divorce initiated by the woman in which she gives a compensation to her husband in return for his consent. See Mir-Hosseini, 1991.

22. This is not true but women choose to believe it; it is one of the excuses that men give in order to avoid commitment.

23. For the formalities, see Sebti Lahrichi, 1985:70.

24. Here I am referring only to those *fatiha* marriages in which the man later can deny the union and evade legal consequences. Of course *fatiha* marriages in rural settings have totally different dynamics; they enjoy social validity and registration is not the determining factor in safeguarding women's status.

References

Afshar, H., ed., 1992, *Women in the Middle East: Perceptions and Struggles*, London: Macmillan.

Anderson, J. N. D., 1958, 'Reform of Family Law in Morocco', *Journal of African Law*, vol. II, no. 3.

Anderson, J. N. D., 1959, *Islamic Law in the Modern World*, New York: New York University Press.

Anderson, J. N. D., 1976, *Law Reform in the Muslim World*, London: The Athlone Press.

Baron, A. M., 1953, 'Mariage et divorce " Casablanca', *Hesperis*, vol.XL, nos. 3–4.

Borrmans, M., 1977, *Statut personnel et famille au Maghreb de 1940 à nos jours*, Paris: Mouton.

Coulson, N. J., 1964, *A History of Islamic Law*, Edinburgh: Edinburgh University Press.

Esposito, J. L., 1982, *Women in Muslim Family Law*, Syracuse: Syracuse University Press.

Geertz, H., 1979, 'The Meaning of Family Ties', in C. Geertz et. al., *Meaning and Order in Moroccan Society*, Cambridge: Cambridge University Press.

Haeri, S., 1989, *The Law of Desire: Temporary Marriage in Iran*, London: I. B. Tauris.

Hijab, N., 1988, *Womanpower: The Arab Debate on Women at Work*, Cambridge: Cambridge University Press.

Hinchcliffe, D., 1968, 'The Iranian Family Protection Act', *International and Comparative Law Quarterly*, vol. 17.

Khomeini, R., 1366 (1987), *Resaleh-e Touzih al-Masa'el* (Treatise on Resolution of (Legal) Issues), Markaz-e Nashr-e Farhangi-ye Reja', Tehran.

Maher, V., 1974, *Women and Property in Morocco*, Cambridge: Cambridge University Press.

Mahmood, T., 1972, *Family Law Reforms in the Muslim World*, Bombay: N. M. Tripatl.

Mir-Hosseini, Z., 1986, 'Divorce in Islamic Law and Practice: The Case of Iran', *Cambridge Anthropology*, vol. 11, no. 1.

Mir-Hosseini, Z., 1991, 'Contrast Between Law and Practice for the Moroccan Family: Patriarchy and Matrifocality', *Journal of Society of Moroccan Studies*, no.1.

Mir-Hosseini, Z., 1992, 'Women, Marriage and the Law in Post-Revolutionary Iran', in H. Afshar, ed., *Women in the Middle East: Perceptions and Struggles*, London: Macmillan.

Mir-Hosseini, Z., 1993, *Marriage on Trial: A Comparative Study of Islamic Family Law in Iran and Morocco*, London: I.B. Tauris.

Muhaqqeq-Damad, S. M., 1365 (1986), *Barrasi-ye Feqhi-ye Hoquq-e Khanevadeh* (Investigation of the Jurisprudence of Family Law), Nashr-e 'Olum-e Eslami, Tehran.

My Rachid, A., 1985a, 'Le project de code de statut personnel', *Le parlement et la pratique legislative au Maroc*, Casablanca.

My Rachid, A., 1985b, *La condition de la femme au Maroc*, Rabat: Edition de la Faculté des Sciences Juridiques, Economiques et Sociales de Rabat.

Nasir, J. J., 1986, *The Islamic Law of Personal Status*, London: Graham & Trotman.

Russell, A. D. and M. Al-Suhrawardy, 1906, *First Steps in Muslim Jurisprudence, Consisting of Excerpts from Barkat al-Sa'ad of Ibn Abu-Zayd*, London: Luzac & Co.

Ruxton, F. H., 1916, *Maliki Law: A Summary from French Translations of Mukhtasar Sidi Khalil*, London: Luzac & Co.

Schacht, J., 1964, *An Introduction to Islamic Law*, Oxford: Clarendon Press.

Sebti Lahrichi, F., 1985, *Vivre musulmane au Maroc*, Paris: Librairie Generale de Droit et Jurisprudence.

3

Islam and Gender: The Nigerian Case

Gloria Thomas-Emeagwali

Introduction

This chapter is divided into two main sections. The first focuses on some theological and other variables associated with Islam in Nigeria and briefly examines the historical context of Islamisation within Nigerian society. The second section discusses specific social and economic dimensions of Islam with respect to gender relations, and the manner in which traditional norms and Islamic injunctions have accommodated one another. This accommodation between religious belief and social reality has become particularly evident with the introduction of wide-ranging economic reforms as part of the implementation of structural adjustment programmes (SAP) inspired by the International Monetary Fund (IMF) and the International Bank for Reconstruction and Development (World Bank).[1]

The impact of SAP, particularly in terms of changes in the life-style and day-to-day activities of Muslim women in Nigeria, has recently been the focus of two surveys carried out in Zaria and Ilorin in the north of the country.[2] Some of the survey findings will be incorporated into the analysis in order to underline the type of choices that Muslim women in Nigeria are facing.

Theological and other Variables

It is estimated that the proportion of the Muslim population in Nigeria is 42 per cent. Given the fact that current demographic estimates for the population as a whole range from 100 to 120 million, and pending more accurate demographic data from the recent census, this would indicate that there are some 50 million Muslims in the country.[3] There is, of course, a spatial dimension to be taken into account, with a great density of Muslims in the northern parts of the country, a medium spread in the central and western parts and a relatively sparse population in the eastern region. Northern states such as Kano, Sokoto, Katsina and Borno have higher densities of Muslims than eastern states such as Anambra, Imo and Abia, for example.

Nigerian Muslims, as is the case of Muslims elsewhere, believe in the supremacy of the Qu'ran and the necessity to be fully acquainted with its contents, preferably learning it by rote. Opposed to a polytheistic spectrum of deities, Islam is fundamentally monotheistic and firmly committed to the belief in a single omnipotent deity, Allah, whose messenger Mohammad is considered to be the last of the prophets. However, this belief is not necessarily shared by all Nigerian Muslims. In fact, between 1980 and 1985 there emerged in some of the urban and predominantly Muslim regions of Nigeria, a heretical sect collectively referred to as 'the Maitatsine' after its founder, Alhaji Mohammad Marwa Maitatsine, challenging this proposition and declaring that Mohammad was not the last of the prophets (cf. Clarke and Linden, 1984). Another issue of great significance to the Nigerian Muslim community is the belief in the wisdom and truth of the Hadiths, the sayings of the Prophet Mohammad, as well as the collective wisdom of the local community of Muslim scholars, the 'ulama. The obligations associated with the Islamic belief system and practice in the Nigerian case involve fasting from before dawn to sunset each day during Ramadan; annual pilgrimages to Mecca by those who are able to do so; observation of the five daily prayers; partial or total seclusion of women in the context of purdah; as well as zakat or almsgiving to the poor (cf. Hiskett, 1984; Trimingham, 1962).

Islam in Nigeria is believed to date back to the eleventh century, and is primarily related to the activities of African clerics who initiated the process of conversion in Kanem-Borno in the north-east of the country (cf. Clarke and Linden, 1984; Kani, 1985). They took up posts as advisers in some of the central Sudanic states, placing themselves in politically strategic positions, and thus helped to further the process of conversion. In the case of western Nigeria, the generally accepted date is the fourteenth century, though its spread appears to have been relatively limited. In fact, the major diffusion of Islam in this region took place after the mid-nineteenth century. Other developments related to the spread of Islam in Nigeria include the expansive commercial activities associated with the trans-Saharan trade routes over the centuries, such as those between Ghana, Mogador, Fez and Awdahast in the thirteenth century; Timbuctu to Mogador and Fez via Teghaza in the thirteenth, fourteenth, and fifteenth centuries; Timbuctu to Tunis and Tripoli via Agades, Ghat and Ghadames as well as Bornu to Tripoli via Bilma and Murzuk in the seventeenth and nineteenth centuries (cf. Levtzion, 1973). In short, Islam in Nigeria in particular, and West Africa in general, cannot be historically conceived outside the context of the extensive trans-Saharan trade which from its inception in circa 1000 B.C.E. facilitated extensive interaction within the West African region and between West and North Africa. In the era before Islam, such contacts evolved in the context of intra-regional and inter-regional specialisation and a network of caravan traders. With the emergence of Islam in Nigeria in the eleventh century there would have been identifiable innovations such as the use of Arabic as a lingua franca; an infrastructure of residential quarters and food centres for itinerant Muslim traders and their interpreters; a well-organised network of caravans; accounting and record-keeping procedures; and credit and brokerage facilities, all of which would help to consolidate and strengthen the significance of Islam in the region.

The *hajj* (the annual pilgrimage to Mecca) also helped to consolidate local ties amongst Muslims and to integrate Nigerian Muslims even further into the *umma* (community) of Islam, a process which continues into the contemporary era. In the 1970s, Nigeria had the second largest annual contingent to Mecca after Indonesia, though during the last decade the number of pilgrims has been declining drastically due to the overall economic recession and the subsequent debt crisis (cf. Clarke and Linden, 1984).

Several explanations have been given for the rapid and extensive spread of Islam in the West African region as a whole, among them the fact that most Muslim 'missionaries' were indigenous Africans; the relatively easy mode of conversion; Islamic accommodation of a largely polygynous indigenous marital system; and the perception of exemplary conduct in role models such as Usuman dan Fodio, Nana Asma'u, Ahmadu Bello and others (cf. Boyd, 1989; Isichei, 1977; Paden, 1986). In the contemporary era the rate of conversion to Islam has not apparently slowed down.

Implications for Gender Relations

In the following discussion, the implications of some of these theological principles for the treatment and condition of women as it relates to marriage, divorce, seclusion and inheritance will be examined. The analysis will simultaneously incorporate some insight into the effects of structural adjustment on women's lives in contemporary Nigeria.

Marriage

Islam has had specific implications for traditional marital relations and marriage patterns in Nigerian society. Pre-Islamic Nigerians were generally polygynous in the context of a regulated system of household production and reproduction (see WIN, 1985). Islam reduced the numerical option to four wives and introduced a few new rules to the marital game (cf. Ogunbiyi, 1969; Pittin, 1979). Since Qu'ranic injunctions call for equitable treatment of all wives, it became a social offence for husbands to be accused of discrimination. By contrast, in the pre-Islamic world-view and philosophy in Nigeria, discrimination between wives was sanctioned and even encouraged. A clear hierarchy of wives based on seniority and age was the norm, a pattern which was not unrelated to the division of labour in the household, whereby junior wives performed more menial duties (cf. Ajayi and Ikara, 1985; Falola, 1986). This is not to deny the fact that the pre-Islamic custom of a hierarchy based on the seniority of wives in polygynous marriages has persisted in some areas. However, this pattern is not generally socially sanctioned and is held to be counter to Islamic prescriptions favouring equality among wives. Moreover, women who are informed of their rights are, at least theoretically, in a position to negotiate a more favourable status for themselves.

In the Zaria survey referred to earlier, 90 per cent of the women had married under the age of 15, a trend which appears to be the norm in a number of Islamic communities in Nigeria (cf. Pittin, 1990). Variables such as social status and class origin are relevant in the overall appraisal of marital trends, and most of the respondents were lower middle class. Their class origin is to some extent reflected in their economic activities, which ranged from petty trade to farming, i.e. sectors where the impact of SAP has tended to be particularly unfavourable to women and their sources of livelihood. Attempts have been made to legislate against the practice of early marriage within the last decade, largely as a result of activist organisations such as Women In Nigeria and in some cases protest on the part of young girls against such marriages (WIN, 1985). It is doubtful, however, whether the on-going SAP and related state policies undermine the practice of early marriage given the real or imagined economic benefits this may hold for parents in terms of absolving them from the need to support their daughters. There is also increased 'feminization of poverty' whereby girls and women may find themselves increasingly dependent and impoverished in the context of subsidy removal on health, education and food items – a trend which also appears to encourage early marriage (see Thomas-Emeagwali, 1991).

However, the Ilorin survey suggests a possible countervailing force reflected in the growing caution on the part of males of marriageable age *vis-à-vis* the issue of starting a family given the economic crisis. Respondents in this survey pointed to a decline in the level of festivities accompanying marriage ceremonies. From the earlier practice whereby festivities spanned a seven-day period, there was now a noticeable reduction to five days and less. Moveover, there seems to be an overall decline in the number of marriages and even an upswing in the incidence of monogamy. There were more cases of simultaneous marriages of daughters and sons in order to reduce cost. One may also assume that economic conditions have been having a perceptible impact on the *mahr* (bride-price) which women are legally entitled to under Islam. However, the data with respect to reproductive behaviour and the size of family units were inconclusive, with evidence for the retention of large families in some cases, and reduced family size in others.

Divorce

Whilst Muslim males in Nigeria are not obliged to state the reasons for divorce, women are expected to do so, but only within the context of the following parameters: a women may sue for divorce should the husband fail to provide for the economic needs of the family, or decides to change his religion, or wrongly accuses her of adultery. If the husband proves to be impotent or, in the case of early marriage, she has become disillusioned with the marriage after attaining puberty, she is also entitled to file for divorce (cf. Schacht, 1957). In spite of this trend, it was noted that most of the respondents in the Zaria survey were in stable marriages of ten years or more, and there seemed to be an overall low divorce rate. By contrast, in the case of Ilorin, most of the women indicated an increase in the rate of divorce. This supports an earlier finding of Barkow (1971), which found that around 50 per cent of the Muslim women in the study were divorced. The Zaria trend notwithstanding – and further research is needed to explain these apparently contradictory findings – there generally seems to be a noticeable ease by which Muslim women in Nigeria move in and out of marriage. Equally important, divorce is generally not associated with social stigma as in pre-Islamic times, and divorced women can and are expected to remarry. Casual observation suggests that the Ilorin case cited is not unique in terms of the region as a whole.

Seclusion

The issue of female sexuality is generally associated with the question of male–female interaction and female seclusion. Purdah, identified as one of the major pillars of male patriarchy, exhibits three variations in the Nigerian case: complete seclusion, partial seclusion and voluntary 'seclusion of the heart' (cf. Abdullah-Olukoshi, 1990). In the latter case, seclusion is symbolic and not based on physical segregation. This situation appears to have evolved as a compromise sanctioning the employment of educated elite women in the civil service and other forms of public activities. Associated with the two other forms of seclusion is a degree of withdrawal from public view, which may be either partial or total – as in the case of the wives of traditional rulers and members of the *'ulama* who tend to serve as role models. As elsewhere in sex-segregated societies, in reality the process of seclusion is largely class-based. Thus, peasant or working-class males in particular can generally ill afford the luxury of non-working wives. A recent study focusing on Kaduna, Bauchi and Kano (with a large proportion of Muslims among their populations), showed that 65 per cent of women in these areas were active in farming and livestock rearing, marketing of grain, spinning, weaving, cooking of fast food as well as in general trade (WIN, 1985).

The growing force of the Tijaniyya brotherhood is important in this context for, unlike the Qadriyya, it does not consider seclusion to be imperative. The Tijaniyya, founded by Abu al-Abbas Ahmad al-Tijani in North Africa during the second half of the eighteenth century, found adherents in Nigeria following the activities of the Senegalese cleric Al Hajj Tall in the nineteenth century (cf. Isichei, 1977). It remains one of the most dominant of the Sufi orders in Nigeria, and may be contrasted with the Qadriyya brotherhood, which has its roots in twelfth century Baghdad where it was founded by Abdel Qadir al-Jilani. They differ from one another in terms of a number of basic issues. For example, unlike the Tijaniyya brotherhood, the Qadriyya is opposed to the appointment of women in positions of leadership and adheres overall to a stricter separation in its ascription of gender roles. The brotherhoods also diverge in terms of praying positions and in their attitudes towards mysticism. However, association with one or the other brotherhood and the concomitant attitudes towards seclusion are also influenced by other variables, such as proximity to urban centres, class origin and educational level.

The recent surveys in Zaria and Ilorin suggest some of the effects which economic conditions can be presumed to be having on the observation of moral imperatives dictated by the brotherhoods. Thus, there is a trend whereby women traditionally associated with purdah have been abandoning the custom. Some respondents pointed to the increasing participation of women in farming, with the effect that the differentiation between those adhering to purdah and those outside of it are becoming more blurred. In the words of one informant: 'Women come out of purdah and mix freely with men in the market because they are looking for money.' Another informant emphasised that in her area she could hardly tell the difference between women who were traditionally in purdah and those who were not. One woman specified that economic difficulties have caused a lot of women to come out of purdah and engage in different occupations, whilst another pointed out that many women who used to be secluded were now engaged in farmwork. For yet another respondent, it was clear that a lot of women who were formerly in total seclusion were coming out 'to find something to do'. An older respondent stressed that times were such that 'she who waited for her husband to provide sustenance would suffer.' In the words of another, 'women in purdah have to fend for themselves and not depend on their husbands.'

It would seem therefore that a large percentage of these women outside of the elite who had until recently remained in either partial or total seclusion are now modifying their behavioural patterns to accommodate the changing economic realities affecting their lives. Those who engaged in the so-called 'silent trade' (i.e. employing another person to carry out public trading activities for them) could no longer do so successfully. They now found themselves unable to compete in the market from a position of seclusion given the increased competition from petty traders 'on the beat' hawking their goods. This trend must also be viewed within the context of rising religious fundamentalism in parts of northern Nigeria, where edicts have been issued prohibiting younger women on moral grounds from engaging in house-to-house trade and the marketing of household products. Pittin has pointed out that there are at present various indications of the fundamentalist offensive, including specific edicts on dress for women, the trend towards the boarding of female students and other forms of physical segregation, as well as the increased emphasis on the part of the state on women's family roles. She argues that these trends must be seen in the context of emerging contradictions between rhetoric and practice and within and between levels of government (1990: 23). One may add to this the proposition that economic imperatives and the fundamentally harsh economic variables associated with SAP, in themselves constitute significant vehicles for undermining the fundamentalist call for total seclusion and sex-segregated labour.

All the women interviewed observed that there was a marked increase in the cost of providing meals for the family. Increases ranged from 300 per cent to 1,000 per cent. Ilorin interviewees specified that items such as eggs, bread and rice were being dropped from their daily diet. They also claimed that their main diet consisted of *amala* and *gari* (yam and cassava derived food products), and meat was not eaten as frequently as before. When asked about the household budget, they claimed that they were operating on comparatively smaller allowances, since in some cases they received the same sum as before or even less. It is in the context of these economic difficulties that modifications have been taking place in terms of what some believe is a prime pillar of

Islam, namely the principle of seclusion. Of course, as pointed out by one respondent, economic difficulties have been affecting women of other religious affiliations as well. Given the nature of class relations in Nigeria both historically and at present (cf. Thomas-Emeagwali, 1989), it is not surprising that, in the words of some of the women interviewed, 'wealthy women are not suffering as much.' Most interviewees reflected a clear recognition of status and class differentiation within Nigerian society, and its implications for women's economic roles.

Many respondents were engaged in petty trade. Some sold *dawa da wake* (a processed cereal), palm oil, or fast food such as *akara* or *kosai* (fried pastry made from beans), *moi moi* (another bean-based condiment prepared by steaming), or consumer products such as detergent, kerosine, sugar or salt. Some admitted to having made as many as five product changes in recent times due to the fact that some goods became uneconomical for resale almost overnight with the intense price fluctuations in the market.[4] A few of the women were involved in tailoring, the making of hats or occasional farm labour. Muslim informants from both Ilorin and Zaria attested to an increase in petty trading in their respective communities with the implementation of SAP, underlining the reality that it is the informal sector in particular which provides largely unskilled women with employment opportunities. The devaluation of the local currency seems also to have brought about a shift in trading patterns. Kano in the north has become an important wholesale trading centre and Saudi Arabia has been attracting a sizeable percentage of local merchants, which implies a trend away from western Europe in particular.[5] The implication of these shifting patterns for women's role in petty trading remains to be seen.

Inheritance

Pre-Islamic Nigerian society generally accorded women usufruct rights to land, but actual control remained exclusively in male hands. The arrival of Islam posed a threat to the traditional patterns of male land ownership by way of introducing new inheritance rights since, according to Islamic law, wives and daughters are entitled to a share in the estate of the deceased male kin. Where Maliki law applies[6] (as is the case among Nigerian Muslims), 50 per cent reverts to the daughter and 25 per cent to the widow. This represents a perceptible difference compared with the pre-Islamic tradition whereby inheritance was exclusively patrilineal, and where the eldest brother of the deceased inherited everything in areas such as Zaria, Tivland and Abuja, for example. Historically, in the northeast, the eldest sons and younger brothers were the legal inheritors. However, there were areas of divergence such as in the

Jos Plateau area in the Middle Belt region, where at the death of her father a daughter could, if she had no brothers, take the corpse to claim all his land which then became the property of her husband and sons.[7] There are also cases in the Central Nigerian region where the property of a deceased male reverted to males from adjacent villages in cases where there were no male inheritors on the father's line.

Thus Islamic law introduced new codes of conduct and legal obligations into aspects of the pre-existing patterns of inheritance though there have inevitably been cases of violation. For example, the Report of the Land Investigation Commission which held public hearings in Kaduna in 1979, includes cases of complaints by women about the misappropriation of their inherited farmland. It has also been documented that traditional rulers, the courts as well as close relatives often connived to deprive women of their inheritance rights (cf. Perchonock, 1985). None the less, at least in conceptual terms, women have generally benefited from new possibilities in terms of legal rights according to Islamic law.

Diop (1978) and more recently Amadiume (1987) have argued the case for a matriarchal foundation for African indigenous societies, proposing that patriarchal elements were later impositions on the older matriarchal system. Amadiume further argues that there was a central female role in production, reproduction, property and status in parts of eastern Nigeria, a trend which she believes might be applicable to other parts of the continent. It would seem though that the collective testimony of oral tradition as reflected in anthropological accounts, court records, interviews and traditional legal systems, contradicts this view in the case of western, central and northern Nigeria in particular. However, it may be that the power of patriarchy in the formation of existing perceptions of societal organisation has been overestimated, and that researchers have generally failed to discern underlying matriarchal tendencies and other indications of female power.[8] Thus, the spread of Islam may well have served to reactivate ancient patterns of empowerment which, for reasons as yet obscure, became submerged with the spread of the patriarchal social system.

Conclusion: The Balance Sheet

Islam gave but it also took away. On the negative side it may be noted that, with the introduction of partial or total seclusion, there has been a relative loss of mobility and independence for some sectors of the female population, in particular those of high social status. This would also be the case with adherents of the Qadriyya brotherhood which, in contrast to the followers of the Tijaniyya inspired sect, restricts women's physical mobility and participation in public life. Islamic injunctions as laid down in the Qur'an and the Hadith are basically patriarchal in orientation. Muslim converts therefore became subjected to new forms of patriarchal reforms, which reinforced women's subordination and thus curtailed the relative freedom of movement they generally enjoyed during pre-Islamic times. Relative economic independence has in some cases been replaced by dependence and tutelage. Nevertheless, the gains in terms of inheritance rights have been quite significant, as has been the increased security with respect to land tenure rights. In fact, by all accounts, the assurance of an inherited share as stipulated in the Islamic legal code – however unequal in comparison to men – has apparently been encouraging conversion among some sections of the non-Muslim female population in Nigeria. It would also seem that women have generally gained respectability in the event of divorce and a breakdown of marital relations, in contrast with the pre-existing situation where divorce was socially stigmatised. Though women generally enjoy less flexibility than men in the initiation of divorce, they are nevertheless not hindered and even encouraged to remarry. The point to be made, therefore, is that Islamisation in Nigeria should be seen neither as the introduction of light in an area of darkness nor as a retrogressive force in absolute terms. The process has in fact been a chequered one and thus merits a balanced and sober evaluation.

The analysis of some impacts of the structural adjustment programme and its concomitant economic implications for Nigerian Muslim women, further illustrates the reality that the influence of Islam has and continues to be multi-faceted. Economic imperatives, in particular the subjection of non-elite women to the harsh realities of changing market forces have induced subtle and less subtle changes in attitudes towards female seclusion and economic activities outside the home. It remains to be seen what effect these changes may have for male–female gender relations, and whether the perceptibly increasing feminisation of poverty will lead to further erosion of the level of relative female autonomy which some female segments – such as petty traders – have tended to enjoy.

Notes

1. It should be noted that Nigeria is among more than 30 African states implementing structural adjustment programmes which have been adopted in the context of large-scale indebtedness to the World Bank and the International Monetary Fund. The programme itself involves the adoption of a largely monetarist policy which implies the removal of subsidies from health, education and other social services; continuous devaluation of the domestic currency, the naira; trade liberalisation and the general consolidation of a free market model as

opposed to a state capitalist model of economic growth. The overall effects of this programme have, for example, included the increased decline in the purchasing power of the populace with the exception of those who actually benefit from the new dispensations given their class connections to the ruling elite or their participation in commodity imports in the context of the liberalised market. For general and specific reference to the on-going structural adjustment programmes see Onimode, 1989.

2. Questionnaires were administered on my behalf by R.O. Lasisi, Department of History, University of Ilorin, and Nurudeen Abubakar, Centre for Nigerian Cultural Studies, Ahmadu Bello University, Zaria between December 1990 and February 1991. Most of the women involved in the survey were working class and lower middle class.

3. At the time of writing the census was in progress in the context of the transition to civilian rule undertaken by the Babangida regime.

4. Between 1984 and 1990, the introduction of SAP and other economic changes caused large price increases. For example, in 1984 a plastic kettle cost 1–1.5 naira and in 1990 it cost 10 naira. In the same period, the cost of a female head cover rose from between 3 and 5 naira to 40 naira; a rosary from 1 to 4 naira; cotton prayer mats from 13 to 80 naira.

5. This trade network is not unrelated to the annual *hajj* (pilgrimage) to Mecca.

6. There are four Sunni Muslim schools of jurisprudence, Maliki, Shafi'i, Hanbali and Hanafi; Shi'a Muslims have their own school.

7. For a related discussion and bibliographical references on this issue see Thomas-Emeagwali, 1988.

8. Though hard-core evidence to support the existence of widespread matriarchal elements in various African societies including Nigeria remains elusive, one should not dismiss the research carried out on this issue. But as Amadiume (1987) herself admits, additional investigations need to be carried out to substantiate the hypothesis.

References

Abdullah-Olukoshi, H., 1990, 'Women in Islamic Societies in the Kano Setting', mimeo, University of Hull.

Ajayi, J. and B. Ikara, 1985, *The Evolution of Political Culture in Nigeria*, University Press Ltd. and Kaduna State Council for Arts and Culture.

Amadiume, I., 1987, *African Matriarchal Foundations: The Igbo Case*, London: Karnak.

Barkow, J., 1971, 'Hausa Women and Islam', *Canadian Journal of African Studies*, vol. vi.

Boyd, J., 1989, *The Caliph's Sister*, London: Frank Cass.

Clarke, P. and I. Linden, 1984, *Islam in Modern Nigeria: A Study of a Muslim Community in a Post-independence State, 1960–83*, Mainz: Grunewald.

Diop, C.A., 1989, *The Cultural Unity of Black Africa*, London: Karnak.

Falola, T., 1986, *The Political Economy of Ibadan*, Nigeria: Ife Press.

Hiskett, M., 1984, *The Development of Islam in West Africa*, London and New York: Longman.

Isichei, E., 1977, *A History of West Africa*, London and New York: Longman.

Kani, A., 1985, *The Intellectual Origins of the Sokoto Jihad*, Iman, Nigeria.

Levtzion, N., 1987, *Rural and Urban Islam in West Africa*, Boulder: Lynne Reiner.

Ogunbiyi, A., 'The Position of Muslim Women' as stated by Uthman B. Fudi, *Journal of West African Studies*, Ife University, 1969.

Onimode, B., ed., 1989, *The IMF, the World Bank and the African Debt*, London: IFAA/Zed.

Paden, 1986, *Ahmadu Bello, Sardauna of Sokoto*, London: Hodder and Stoughton.

Perchonock, N., 1985, 'Double Oppression' in S. Bappa et al. *Women in Nigeria Today*, London: Zed Books.

Pittin, R., 1990, 'Selective Education Issues in Gender, Class and Ideology in Northern Nigeria', *Review of African Political Economy*, no. 48.

Pittin, R., 1979, Marriage and Alternative Strategies: Career Patterns of Hausa Women in Katsina City, Ph.D. thesis, University of London.

Schacht, J., 1957, 'Islam in Northern Nigeria', *Studia Islamica*, vol. viii.

Thomas-Emeagwali, G., 1991, 'Development at Risk', *Woodstock Road Editorial*, St Antony's College, Oxford, no. 7.

Thomas-Emeagwali, G., 1989, 'Class Formation in Pre-colonial Nigeria', in D. Miller, M.J. Rowlands, C. Tilley (eds), *Domination and Resistance*, London: Unwin Hyman.

Thomas-Emeagwali, G., 1988, 'Women and the Pre-colonial Nigerian Economy', paper presented at the Annual Conference of the African Studies Association, Chicago.

Trimingham, J.S., 1962, *Islam in West Africa*, Oxford: Clarendon Press.

Women in Nigeria, 1985, *The WIN Document*, Zaria.

4

Separate but more than Equal: Muslim Women at the Cape

Rosemary Ridd

Fatima

'How did you cope as a western woman?', I was asked by a Scotsman when he learned that I had lived for two years among Muslims in South Africa. What sort of restrictions and privations had I had to face?

I thought back to Cape Town. I thought of my old friend, Fatima, and a particular incident came to mind, which serves to challenge the stereo-typical image of Muslim women that is so often encountered in the West. That day someone at the university had lent me a clapped-out old, red sports car: an open-top, two-seater model. With some excitement I had driven it back to District Six, the inner city area of Cape Town where I lived, and I had taken it along to show Fatima. It was early evening and the *maghrib* prayers had just finished when I reached her house.

We decided on a drive to Bo-Kaap, just the other side of central Cape Town. This was where she had been brought up, and she still had fami-ly and many friends there. Fatima seemed to know everyone, both in Bo-Kaap and in District Six: a woman of large frame and even bigger personality, she gave all who knew her the sense of reassurance that whatever apartheid might do to them, the spirit of their community would never die.

Bo-Kaap – or Upper Cape – is well named, for the gradient of its streets seems almost vertical as one travels up from the shopping streets of Cape Town. It is also known as the Malay Quarter, for here is a tight-knit Muslim community, with small historic houses that the Malays had made their homes in the nineteenth century after the emancipation of the slaves. Fatima had moved to District Six when she married Manie (Abdurahman) and there she lived in a Black community where people distinguished themselves as *die Christe mense* and *die Slamse* (the Christian people and the Muslims).

85

Fatima called out to Najwa, her 14-year-old daughter, and to Najwa's friend, Soraya. Both girls were already in their night-dresses. Now they were instructed to put cardigans on quickly and to squeeze into the back of the car, the area meant for luggage, while Fatima got into the passenger seat next to me. We drove through District Six, across the city centre, and then prepared for the ascent up Leeuwen Street. The car lumbered with the weight, and just as we were turning left on to the flatter surface of a side street the exhaust pipe came away and clattered along the ground. Fatima reassured me that her friends would see to it. I stopped the car and she disappeared into someone's house.

The three of us waited. There was no sign of Fatima, and after about half an hour we began to complain of cold and to debate about which front door we might approach to find her. Then Najwa called to a small group of men lounging on the street corner across from us and asked them if there was anything they could do about an exhaust pipe. The men went off and returned with some thick string which they used to tie the cylinder back on. Fatima re-emerged soon afterwards, bounced back into the car and, with the rest of us feeling we had had enough for one evening, we went home.

My main concern that day had been about the car; it was also beginning to leak petrol. Was I going to have to pay a garage mechanic to put it right or could I return to its owner a car that had been mended with a piece of string? It was only now, as I was talking to the Scotsman back in England, that it occurred to me that none of us had worried much about the safety of myself or two young Muslim girls who were out in the street in their night-dresses. I happened to meet the same man again a few weeks later and we fell into a similar pattern of conversation about South Africa. Again he talked about the restricted lives of Muslim women. I thought back to Cape Town when I had felt freer then I had ever done in England, but I said nothing.

Gender Separation Versus Race Segregation

It would be quite wrong to suggest that life in District Six was without its risks, for this was a neighbourhood ruled by street gangs. The domain of male and female was clearly demarcated: the street was men's territory; women's place was in the home. A woman put much store by her respectability, and it was not done for her to usurp men's space. But if the circumstances arose where she did find herself in the street at night she could reasonably expect to be respectfully treated by the local men, especially if they knew her family. However, for women's place to be in the home was no relegation. The home was a power centre from which women established their position in the community. Far from being in the background, Muslim women in District Six were in the centre of activity, vocal in their authority and often conspicuous in their dress.

This separation of male and female into different spheres takes us to the heart of western difficulties with Islam. It runs contrary to so much that western feminists have struggled for. Although in the West we have tried to recognise the value of women's domestic work and the need to give women a choice between being a home-maker and having a career (and, indeed, the choice of both), our attention has focused primarily on the problems for women of becoming integrated into the public world that has been so long dominated by men. It appears to be generally difficult for western feminists, even anthropologists, to look at Muslim societies in their own terms and to recognise the possibility that women can also enjoy autonomy and fulfilment within their own sphere.

The division of people into separate spheres of life is an issue particularly apposite to South Africa. This is a country where for 40 years Christianity in the form of the Dutch Reformed Church sanctioned and upheld a political system that divided people into rigidly defined racial groups for what it called 'separate development' on the grounds of the racial superiority of White over Black. As a result, a large part of the African population was forced on to 13 per cent of the land surface in scattered parts of the country while the Whites, comprising 16 per cent of the population, held on to the bulk of the land together with most of the mineral resources.

While there are some African Muslims, and a few White Muslims, in Cape Town, the great majority are Malay and Indian.[1] Malay Muslims have antecedents going back to the seventeenth and eighteenth centuries, when they came to South Africa as slaves and political exiles at the time of the first White settlers. They were a heterogeneous population derived from various parts of the Indian Ocean area, where the Malay language was a lingua franca. Indian Muslims came later, at the turn of the nineteenth century. They were traders, mostly from the area around Bombay.

Under apartheid law, Malay Muslims were classified as part of the so-called Coloured or mixed race population group that was not allocated a separate homeland, but lived alongside Whites as a marginal group. Spheres of living here were determined by a range of legislation that delimited separate residential areas (through the Group Areas Act), separate public facilities (the Separate Amenities Act), and different administrative and education systems. White and Coloured still intermingled on the street and interacted in the work-place, but they met at different levels in a social hierarchy that determined the dominance of the one group and the dependence of the other.

Malay Muslims had lived for many generations as a minority group (of about 10 per cent) within the predominantly Christian Coloured population. In District Six they lived cheek by jowl with *die Christe mense*, as the Christians were known, and although they made religious and social distinction between them, they were also conscious of being brought up together in a larger common community.

In the 1960s the South African government had made moves to separate Malays from Christian Coloureds into different Group Areas but it was not successful. Apart from Bo-Kaap which is almost exclusively a Malay area, Nationalist plans faltered when officials were forced to accept that the two groups were too closely inter-connected to be able to separate them (Western, 1981: 130).

It did, however, divide off the Indian Muslims. This was less difficult to achieve because, despite their common religion, Indians had remained a more exclusive group than the Malays, bound together by a common sense of origin, arranged marriages and business links. Both Malays and Indians are Sunni Muslims, the former mostly following the Shafi'i, the latter mostly the Hanafi, schools of jurisprudence.[2] While Muslims insisted that this made no difference to their belief or religious practice, it did increase the tendency for each group to favour different mosques and to keep to separate social networks. In District Six there were three Shafi'i mosques and one rather grander Hanafi mosque supported mainly by Indians. With the removals following the Group Areas Act, Indian Muslims were moved out of District Six to three designated townships on the Cape Flats: Rylands Estate, Gatesville and Cravenby.

These were some of the darkest days of apartheid. By the 1970s, the separation of Coloured from White into Group Areas was almost complete, after the removal of thousands of Coloured families from older residential areas to the rapidly growing townships on the Cape Flats. Nowhere in Cape Town could one be more aware of apartheid than in District Six itself where an entire community was being destroyed, the buildings pulled down to make way for its redevelopment as a White area. During the two years that I lived there (1976–8) the most densely populated part of District Six – about two-fifths of the area – had already gone. Those who still lived there were clinging on to the past, to a community life that would soon be destroyed completely, determined to maintain it to the end.

This was a community life that went back long before apartheid. District Six grew up in the second half of the nineteenth century, but for the Malays the sense of community in Cape Town went back further, at least to the early part of that century when Muslims were first granted freedom of worship and began openly to organise themselves. For more than a century and a half a ghettoised community had shut itself off from the prejudice and discrimination of White South Africa.

I have written elsewhere about the position of District Six women in general, Christian and Muslim, and I explained how it was that women assumed their central role (Ridd, 1981). Here, in this chapter, we see how this centrality was particularly relevant to Muslim women who made the home an enterprise and derived status out of their twin responsibilities as custodians of their religion and of the local Malay traditions of their community.

These Malay women in Cape Town present an interesting contrast with the Egyptian Muslim women depicted in this volume, where women's relative strength comes from circumstances in which religion may not be the main factor impinging on people's lives. The Cape Town community was proudly Muslim. We may argue that these women derived abnormal strength from abnormal circumstances. This was true, for women in District Six were in some respects *more* than equal to the men. But their position also suggests that Muslim women's equality with men does not have to be incompatible with Islam. Islam, while it teaches the separation of male and female roles, also teaches mutual respect between the sexes.

The position of women in Islamic society has been the subject of discussion for much of this century, largely as a result of contact with the West. Recent discussion, fomented in great part by the 1979 Iranian Revolution, has centred largely on whether Islam in its pristine form gave women equality with men, or whether it made women subject to male authority (cf. Muttahari, 1981; Siddiqi, 1986). Recent contributions from Leila Ahmed (1992) and Fatima Mernissi (1992) both argue that the controls placed on women in Islamic societies under the Shari'a should be seen as cultural accretions that came after, often soon after, the death of Muhammad. They further argue that the Prophet set an example in his own life by enabling women to live much more freely than they had been able to do in pre-Islamic times, and by protecting them from those who would abuse them.

Repostes come from both western critics of Islam and from more traditional Muslim writers who pick out particular Qur'anic verses and also Hadith (sayings of the Prophet) that point to male authority. One of the most frequently quoted verses from the Qur'an (sura 4: verse 34) states:

Men are the protectors
And maintainers of women,
Because God has given
The one more (strength)
Than the other, and because

They support them
From their means.
Therefore the righteous women
Are devoutly obedient, and guard
In (the husband's) absence
What God would have given them to guard.

Malay women in Cape Town did not deviate from this prescription. But although they expected their husbands to provide financially for the household, this did not prevent them from being vocal in the home and the community, or from earning additional income, whether as wage earners or as small business women. They were conscious of the example of Muhammad's first wife, Khadija, who had been a business woman in her own right.

In District Six we are looking at a community where few opportunities beyond its boundaries were open to men or women. It was not Shari'a law, but apartheid law that restricted people's lives. Where the Malay community did impose restrictions upon women, these were invariably 'restrictions' that I, as an outsider, observed rather than anything that Muslim women were themselves particularly concerned about. Usually they reflected the separation of male and female spheres, where Muslim women considered it was not appropriate for them to behave like men. We will consider some of these 'restrictions' when we come to look at women's religious practice.

Here I shall explain *why* it was that women should have been so central to the community and *how* this position was maintained through women's control of the home and through the responsibilities they took on, both in their religious practice and the encouragement of local Malay tradition. I shall go on to give some historical perspective to this situation before completing this analysis with some intimation of changes that were coming, not only with the end of District Six, but with the end of apartheid and a ghettoised Malay community.

We are looking here at a way of life wrapped up in the folk tradition of a ghettoised community. By the 1970s it was already being challenged by a new, more educated and more affluent generation that was trying to dissociate itself from what it saw as the ignorance of the past. Change from the old order to new ideas about what it meant to be Muslim was reflected in the use of terms. Here I try to keep to the spirit of the old community life by using what were described as 'Malay terms'. By Malay, people did not refer necessarily to the language or culture of a foreign land, but to the traditions of their own community in Cape Town. Some terms were of Malay origin, like *labarang* (festival), *pwasa* (fast), and *soembine* (pray); others were derived from Arabic, such as *karamat* which is rendered *kramat*, meaning the shrine of a saintly person. Muslim, in the old Malay community, was spelt and pronounced 'Moslem'. In the 1970s a person could be quickly marked out as being part of the traditional or the new order by which of these terms he or she used. People in District Six said 'Moslem', and for the rest of this paper I shall adhere to this form, until the concluding section where it is more appropriate to return to Muslim.

Change would have to come. The Malay community in its traditional form had done its job in protecting a vulnerable population group for at least a century and a half before apartheid. Social change would have its effect on gender relations. But this must be the subject of another study. Here my purpose is to look at the traditional Malay community to explain why and how women played a prominent role.

Household Entrepreneurs

The separation of men and women into different spheres of living was likely to have been more conspicuous among Whites in Cape Town than among Moslems. White South Africans, particularly Afrikaners, had firmly resisted western feminist influences. The male sphere was rooted in the work-place, politics and sport. For the most part (excepting, that is, poor Whites), White men could expect secondary education and training and to aspire to a career. The female sphere was the private life of the home. With Black servants to do much of the domestic work, Afrikaner women were revered in their role of nurturing the family and fostering the culture and identity of *die volk* (the people) (Moodie, 1975: 17–18). For White women in general it was acceptable to do social work in their own community or for non-Whites, but few stepped outside that area into the public sphere.

For people in District Six it was different because there was no public sphere. Here the division between private and public spheres is not the one normally understood by western scholars, where the home is associated with the private domain, and everything outside this space is perceived as the public area. In District Six, because the home was so central to people's lives, the influence of women extended from there into the community. Women's networks tended to be more apparent, while men's networks, built up in the street and the mosques, were more muted, more withdrawn from public view. Thus, to the people of District Six, the term public sphere was largely perceived in terms of being foreign territory associated with the White man's world.

In the 1970s people considered themselves privileged if they had completed their primary schooling, and only a tiny elite ever reached the professions. Most District Six men and women had no expectations of a life outside the community. Lack of education reduced job opportunities and, for many years, work had been restricted by the government's policy of job reservation (the protection of specified blue-collar jobs for poor Whites). It was common in District Six for men to have irregular or insecure employment, or to have no work at all. District Six had its own street culture with its organised gangs, its *skollies* (thugs) and *ou rookers* (old smokers).

In this context, the home and community were central to people's lives. They provided people with sustenance, self-respect and a refuge from apartheid. Women in District Six were strong: they had to be. They were often the most vocal members of the community, speaking on behalf of men as well as for themselves. In nearly every household I knew the woman of the house was visibly in charge. Her responsibilities for keeping the house clean and for feeding the members of her household were endowed with much importance. It was essential to her sense of honour that her home should be immaculate, and seen to be so. Some women kept their front doors ajar after polishing the corridor so that passers-by could look in, so intensely did they feel the need to demonstrate that non-White they may be but their standards were as good as those of any White.

While the housewife might organise other women and girls in the household to help her with the cleaning, the cooking she made her responsibility alone. Cooking could take all day and it required skills which made her indispensable. In a community where the only public places were sleazy cafés that served those without a home to go to, the 'pot of food' provided by the woman of the house was far superior to anything obtained outside.

Beyond these tasks the woman controlled the household budget. In some cases she herself was the principal breadwinner, but if there were a husband and children at work they were expected to hand their monthly wage-packets over to her and they would receive pocket-money in return. Young girls who had left school to work in the factory said that this was what they had been brought up to expect and, besides, their mother put some of this money aside to pay for their wedding. Older boys saw their wages going to support their younger siblings who would, throughout their lives, address them respectfully as *boeta* (older brother).

All this applied to Christian as well as to Malay Moslem women, but for the latter there were particular reasons why, within their more ghettoised environment, the woman took on a central role. In the first place, as a Malay, she was invested with specialist knowledge, particularly in her style of cooking. Although Malay cooking was not as exotic as White South Africans often thought, it did have a distinctiveness, and a variety of characteristic items, that set it apart. Although *roti* (unleavened bread) and curry, *bredie* (stew) and *koeksiesters* (spicy doughnuts), for example, could also be produced by Christian women in District Six, the authentic product was associated with Malay homes.

Secondly, the Malays, both men and women, had developed a degree of self-reliance within their community network and an aptitude for business. Traditionally they were known for their artisan skills – as stonemasons, cabinet-makers, coach-makers, tailors, fishermen – and for their street trading as hawkers of fish, and fruit and vegetables. By the 1970s it had become more common for men to take office work or even to enter the professions, but the tradition of local skills and co-operative action still remained. It was not uncommon, for example, for a man who bought a plot of land, to get his friends to rally round, contributing their skills and their free time at weekends to build him a house. No payment needed to be made for there would be other occasions when the beneficiary would be called upon to give his services.

The self-sufficiency of the Malay community gave Moslem men a dignity that was quite often denied to *die Christe mense*. It also endowed Moslem women with a degree of independence through the collective will to cope with hardship. Women shared with their men a reputation for making money by independent means, whether as dressmakers or cooks, or, in the old days, as washerwomen or flower sellers. They found their clientele among Whites in Cape Town as well as within their own community, but mostly they worked from their own homes. There were women in District Six who made a living from selling traditional Malay fare. This came hot from the kitchen and was either taken around from door to door, or customers sent their children to the Malay woman's home to buy.

Janap, a mother of six in her middle fifties, had been particularly successful. Her husband had been a butcher's apprentice until Janap had pushed him into setting up his own business, and then she managed his accounts. With the profits the family had moved out of the slums to a house in the well-to-do area of Walmer Estate, adjacent to District Six, and with the money that she had earned over the years from selling *koeksiesters* and *samosas* she paid a substantial sum for interior renovation and redecoration. In this case again much of the labour was given free by Moslems with whom she had a reciprocal relationship.

While some Moslem women worked outside the home for a wage packet, typically in the factory, others made the home itself a business enterprise. Not only could this be achieved by selling products from the kitchen, but also by extending the membership of the household. Women enlarged their households, and their spheres of influence, beyond the immediate family by taking in relatives or others from the community. These people, if they did not give the woman of the house their full wage packet, would contribute a substantial part in return not just for food and lodging, but also for the privilege of being incorporated into the household, under the protection and patronage of the woman.

Janap had had several protégés who had extended her household of husband and six children. One had been a niece who had lived with her for several years and who, when she left school, had been expected 'to work for' Janap, that is, to hand over her full monthly wage packet. Janap, for her part, had seen to it that her niece was married to a suitable man (another poor relative of the family), and had paid for the girl's wedding.

In Janap's house there was an old man, a distant cousin of her husband's, who gave Janap his pension in return for his meals and a small room in the back yard. There was also Noor, a Christian convert to Islam who had done much of Janap's interior decorating and now continued to do odd jobs for her in return for a few meals each week and the introductions Janap gave him into her social network. And there was Yusuf, who, although he lived with his sister, for some reason had no woman to cook for him. He ate most days at Janap's house, and in return he brought her a generous weekly quantity of groceries and acted as chauffeur whenever she and her eldest daughter, Soraya, wanted to visit friends. Yusuf had been thwarted in his designs on marrying Soraya, but still allowed himself to hope. Soraya hated him and pressed her mother to exclude him from the household. But Janap was a pragmatic business woman. 'One hand washes the other', she would say, miming the action with her hands.

Custodians of the Faith and Malay Traditions

In their daily religious practice it was not uncommon for women to act on behalf of all the members of their household, particularly when it came to prayer. Janap was the only one in her house who did *soembine* (prayed) the obligatory five times daily and, while she would have preferred it otherwise, she considered that she took this responsibility for everyone under her roof. The same principle held during Ramadan. As the month of Ramadan approached, the whole household prepared itself psychologically for the fast. On the first day Janap ensured that every-

one was up at half past five for breakfast before dawn. She herself would have been up an hour earlier to prepare the meal. After a few days the number dwindled as her husband and younger children gave up fasting. Janap kept going even when she became ill with exhaustion from her extra household duties. Her eldest daughter stopped, as prescribed by the Qur'an, only while she was menstruating. Thus Janap upheld the honour of her family, helped to strengthen the identity of Malays within the larger Coloured community, and also gained for herself merit in the afterlife when her good deeds would be weighed up against her bad.

A born Malay who did not practise the religion did not cease to be a Moslem or a member of the community. All that was necessary was that he or she accept the basic statement of belief in Allah and in Muhammad as His Messenger. This was automatically assumed and no one would be indiscreet enough to deny the *kalimah* (*shahada*, Arabic for faith). It was said that even the most hardened gangster was a believer for, 'if he swears by Allah, he must believe.'

There was a good deal more tolerance shown towards men than towards women for anti-social behaviour. Mothers expected their daughters to lead disciplined lives while they allowed their sons out on the street to do as they would on the grounds that men, by nature, could not be controlled, nor could they control themselves. Thus Haji Kooli, a Malay woman in late middle age from one of the poorest parts of District Six, used to sigh over her youngest son, Boobi (Abubakar), who rarely worked, drove an old van without a driving licence and hung out with the local gang with whom he smoked *dagga* (cannabis) and openly drank cheap wine or brandy in the street. She accepted this with resignation for most of the year and only in Ramadan, when her friends reported seeing him drunk on the street, did she attempt to remonstrate with him.

Although more was expected of women, it was still inconceivable that any should become *moertat* (*murtad*, Arabic for apostate). The one exception when they automatically became *moertat* was if they married out of the faith. A Moslem man could marry out provided the woman was of a 'religion of the Book' (i.e. a Christian, Jew or Zoroastrian), because he remained a Moslem. But a Moslem woman who married out was considered lost to Islam, her religion defined by that of her husband. Marrying out in District Six meant marrying a Christian Coloured. From an early age Moslem girls were warned of the dangers. In the old days they were told how, when she died, the body of an apostate woman would be dragged through the streets of District Six on a stretcher pulled by pigs. The punishment for marrying out was becoming an outcast.

One such woman lived next door to Janap. Ten years earlier she had married a man who was suitable in every way except for his religion, and now they had three children. Although she still insisted she was a Moslem there was no softening of attitudes towards her: she was *moertat*. Her father, an otherwise affable and gentle old man, had not seen his daughter in all those years. Janap expressed pity for her but was reluctant to allow her own younger children to play with her neighbour's children though they were of similar age. 'She does not know what she is', was Janap's explanation. In District Six, a person who lacked a clear social status was disparaged as *deurmekaar* (mixed up).

Tragic though these circumstances were, they were rare. Moslem girls did not marry Christian men, partly no doubt because of the penalty, but also because of the attraction of becoming a married Malay woman. There were of course the responsibilities, but these did not diminish a Moslem woman's life. Fatima was evidence of this. With all her energy, she was not so much typical as archetypal; the quintessence of what a Malay woman could be. Indeed, the attraction of being a married Malay woman was evidenced in the relative frequency of marriages made between women from the Christian Coloured community and Malay men. The woman was expected to 'turn Malay', and in most cases she entered into the marriage for that specific purpose. In an environment where to be deemed to be Coloured made identity equivocal, there was much pride, especially among the poor, in being a Malay.

There were expectations laid upon those who 'turned Malay' to learn to practise the religion and to participate in the traditions of the community. Those who explicitly failed to do so risked losing all social identity and being *deurmekaar*. The Malay community from the viewpoint of one such woman I knew was one of doors slammed in her face. But for those who made the effort to become integrated the doors were opened. Haji Kooli had been a convert. Some thirty years earlier she had married a Malay hawker. He had done nothing to help her, apart from giving her the status of a Malay wife, and, indeed, after a few years he ran off and left her with three small sons. Haji Kooli had created her own position in the community and later married a Christian man who 'turned Malay for me', as she put it. They had three daughters. Later Haji Kooli took a job as an office tealady and from her wages she saved the money to make the pilgrimage to Mecca (her husband went a year or two later), and so gained the status and title of Haji (derived from the Arabic *hajj*, pilgrimage).

The relative ease with which Christian women could become integrated into the Malay community says something about what it meant to be Malay. Whites in Cape Town generally saw the Malays as the remnants of a racial group that was brought to the Cape during the slave period and mixed with others, especially Christian Coloureds, to become racially mixed themselves. Malays in District Six generally accepted this (more educated Moslems did not), but they gave little attention to their distant past. For them to be Malay meant being a Moslem and participating in the life of the community. These two things went together. Women ensured this, protecting the Malay community with a culture of local tradition that surrounded religious practice.

Local traditions were broadly of two types. One was linked with the Islamic calendar: for example, with the month of Ramadan, with the two *labarangs* (*eid*, Arabic for festival), with the Prophet Muhammad's birthday, known in Cape Town as *moulood* (from the Arabic *maulid*). The other type was linked to personal *rites de passage*: to marriage, to death, to preparation for the pilgrimage. In these, women's centrality came out of their responsibilities for giving hospitality, for providing food and for reinforcing the sense of community among Malays.

Some traditions focused on the family. One such tradition was *kers op stiek* (lighting the candle) on the 27th night of Ramadan. More properly it is *lailat al-qadr* (Arabic for night of destiny), commemorating the night when the Qur'an was first revealed to Muhammad. Houses in District Six had to be thoroughly cleaned by that night for the angel Jibra'il (Gabriel) to come to inspect. The angel was welcomed by children lighting candles around the house when the fast was broken for the evening meal. It was an evening of anticipation for the end of the fast.

Most traditions involved women giving hospitality in the home or were community events in some larger building. *Rites de passage* were often accompanied by news of the event taken around from house to house. When a death occurred it used to be the *malboet* (a male mosque official) who carried the message to each household in the neigbourhood with an invitation to the funeral that same day. That particular tradition had gone by the 1970s, but still *goedjarjies*, (intending pilgrims) went around to each home to announce their intention of going to Mecca and, in preparation for this, to ask forgiveness for any offence they might have given in the past. (Those they had visited would then return the visit before the *goedjarjies* left on pilgrimage, to give them their blessing.) Similarily, a young woman and man intending to marry each took a small retinue of bridesmaids or supporters with them to invite people in their vicinity to the wedding. Such visits were formalised with old-fashioned, formulaic language, Malay words mixed with Afrikaans. The visitors might be male or female, but it was often women who received them and who were the more conversant with the appropriate procedure.

When it came to big gatherings – especially weddings – women's organisational skills were applied on a large scale and often collectively with others. The cost too was spread out with donations of food made, usually by men with business interests. Thus the meat might come from a Moslem butcher; fizzy drinks, rice, sugar and so forth from those with shops or contacts in the right places. Women were generally the co-ordinators.

The feast was in fact two feasts: bride's and groom's family each held their own, and guests could move between them. The bride's was the more eventful. Guests came to see the bride who appeared in the course of the afternoon in several different bridal costumes (one of which was the western bridal dress), to watch for the arrival of the groom to inform his bride that they were married, to eat and drink, and then to sing traditional folk songs in a mixture of Afrikaans, old Dutch and Malay. Women were often the more proficient with the words; some attended a wedding every week, mainly for the singing. At the end of the proceedings bride and guests await the arrival of the Hajis. About three respected women, friends of the groom's family, dressed in their *moedering* (fine clothing in which they had returned from the pilgrimage to Mecca) arrive to take the bride away.[3] The bride must make an effort to cry as she is 'dragged' away from her family to her new home. Guests follow, arriving at the bridal chamber singing praises to the Prophet and keen to see the furnishings the groom's family had provided before the groom arrives. This is what the marriage was all about: it was a community event in which women played the central role. It was some little time, however, before it occurred to me that at the wedding ceremony itself – the *nikah* – women were altogether absent.[4] The bride herself was not present for the marriage contract; she was represented by her father or another man acting as *wakiel* (Arabic for guardian). So much attention was directed by women to the festivities that followed the *nikah* that the ceremony itself was rarely spoken of. When I raised the matter of their exclusion from the *nikah* with Moslem women themselves, they indicated that they saw no reason to be there: this was the men's domain.

The same pattern of gender division applied to *moulood*, the celebration of the Prophet Muhammad's birthday. Here the more specifically religious celebration – the *salawat* (prayers) to the Prophet – was attended by men in the mosques in the evening. But the main attraction in the community was the *rampie sny* organised by the women in the mosques in the afternoon. Hajis dressed in the *moedering* and young girls dressed up like bridesmaids sat on the carpeted floor of the mosque, singing praises to the Prophet while they cut up orange leaves to be mixed with rose water and other scents and then put into satchets of brightly coloured tissue paper. These *rampies* were then given to the men or kept by the women themselves for their wardrobes where they were used like lavender bags. Such a tradition no doubt derived from South East Asia where the *rampie* is a tree bearing long, strong-smelling fronds. In Cape Town, where there was no such vegetation, orange leaves became the substitute, and because they had no scent of their own, this was added. In the old days *rampie sny* was more than a social occasion: it was a time to transact the business of match-making, when older women arranged alliances between their sons and daughters. This practice has since faded out, and young people generally choose their own marriage partners.

The traditions around which much of the life of the Malay community had focused up to the 1970s were beginning to go, and women felt the ebbing away of a way of life. Motjie Beira and Haji Kooli attributed this to the moral decline among the young:

> We like to uphold all the old customs. But the younger ones, they seem to think it's not necessary, that it's a waste of time. But I don't take notice of that. They must go to church (mosque), they must *trawig*,[5] and they must make *salawat* (prayers) five times a day, and they must visit the *goedjarjies* and they must go to *gadats*.[6] We do it all in the name of Allah, and for the Prophet, and for all the other prophets.

Out of Slavery

Two principal questions have been posed in this paper: one about *why*, the other about *how*, Moslem women in District Six should have played the central role they did in their community. It would be tempting to answer these questions simply by arguing that Moslem women do not always conform to western stereotypes. But their position in District Six requires more to be said to explain why and how women have in some respects been *more* than equal to men.

We have seen *why* Moslem women were to the fore in District Six in the context of an apartheid society where Black South Africans, deprived of much participation in the public sphere, focused their lives on the home and community. *How* women maintained their position has been shown in the responsibilities they took on in the domestic sphere and in their commitment to religious practice and local tradition. The centrality of women in District Six, however, should not be seen as an inevitable outcome of oppression. There are a good number of studies of other societies where people living in conditions of political and economic deprivation show quite a different response in their pattern of gender relations; where men, resentful of their treatment by government and frustrated by blocks to life fulfilment, attempt to compensate for these feelings by exerting control over women.[7]

This did not happen in District Six. The explanation for this can, I would argue, be found in history; specifically in the duration and stability of the Malay community, and in the very way in which it came into being. This community can be traced back to the end of the slave period, to Cape Town at the turn of the eighteenth century. From the beginning the community appeared to need women to be active and strong in building up a sense of group identity and appears to have allowed women the freedom they required to play their role. This role became accepted as the norm without being seen to be threatening to men.

The stress here is on 'appears' to have allowed, for we have very little historical information about the formation of the Malay community during this period, and nothing has been written about gender relations. During the slave period, before the Malay community became established, there are no records at all from slaves themselves, except for one letter written by a slave.[8] And even in the nineteenth century most of what we have on Malay Moslems are the observations of White South Africans and European visitors. We can, however, surmise from the limited evidence that Moslem women played an active part in the nineteenth century Malay community.

Until relatively recently, it was assumed by White South Africans that the Malay community came into being at the Cape with the arrival of slaves. During the past couple of decades historians have countered with arguments that this community developed much later (cf. Ross, 1983; Shell, 1974). The slaves were a heterogeneous population brought from all round the Indian Ocean area (all part of the Malay world) who had, as Robert Ross (1983) has described, an 'atomised' existence at the Cape (cf. Armstrong, 1979; Boeseken, 1977; Bradlow and Cairns, 1978). While many of the slaves came from areas where there was contact with Islam, few were themselves Moslem. Islam existed at the Cape in small pockets among the slaves, often around a local teacher. The most prominent of these teachers are to this day commemorated at *kramats* (shrines) at the Cape. Thirdly, there were very few women brought as slaves; those who were, were likely to have been appropriated by their owners for sexual use. Marriage among slaves was proscribed and any liaisons that did form were liable to be broken up with the selling of one or the other of the partners. Authority, where it existed among Moslem slaves, was focused on spiritual teachers, men following a Sufi *tariqa* (path, tradition), who attracted followers around them. Women, it appears, would have been largely absent.

The beginnings of a Malay community, towards the end of the slave period in the late eighteenth century, has been attributed to an increase in the number of manumitted slaves, known as Free Blacks, who were able to move around and propagate the faith, and secondly to the charismatic figure of Imam Abdulla Abdus Salaam, who became popularly known as 'Tuan Guru' (Mister Teacher). He brought Moslems together as a single group and was their first *qadi* (chief imam). We should also note, however, that by this time too there were more women, most of them born at the Cape to slaves and Free Blacks (cf. Davids, 1980; Ross, 1983). (The Moslem community was known as Malay, we are told, not because of place of origin but because Malay was a lingua franca of the slaves, together with creolised Portuguese and Dutch. Malay and Portuguese were the principal trading languages of the Indian Ocean area (cf. Bradlow and Cairns, 1978)).

The turn of the century saw the first mosque (Auwal Mosque in the Bo-Kaap) in 1798, established in anticipation of the granting of freedom of worship in 1804 by the new British colonial government at the Cape. Achmat Davids, an historian from Bo-Kaap itself, writes of the Auwal Mosque as providing a religious and social focus for the new community for nigh on 50 years until other mosques provided alternative foci (1980: 94).

The formal history of Malays in this period is one of the imams – successors to Tuan Guru – and of disputes between rival male figures in the community. The names that have gone down in history are those of men, except for two women, Trijn and Saartjie van de Kaap. Trijn, a manumitted slave, owned the property (inherited from her husband) which was turned into the Auwal Mosque. In 1809 she transferred this property to Saartjie, her daughter, who was married to the second *qadi*, Achmat van Bengalen. Davids, describing Saartjie as a 'remarkable woman', writes:

> It is in her that the ownership of the Auwal Mosque is vested to this day. Born in slavery she played a subdued but vital role in the history of the Cape Moslem community. Her foresight perpetuated the wishes of Tuan Guru and ensured the existence of the Auwal Mosque to this day (1980: 107).

Saartjie herself was not a community leader, but a woman acting behind various leading men, not just her husband. Other women would follow her as imam's wives, holding respect and exercising influence in the community; they would be known as the *motjie imam* (lady imam), and would exercise authority within their own sphere, among other women.

While the importance of Saartjie as a property owner and influential Moslem woman should not be under-estimated, it is not so much in the lives of individual women as in the role played by Moslem women as a gender group that I believe we may find a basis for their strength in the next century. However, with very little information on which to draw, we can only make some tentative assumptions.

First, women would have played an important role in the establishment of the home and local community life. The early part of the nineteenth century was a time when members of the Malay community increased dramatically in number as outsiders – mainly freed slaves – converted to Islam, attracted by a cultural identity and a home. Davids writes about some of the cultural practices which came to be seen as Malay traditions originating or becoming consolidated into the community life at this time (1980: 94–95). He refers to *rampie sny* and *merang* – a religious ceremony followed by feasting – as particular examples. We can include several others: for example, the wedding feasts would have begun about this time, when Moslem marriages were first permitted (although never, to this day, given legal recognition), and the traditions associated with the *goedjarjies* would have been established when some Moslems found the means to make the pilgrimage. Davids does not discuss gender roles, but we may assume that women had much to do with the hospitality and provision of food that surrounded religious occasions, and that they indeed provided the core for a community life that was attracting new members.

Secondly, in all the descriptions we have of nineteenth century Malays there is nothing to suggest that Moslem women retired into the background. On the contrary, they were conspicuous. Robert Shell (1978), writing about the famous water-colourist of the 1820s and 1830s, H.C. de Meillon, notes that all men and women 'of colour' were determined at this time to shed their slave origins and to express this in any finery they could afford in their clothing. Moslem women were no exception. Shell quotes J.S. Mayson on Malay women, writing in the 1860s:

> Their dress, which on gala days is of silk or expensive material, but ordinarily of cotton, differs from that of European females in having a short spenser of a different colour from the wide skirt to which it is attached – their well chosen and somewhat showy attire adding a charm to their personal graces. Their figures are fine, and their features are not devoid of comeliness (1978: 9).

In the 1860s, when Abu Bakr Effendi, a *mufti* from the Ottoman Empire, was brought to Cape Town to resolve disputes among the Malays, women were prevailed upon to dress more modestly. Some compromise was reached, but the love of conspicuous apparel continued, especially in the clothing women wore on their return from Mecca.

Thirdly, women shared in the work ethic for which Malays developed a reputation in the nineteenth century. Visiting the Cape in 1861,

Lady Duff Gordon described the industriousness of the Malays as small entrepreneurs who had built their lives up from slavery. She relates the achievement of an elderly couple who together run 'a fruit shop of a rough sort, with "Betsy fruiterer" painted on the back of an old tin tray which hangs by the door of the house. The couple were now worth upwards of 5,000 and supporting a son who was studying in Cairo' (1927: 43). It was probably more common, however, for husband and wife to work on separate enterprises, the wife earning from domestic chores as seamstress, cook or washerwoman.

Earlier in this chapter, I referred to the maintenance of gender roles among White South Africans, especially among Afrikaners, where women are revered for their role in the home and community where they protected the cultural identity of *die volk*. To an extent Malay women had a comparable function, except that theirs was a singularly more assertive role. They have not been kept in the home so much as made the home their enterprise.

Changing Gender Roles in a New South Africa

As long as Malay Muslims were shut off from the public sphere of life in South Africa their community remained ghettoised. By the 1970s change was becoming evident. New opportunities were opening up and the old folk traditions that had protected the Malay community were losing their relevance. When secondary education up to the age of 16 was made compulsory for Coloured children in the 1960s a new generation began to grow up with different expectations from their parents. While their education system was markedly inferior to that for Whites, and was much disrupted in the late 1970s and the 1980s, the days were fast going when a man or woman from District Six was proud to have completed only primary schooling.

Higher education at the segregated University of the Western Cape and other training centres allowed Muslim and Christian Coloureds to move in greater numbers into professional jobs, especially school teaching, where the Nationalist government needed Coloured teachers for Coloured schools. Muslims, who had hitherto shown suspicion towards secular education, now outmatched their Christian neighbours in their efforts. For those who did not reach the professions, a shortage of White workers for office jobs in the 1970s opened the way for Coloureds to fill the gap.

Education and training among Muslims, mostly outside District Six, brought disparagement for the poverty of the past and for those who still lived the old way of life. Malay traditions became associated with the slums. Janap even insisted that the term *Slams* (pl. *Slamse*) which was often used for the Malays (and derives from the word Islam, via the colloquial Dutch *Slammaier*) refers to 'people of the slums'. At the same time, White South Africans in Cape Town of liberal inclination were beginning to replace their prejudices against the Malay Muslims (*sic*) with interest, indeed fascination, in their culture and traditions. Educated Muslims (sic) now saw themselves being stereotyped by well intentioned but condescending Whites who seemed to want to keep them in the nineteenth century, and they reacted angrily against the timeless folksy image of them put out in coffee-table books and in the media. 'We are not Malay; we are Muslim', they would retort. Arguments were put forward as to why Malay was a misnomer, and how culture interferes with the practice of the true religion.

The acceleration of political protest against apartheid in the late 1970s and in the 1980s reinforced the movement out of the ghetto as a plethora of new organisations, many of them dating to 1983 and linked to the United Democratic Front, gave Christian and Muslim new roles, especially for men. During this time the Muslim population was opening itself up to a wider Muslim world through contact with religious scholars who came to South Africa on lecture tours from India and Saudi Arabia, and there was foreign investment in new centres of Islamic education.

In 1991 Muhammad Haron, at the University of the Western Cape, began an article for *The American Journal of Islamic Social Studies* with the statement: 'The field of Arabic and Islamic studies in South Africa remains, with few exceptions, virgin territory'(363). His article reflects a dissatisfaction with the continued sense of isolation from the centres of the Muslim world, but also significant moves and a determination to change this situation (cf. Haron, 1988).

The effect these changes will have on gender relations has yet to be investigated. Most research interest at present is devoted to the place of Muslims in political organisations and their place in the future South Africa. There is much debate over whether Muslims should work with non-Muslims in the struggle for change, whether they should fight separately on Islamic principles, or whether they should keep out of politics and concentrate on religious concerns (cf. Esach, 1988; Naude, 1985; Nkrumah, 1989).

District Six has now gone. The Malay Muslims who lived there have been scattered over the townships of the Cape Flats. The small, ghettoised community is no longer, but the earlier reaction against all things Malay has since become more muted as people recall with some nostalgia a world destroyed by apartheid.

Time will tell how Muslim women will fare in a new political order. However, if the Malay Muslims are to become incorporated into a broader South African society, the problems for Muslim women may come not from the strictures of their religion but from the secular state in which they must compete with men for a public voice.

And what of Fatima? During the time I lived in District Six the area was only partially demolished. Soon afterwards the bulldozers came back to complete the job and Fatima's house was among those that were destroyed. She and her family were rehoused by the City Council in a township on the Cape Flats some 15 miles away. For Fatima it was the end of her way of life. Barely forty, she suffered a stroke that left her partly paralysed. Fatima, who had been the quintessence of the fighting spirit of District Six, was now largely housebound and unable to communicate with people except indistinctly. Her way of life had gone, but it would not be forgotten.

Notes

1. The Muslim population for the Cape Province in 1970, as shown in the South African census, was broken down as follows: Malays 117,673, Indians 9,785, Whites 412. No separate figure was given for Africans. The Muslim population for South Africa as a whole in 1970 was 269,911 (134,087 Malay, 125,987 Indian, 8,892 African, and 945 Whites).

2. There are four Sunni Muslim schools of jurisprudence, each named after its respective founder: Shafi'i, Hanafi, Hanbali and Maliki. Shi'a Muslims follow their own legal school.

3. Haji Kooli's *moerdering* comprised her *abaya* (a shiny, embroidered cloak over a long dress of the same material), and the *medoura*. The latter is a long chiffon scarf, embroidered with gold or silver thread, intricately folded about the head. This more than any other garment marks out the woman who holds the title of Haji.

4. Women's exclusion from the *nikah* is not prescriptive, but (common to most Muslim societies) is a tradition that proved to be binding. At one large Muslim wedding – Indian rather than Malay in this case – held in two great halls of the exhibition centre, I was seated in one of the halls when I heard that the *nikah* was actually going to take place in the other. Curious, I made my way to the back of the other hall where many people were seated at tables and the *nikah* was about to begin in a space at the far end. Holding on to my camera, I was taken for a press photographer and called to the front to take photographs. No one appeared to be embarrassed about my presence in the midst of the *nikah* except myself. In some parts of the world, Britain included, a Muslim bride does sometimes attend the *nikah*.

5. This term, derived from the Arabic *tarawih*, refers to an extra-canonical prayer during Ramadan.

6. Prayer meetings held in people's homes on Thursday evenings during which women served *gadat melk* (milk) and cakes.

7. See, for example, Edgerton's study of Catholic women in Northern Ireland,

and Roussou's on Greek Cypriot women, in Ridd and Callaway, 1986.

8. The letter was written in Buginese, a language from the East Indies (see Ross, 1983: 14). Ross contrasts the Cape with the American Deep South where much more information is available.

References

Ahmed, L., 1992, *Women and Gender in Islam*, New Haven & London: Yale University Press.

Ardener, S., ed., 1981, *Women and Space: Ground Rules and Social Maps*, London: Croom Helm; 1993 revised edn, Providence & Oxford: Berg Publishers.

Armstrong, J. C., 1979, 'The Slaves, 1652-1795', in R. Elphick and H. Giliomee, eds, *The Shaping of South African Society 1652-1820*, Cape Town: Longman Penguin Southern Africa.

Boeseken, A., 1977, *Slaves and Free Blacks at the Cape, 1658-1700*, Cape Town: Tafelberg.

Bradlow, F. R., 1978, 'The Origin of the Early Cape Muslims', in F. R. Bradlow and M. Cairns, eds, *The Early Cape Muslims*, Cape Town: A. A. Balkema.

Bradlow F. R. and M. Cairns, eds, 1978, *The Early Cape Muslims*, Cape Town: A. A. Balkema.

Brandel-Syrier, M., ed., 1971, *The Religious Duties of Islam as Taught and Explained by Abu Bakr Effendi*, Leiden: E. J. Brill.

Davids, A., 1980, *The Mosques of Bo-Kaap*, Cape Town: The South African Institute of Arabic and Islamic Research.

Duff Gordon, K. L., 1927, *Letters from the Cape*, London: Oxford University Press.

Edgerton, L., 1986, 'Public Protest, Domestic Acquiescence: Women in Northern Ireland', in R. Ridd and H. Callaway, eds, *Caught up in Conflict: Women's Responses to Political Strife*, Basingstoke: Macmillan.

Elphick, R. and H. Giliomee, eds, 1979, *The Shaping of South African Society 1652 – 1820*, Cape Town: Longman Penguin South Africa.

Esack, F., 1988, 'Three Islamic Strands in the South African Struggle for Justice', *Third World Quarterly*, vol 10, no.2, April.

Haron, M., 1988, 'Islamic Dynamism in South Africa's Western Cape', *Journal Institute of Muslim Minority Affairs*, vol. 9, no. 2, July.

Haron, M., 1991, 'Arabic and Islamic Studies in South Africa', *The American Journal of Islamic Social Studies*, vol 8, no. 2.

Mernissi, F., 1992, *Women and Islam*, Oxford: Basil Blackwell.

Moodie, T. D., 1975, *The Rise of Afrikanerdom*, London: University of California Press.

Mutahhari, M., 1981, *The Rights of Women in Islam*, Tehran: WOFIS (World Organization for Islamic Services).

Naude, J.A., 1985, 'Islam in South Africa: A General Survey', *Journal Institute of Muslim Minority Affairs*, vol. 6, no. 1, January.

Nkrumah, G. G., 1989, 'Islam: A Self-Assertive Political Factor in Contemporary South Africa', in *Journal Institute of Muslim Minority Affairs*, vol. 10, no. 2, July.

Ridd, R., 1981, 'Where Women Must Dominate: Response to Oppression in a South African Urban Community', in S. Ardener, ed., *Women and Space: Ground Rules and Social Maps*, London: Croom Helm; 1993 revised edn, Providence & Oxford: Berg Publishers.

Ridd, R. and H. Callaway, eds, 1986, *Caught up in Conflict: Women's Responses to Political Strife*, Basingstoke: Macmillan.

Ross, R., 1983, *Cape of Torments. Slavery and Resistance in South Africa*, London: Routledge and Kegan Paul.

Roussou, M., 1986, 'War in Cyprus: Patriarchy and the Penelope Myth', in R. Ridd and H. Callaway, eds, *Caught Up in Conflict: Women's Responses to Political Strife*, Basingstoke: Macmillan.

Shell, R., 1974, *The Establishment and Spread of Islam at the Cape from the Beginning of Company Rule to 1838*, unpublished B.A. Thesis, University of Cape Town.

Shell, R., 1978, *De Meillon's People of Colour*, Johannesburg: The Brenthurst Press.

Siddique, K., 1986, *The Struggle of Muslim Women*, Kingsville, Md.: American Society for Education & Religion.

Western, J., 1981, *Outcast Cape Town*, London: George Allen & Unwin.

5

Mixed Motives: Islam, Nationalism and *Mevluds* in an Unstable Yugoslavia

Cornelia Sorabji

Changing Political Contexts

This chapter concerns a complex society at a particular, complicated and critical moment in its history, and focuses on one ritual, the *mevlud* (from the Arabic *mawlid*, denoting the calendar date of the Prophet's birthday), as performed by local women at that critical moment during the summer of 1990. Sarajevo was then the capital of the socialist republic of Bosnia-Hercegovina which formed part of socialist federated Yugoslavia. But multi-party elections were on the way and years of weary contempt, boredom and silence on the topic of politics had been replaced by enthusiasm for the novel recreational activity of comparing political parties and possibilities. For Bosnia's multi-national population of Muslims, Serbs and Croats (approximately 44 per cent, 31 per cent and 17.5 per cent respectively), the freedom to discuss and the perception of new opportunities were exciting. But with the opportunities came dangers, and with the excitement a tinge of wariness. Streams of disputatious verbiage were emanating from a rapidly multiplying number of political parties. While several of these included the word 'democratic' in their titles, their exact aims were for the most part ill-defined. All that many prospective voters knew about them was that they were Serb, Croat, Muslim, or non-national in orientation. National awareness was riding high on optimism about economic progress and EC membership, but also giving birth to the beginnings of anxiety about potentially aggressive nationalisms.

Accompanying the political tension was religious revival. This was true of Bosnia's Serbs, Croats and Muslims, and of their respective faiths, Orthodoxy, Catholicism and Islam. But in Muslim dominated Sarajevo it was Islamic activity that was most in evidence and as part of this general revival the women's *mevlud* rituals were attracting numbers which far outstripped those I had witnessed while doing fieldwork in the mid-1980s. At one level Islamic activity was spreading and uniting the Muslim population, yet underlying this unity of purpose lay the 'mixed motives' of the title. For while all *mevlud*-goers understood their participation as religiously motivated, their understandings of Islam's implications and its relevance to Muslim national identity were varied. The *mevluds* did not then become a simple banner of national and religious unity *vis-à-vis* the Serbs and Croats, nor a banner of any particular religious or political outlook; rather they took on a subtle and variegated hue which was sometimes disturbing to their participants. Women who attended *mevluds* in increasing numbers did so partly in celebration of the end of socialist disapproval and partly in search of national/religious unity as a form of new security and meaning in the context of communist collapse. But in the place where they had most hoped to find this unity they also found discord and conflict. What was the revival, who owned it and who had authority to lead it were questions that made the *mevlud* not only a Durkheimian vehicle for the expression of solidarity, but also an arena for clashes over the nature and basis of that solidarity.

One aim of the present paper is to describe something of the emotional texture of a situation full of uncertainty and confusion. Anthropology has become self-critical of a tendency to treat its subject matter ahistorically, and this self-criticism has resulted in a tempering of the discipline's traditional study of 'the other' as self-contained and unchanging. Yet while the dynamism of changing times has been increasingly addressed, the anthropology of turbulent times, of major social upheaval, remains a small domain. Given the difficulties inherent in attempting to say anything clear about situations characterised by uncertainty and insecurity this is perhaps unsurprising. However, the widespread unrest which has accompanied the demise of one-party communist rule in the ex-socialist bloc begs anthropological attention. Where war has found a firm footing, its cultural effects may form the focus of study (cf. Lan, 1985; Wilson, 1991), but in 1990, Yugoslavia had not yet been subjected to the grim certainties of war.

A second aim is to provide some counterpoise to anthropological studies of women which tend to emphasise the ways in which they express themselves and pursue goals as women. This is perhaps especially notable in anthropological studies of religious and ritual behaviour, and understandably so. Since ritual events more than any other type of event are anthropologically held to say, mean and do things for those who participate in them – rituals reflect social structure, reinforce ideologies, uphold or subvert power structures and so on – women's rituals are most often viewed as events at which women say, mean and do things about themselves as women. Whether religion is used as a direct means of negotiating with men (for example, Somali women's use of spirit possession as a 'weapon of the weak'; cf. Lewis, 1971), or to unite women through a ritual focus on specifically female roles and values (for example, Turkish women's *mevluds*; cf. Tapper, 1983), what many such studies share is an emphasis on the ways in which women's rituals are constructed and understood as specifically female, as countermodels, complements or reactions to male ideologies. The stress is on female unity and solidarity and/or on women's negotiation of their gender role in society.

Less emphasis has been placed on gender negotiation and expression in the rituals of Muslim men. This discrepancy need not lie purely in the eye of the anthropological beholder. Given that for many Muslim women rituals represent one of the few occasions for which they can legitimately demand 'time off' from the patrilineal household and their allotted duties within it, it is unsurprising if such events are felt by the participants to be meaningful, at least in part, precisely because they are gatherings at which women and only women come together for an important spiritual purpose. At the same time many such rituals do focus on roles and values felt to be specifically female (and the Sarajevo *mevlud*, like its Turkish counterpart, includes celebration of the childbed and motherhood of the Prophet's mother; cf. Tapper, 1983). Yet women are not only women, but also people of diverse education, income, occupation, status, belief and temperament and as such, like men, capable of using ritual to assert or negotiate things other than and as well as their role as gendered individuals; and of using ritual gatherings as forums for the expression of conflicting views and values. In the Sarajevo summer of 1990 the prominence of such 'mixed motives' made them hard to ignore.

The misunderstandings and minor hostilities tangible at *mevlud* gatherings occurred against a background in which ethnicity and religion were inextricably linked, a context in which religious rituals, Muslim, Orthodox or Catholic, were felt to have relevance for national identity and thus at some level a bearing on the political future. They also occurred against a cultural background in which personal and nuclear family autonomy were jealously guarded and open affronts against them avoided. Increased *mevlud* participation drew together women of assorted backgrounds and posed dangers for the preservation of polite restraint.

Thirdly, the presence of representatives of a small, loose, urban network of religiously educated young women caused tension. In the 1980s a quiet brand of Islamic reformism had been attracting small numbers of young people and as the end of one-party rule was pronounced nigh they became more vocal and visible. These reformed Muslims were more knowledgeable about and more inclined towards the wider Islamic world than the non-reformed. The meeting of the two, and particularly of the reformed with older traditional female religious leaders, was problematic.

Nation and Faith, Town and Neighbourhood

The Muslims are Serbo-Croatian speaking Slavs of the Islamic faith, descendants of those Bosnians who converted after the Ottoman invasion of the fifteenth century. Under Tito their status as a nation rather than a mere religious grouping was recognised (although this status has been disputed by Serb and Croat voices, and never more so than in the historiographical fervour of the 1990s). In the ordinary language and perceptions of Bosnian Serbs, Croats and Muslims, ethnicity and religion are inextricably linked. A Serb is Orthodox and vice versa, a Croat is Catholic and vice versa, and a Muslim is a Muslim and vice versa. In fact, the terms often applied by Bosnians to Bosnians are Srbin, Katolik and Musliman. While the Communist Party drew a distinction between 'Musliman' with a capital M (national) and 'musliman' with a small m (religious), thus making it theoretically possible to be a Musliman of the Catholic faith or a Serb of the Muslim faith, to the ordinary Bosnian this idea made very little sense.

Islam thus serves to distinguish Muslims from Serbs and Croats but it also potentially ties them to the wider Muslim world transcending the bounds of Bosnia. These two aspects of Muslim identity – distinction from other Yugoslavs and co-identity with the *umma* (community of Muslims) – have been stressed with varying degrees of intensity at different historical moments and by different sections of the population. They by no means exhaust the range of Muslim self-definitions of identity but in 1990 became one axis along which *mevlud* participants found conflict.

Sarajevo's town centre boasts a mixture of Ottoman, Austro-Hungarian and twentieth century architecture and is a domain in which Muslim, Serb and Catholic meet and interact at work, at school and in the shops, markets and cafes. Urbanisation throughout Yugoslavia has meant that the town's population has grown steadily over the past thirty years and the area known as 'New Sarajevo', a wasteland of dreary apartment blocks, is ever-expanding. These blocks are built by business enterprises and inhabited by employees of the firms so that Muslim, Serb and Catholic live alongside each other. In contrast to the town centre and

New Sarajevo, the old Muslim neighbourhoods (*mahale*) on the hills of the valley of the Miljacka river are felt to be, and preserved as, Muslim in a way that the rest of the town's space is not. A mass of steep winding cobbled streets lined with small houses, their courtyards and gardens hidden from the street by high fences and gates, small neighbourhood mosques dotted around, these neighbourhoods are places where people use Arabic and Turkish greetings (*salaam 'aleikum, merhaba, aksam hajrula*), instead of the standard Serbo-Croatian greetings (*dobar dan, dobar vecer*) of the town outside. For Sarajevans, whether they live in an old style neighbourhood or not, the *mahalas* with their gossip, their old women in *dimije* (flowing, baggy trousers), their Turkish greetings and their constant to'ing and fro'ing are both comical and a prized embodiment of Bosnian and of Muslim tradition.

The neighbourhood is a world apart, and in many ways a world of women. Men work outside the home and are not expected to hang around socialising – they should go out to the cafes and bars. Neighbourhood women attend each other's household rituals such as the *tevhid* (death rituals) and the *mevluds*, drink coffee together, borrow money and goods from each other, help one another with tasks ('you sew my quilt, I'll roast your coffee') and exchange small amounts of cooked and uncooked food. Nonetheless, it is not a 'private' world of women as opposed to the 'public' world of men and the town centre. What distinguishes the *mahala* from the town outside (and particularly so in the mid-1980s) is that it is the domain of Islam and Muslim identity, while the town is where one plays down national/religious identity. It is in such neighbourhoods that most *mevluds* take place, and from such neighbourhoods that many of the participants traditionally come.

Unity and Distrust

The social, economic and ritual interdependence of neighbourhood women is evoked by the saying *znanje, imanje*, (knowledge is wealth) – if you can't afford a new sofa before the imminent price rise or don't know how to mend a quilt, knowing people who can help is just as good. While no proverb expresses the idea that knowledge is power, the concept is perhaps even more relevant to neighbourhood life. Nuclear family households keep their comings and goings, incomes and courtships secret from one another and even within the nuclear family privacy and autonomy are guarded: husbands and wives may well not reveal the exact state of their finances to each other, daughters will not tell their mothers about boyfriends. This level of secrecy requires skillful gamesmanship and in many respects merits the title of game. Frequently, for example, the woman concealing the cost of her new curtains knows perfectly well that her neighbour knows, and the neighbour knows that the women knows she knows. The point, however, is that privacy must not be ruptured by an open and offensive statement of the facts. At the same time there are secrets which are really supposed to be secret because neighbours, however friendly and helpful, are also potential malefactors who might spread damaging gossip (cf. Rheubottom, 1985, on Macedonia). People are on the defensive, those who 'have to know everything' are roundly condemned – although never to their faces since open conflict and insult must be avoided – and an atmosphere of secrecy, gossip, defence and counter-attack is pervasive.

In examining the witchcraft beliefs of the French Bocage, Favret-Saada (1980) suggests that while Bocage neighbours distrust each other greatly, their sense of co-identity and of distinction from other Frenchmen is profound. The suspicious and clandestine environment of the *mahala* similarly serves to unite its (Muslim) inhabitants *vis-à-vis* Serb and Croat outsiders, tying them together through a web of knowledge and power as well as through the functional interdependence of social coffee visits, lending, borrowing and mutual aid. In this 1980s context outsiders were different, but also distant and therefore people with whom one could have cordial relationships without worrying too much over the consequences. At the *mevluds* of 1990 open disagreement between Muslims lay only millimetres beneath the skin of ritual unity and was, I suggest, perceived as a threat both to personal integrity and to Muslim unity.

A Diversity of Women

Under the Austro-Hungarians (1878–1918) and within the inter-war Kingdom of Yugoslavia, Shari'a courts had continued to function in Bosnia. However, following the Second World War and the advent of socialism they were abruptly abolished. I have argued elsewhere (Sorabji, 1988) that in itself the disappearance of the Shari'a courts had a less disruptive effect on Muslim marriage and inheritance practices than might be expected, partly because many Shari'a provisions such as polygamy and cousin marriage were rarely exploited even under Ottoman rule, and partly because informal arrangements made between kin could circumvent secular legal rulings. The point to be stressed here is that, unlike some of the other women presented in this book, Muslim women neither live under the jurisdiction of the Shari'a nor have recourse to its courts.

In terms of education women vary markedly, the principal determining factors being age and rural versus urban background. Women raised before the Second World War in Sarajevo may have received religious and secular education, while those who were raised in the countryside and later migrated to town are likely to have received religious instruction from parents and the local *hodza* (religious teacher) in Islamic prayer and custom and the life of the Prophet (but not Arabic language), but unlikely to have received much secular education. They may therefore be illiterate or semi-literate. After the second world war, primary education began to be made available and compulsory to all. While some rural parents still keep their daughters away from school, urban Muslims prize knowledge and learning both as a route to a more prosperous future and as intrinsically valuable within an Islamic frame of reference. Most therefore want their daughters to continue into secondary schooling and perhaps even move on to university. The younger the woman and the more urban her background, the more secular is her education likely to have been. On the other hand, standards of religious education have declined. While post-war children may have been sent to the *mekteb* (Qur'anic school) for part-time instruction in the basics of Islam, it is optional. Children attend after school hours, and few parents are as strict and concerned about success there as they are about success in secular education. The result is that anyone raised before the Second World War is likely to have more religious education than anyone raised after it. (The exception to this case is that of the reform style Muslim women of whom more will be said below).

The range of jobs on offer to women is similar to that of any European city – cleaner, shop assistant, clerical worker, secretary, teacher, lawyer, journalist, and so on. But access to such employment depends on qualifications and connections and many women with children prefer to be at home if this arrangement is financially viable. The need for qualifications and the preference for being at home with the children mean that, in spite of the difficulties of finding a first post, overall younger women are more likely to be in formal employment than their seniors. The latter may, however, engage in small-scale income-raising activities such as rearing chickens and selling eggs to the neighbours, rearing goats or a cow and selling the milk, or weaving rugs and knitting traditional patterned socks for sale in the tourist shops or to acquaintances.

The *mevluds* of the mid-1980s were for the most part attended by elderly or middle-aged housewives with variable levels of personal religious observance (from regular prayer and annual fasting to occasional prayer and fasting the odd day of Ramadan), but usually with enough religious education to know the words of at least some of the relevant prayers (those they did not know they could mumble along to). *Mevlud* holders were relatively well off or considered to be rich (one ritual I attended was held by a family jokingly referred to as the 'Carringtons', in reference to the American TV soap 'Dynasty' which was popular at the time). But the majority of attenders were neither rich nor poor by local standards. They included women married to skilled or white collar workers, owning their own small homes or in possession of company apartments and hoping that their children would rise somewhat beyond them in educational and income terms.

Small grand-daughters, pre-school but old enough not to cry or disrupt the proceedings, were sometimes brought along and always praised and smiled upon in a manner which reinforced their interest in *mevluds* and religion. Young unmarried women, however, were rarely present. Often their college or work commitments would have kept them away, but in any case there was little cultural expectation that they should attend the *mevluds* of any but the closest neighbours and kin. What is appropriate to a *zena* (woman/wife) is not necessarily appropriate to a *cura* (unmarried girl). While the latter was generally expected to have a belief in Islam and to practise Islamic virtues of hospitality, generosity, public modesty and so on, she was not expected to spend much time at rituals. A young woman who did so would be praised, but at the same time most agree that a girl should *hoda* (walk about/have fun) while she had the chance since marriage would put a stop to all that.

Conducting and reciting at the *mevlud* could be anything from five to fifteen *bulas* (female religious leaders, a word of Turkish derivation). *Bulas* were generally middle-aged or elderly women who had no small children to keep them at home and who had for the most part been educated at the female *medresa* (traditional school) before its closure in 1952. They were officially employed by the Islamska Zajednica, the religious establishment which existed under agreement with the socialist authorities. They were, however, a traditional, pre-socialist part of the Sarajevo landscape, and in practice their services at a *mevlud* were very rarely solicited via the Zajednica. Hostesses who knew them personally or by word-of-mouth invited them directly, and paid them handsomely in blue envelopes discreetly slipped into their hands as they left.

The mid-1980s relationship between *bula* and non-*bula* was one in which the former provided religious services which helped to keep Islam alive for women who, caught up by the demands of modern life and of socialism, were less religiously observant than their ideal self-image may have demanded. While there were some caustic comments about the *bulas'* motivation (the blue envelopes contained far more money than a woman could earn from office work or selling eggs), for the most part they were respected figures in front of whom speech was modified to exclude anything too raucous or earthy. In return, the *bulas* kept Islam alive without trying to rejuvenate it or to demand too much religious observance from women unable or unwilling to give it. They provided information on and preached Islamic practices such as Ramadan fasting, the recitation of Qur'anic texts suitable to particular occasions, the *hajj* (annual pilgrimage to Mecca) and so on, but did not command that women cover their heads in public, avoid seaside bathing or remonstrate with husbands who enjoyed a drink or more (alcohol consumption is high among men). Such practices might be mentioned in a favourable light but were not imperative.

In 1990 this balance was unsettled by the arrival of two new types of women on the *mevlud* scene. Firstly, there were women with less religious knowledge or experience than the typical *mevlud*-goer, women whose enthusiasm was stimulated by a political context in which the disapproval of atheist authorities was no longer relevant, in which religious expression seemed to be an expression of the changing times and of the new freedoms which western-style democracy would bring, and in which the assertion of religious/national identity appeared more vital than before. Secondly, there were young women and young *bulas* (or *mu'alimas*, the Arabic term with which the Zajednica wanted to replace *bula* and which many of the young preferred) with a less traditional and more radical vision of Islam than their elders.

The Reformed

Everyone had felt that 1980s Yugoslavia was in decline. Tito's death was followed by a decade of rising unemployment, falling wages, massive inflation and a general feeling that the system was going awry and new solutions had to be found. To some of the young within this 'apocalypse culture' (Ramet, 1985), Islam, a religion astir in the Middle East, became an appealing solution. As one young woman told me: 'It's modern to be Muslim'. The female *medresa* had re-opened in 1978 and provided an alternative education to that offered at secular secondary schools. Many of its early pupils were from relatively poor rural families attracted by the fact that the *medresa* provided accommodation, subsidised meals and bursaries. Others were urbanites drawn to Islam. In and around the male and female *medresas* there grew up a small subculture of committed young Muslims, anxious to learn Arabic and as much about Islam and the Islamic world as possible. Some of the young women had adopted Islamic-style dress which displayed their standpoint to the world, and all avoided the revealing sort of Western fashions – short skirts, sleeveless tops – favoured by their fashion-conscious peers.

In socio-economic terms there was no rigid divide between these reformed Muslims and others, but there was a tendency for them to be the offspring either of families of *hodzas, bulas* and dervishes or of families with above average but not high income levels. Parents might be professionals or mechanics, plumbers and skilled craftsmen – people who could earn money moonlighting or in small-scale private businesses. These young Muslims themselves tended to have or aspire to higher levels of education than their peers. Those who were not at the *medresas* or the Islamic Theological Faculty might be at university studying oriental languages, law, medicine, computer technology, architecture or the like.

The principle that Muslim equals muslim was meaningful to and accepted by all. But reformed Muslims placed an additional emphasis on the need to actively choose rather than simply be born into Islam. Thus the strange conversation I overheard between a friend of mine and her nine-year-old cousin. The boy, sensing that the topic was a sensitive and meaningful one to my friend, asked, out of curiosity and mischief it would seem, whether he was a Muslim. The normal answer to such a question from a child would be a simple: 'Yes, of course, what else are you but a Muslim?' But my friend paused and asked him: 'Well, do you think you are?' Curiosity and mischief showed in the reply he gave while scanning his cousin's face: 'No'. 'Well then, you're not', said my friend.

These varying attitudes were also apparent in my own relationships with traditional and reformed believers. The former accepted me as an English Protestant, whatever this may have meant for them, and were occasionally interested in the customs and rituals of my home. The idea that I might convert to Islam was one usually raised in the context of kindly jokes about my marrying some nice Muslim boy and settling in Sarajevo for good. It was more through affection and jest than through any real wish or hope that I would convert; in their eyes I was what I was and that was more or less the end of it. For the reformed on the other hand, just as Muslim birth and provenance did not guaranteee full Muslim identity, non-Muslim birth and provenance was not a total barrier to it. They knew and respected the fact that I was an English Protestant, but Cat Stevens, Boney M and Anthony Quinn had all been Christians too and they had converted. Islam was a universal religion and there was always the possibility, and sometimes the hope, that I too would convert.

The relationship between this subculture and the Muslim community within which it existed was a delicate one. The reformed felt that Islam was theirs in a way that it was not fully the religion of the non-reformed. Thus one male reformed Muslim told me of the Ramadan *bajram* (feast) greeting he had received from a neighbour, scornfully adding: 'How can he wish me a happy *bajram*? He hasn't fasted Ramadan, so *bajram* isn't his to celebrate.' Yet since many of the reformed Muslims came from families more traditional and less observant than themselves, they could hardly turn their backs on or polemicise with negligent Muslims. At the same time they had to respect, albeit sometimes grudgingly, those elderly Muslims who, although often believers in bits of what the young saw as superstition, sometimes illiterate and certainly not schooled in Arabic or Islamic theology, nevertheless prayed five times a day and fasted Ramadan. Reformed Muslim women therefore tended to avoid the company of those non-reformed who were neither kin nor neighbour and to look forward to an early marriage (a practice supported by reference to the Hadith, the Prophet's sayings) which would take them out of the sphere of their own nuclear family and allow them to create a family environment and lifestyle more in keeping with their beliefs.

From the point of view of the non-reformed it was hard to find anything concrete to object to in the behaviour of the reformed. Unless one was an out-and-out atheist (which very few, even within the ranks of the Communist Party, were), what could one criticise about learning Arabic, daily prayer, and mosque attendance? Such things were self-evidently admirable. However, the reformed Muslims' strictness and seemingly snobbish avoidance of the non-reformed made the latter uneasy and resentful. It led to comments that while these paragons might look perfect on the outside, only God knew what was in a person's heart. And furthermore, some would point out, even if they did not themselves pray five times a day, their grandmother or other kin did, and they could therefore expect to be treated more civilly by reformed Muslims. It was a tension that I sometimes found myself caught in the middle of. My non-reformed friends and acquaintances were unsettled by my relationships with the reformed, worrying about whether the latter were criticising them to me or turning me against them. My reformed friends worried that the non-reformed were giving me an inaccurate picture of Islam which I would then spread abroad. If this made me uncomfortable it was far more unsettling for my assorted acquaintances. In a society where ethnic unity is to be maintained, open hostility to be avoided and where insult is always suspected, conflict over a matter as sensitive and central as Islam was disturbing to all.

In 1990, the tension came out into the open as the predominantly young reformed on the one hand, and the religiously observant or religiously negligent non-reformed on the other hand, found themselves face to face (with the *bulas* caught in the middle). In the 1980s, reformed Muslims had for the most part kept themselves to themselves and left the *mevluds* alone as traditional rituals primarily attended by older women and conducted by older *bulas*. Many non-reformed women raised after the Second World War had left these occasions alone because they felt unfamiliar with the ritual environment, ignorant of the prayers, put off by an atmosphere of socialist disapproval or simply indifferent to this piece of tradition. Now both types of women started adding their *mevlud* efforts to those of the traditional *mevlud*-goers, injecting new and various aspirations, understandings and hopes into the proceedings in a way which threatened the old balance between *bula* and non-*bula*. It made women vulnerable to the sort of open criticism and attack customarily avoided, and questioned the very nature of Muslim religious and national unity.

Mevluds

As indicated earlier, *mevlud* denotes the calendar date of the Prophet's birthday. In Bosnia, it also denotes the text of a poem celebrating this event and honouring the Messenger (there are several such poems in Serbo-Croatian and in Turkish), and, thirdly, a ritual including recitation of such poems. (For clarity's sake it is only in this latter sense that the term is used here.) By extension the term *mevludski* programme denotes a gathering at which the intention is to celebrate and honour the Prophet through recitations of religious material.

If the word itself has several related denotations, it is also true that no single *mevlud* is identical to another. The rituals vary in textual content as well as in venue, grandeur, pretext and participation. All *mevluds* are held to mark some particular event, be it the calendar date of the Prophet's birthday, the return of a son from military service, the building of a new house, the anniversary of a relative's death or some other occasion. Those organised by men are most often held in mosques, *tekijas* (dervish lodges) or other non-household venues, and are generally open to women as long as sufficient space is available to ensure some degree of physical distance between the sexes. Women's *mevluds* are held in the home and open only to female friends, relatives and neighbours of the hostess, some of whom will have been specifically invited, while others who could not be contacted directly hear about it on the grapevine. Invited or not, any woman who has some relationship with the hostess will be welcomed. For the understanding is that she has attended out of respect and affection for her hostess, and in order to join her prayer and thanksgiving with hers. In this respect, the *mevlud* is similar to the other major collective rituals performed by women, such as the *tevhid* ritual held for the recently deceased. But a number of disimilarities help to illuminate why the *mevlud* is capable of becoming the sort of arena for individual expression and a testing ground for competing views that it appeared to be in 1990.

While those who attend the *mevlud* are held to be doing so for the hostess' sake, they are also held to be getting something out of it for themselves. Reflecting this understanding, the *mevlud* sweets given to participants on departure are treated more as going-home gifts than as thanks and payment – the meaning explicitly attributed to the *kifla* (bread loaves) distributed to *tevhid* participants in the closing stages of that ritual. Part of the something *mevlud* attenders are getting is *sevap* (religious merit, deriving from the Arabic *sawab*). Although local ideas on the nature of *sevap* are sometimes sketchy, underlying all exegesis on the matter is the idea that it accrues to actions which are good but not necessary religious duties. Thus one gets no *sevap* for saying daily prayers, but much from fasting the ten days of *muharrem* (the first month of the Islamic calendar). The *tevhid* is not formally accounted a religious duty, and women say that one might equally well pay for a *hatma* (an entire reading of the Qur'an) to be recited for the deceased at the mosque. However, evidence suggests that the *tevhid* has been growing in popularity in recent years. Newcomers to Sarajevo, and in particular Muslim gypsies, have been adopting the custom (cf. Bringa, 1991). In practice, most Sarajevo Muslim women treat the *tevhid* as something which should be done if at all possible, for somehow it would be a bit shoddy to opt for the *hatma*. The *mevlud*, on the other hand, is decidedly optional. The cost of hosting such an event is far greater than the *tevhid* and beyond most family's reach, and the returned son, the completed house or the anniversary of death are deemed less in need of prayer than the recent death of a relative.

The *mevlud's* optional nature allows for *sevap* and, along with the lesser sadness and seriousness of the event marked and the greater flexibility of the elements of the ritual, for beauty and enjoyment. Women express a pleasure in *mevlud*-going which would seem out of place in the context of a *tevhid*. In later discussions of the event, they are more likely to classify it as *lijep* (beautiful), and to dwell on the factors that made it so – the quantity and quality of food served, the number of women and *bulas* present, the attractiveness of the participants' clothing, the beauty of the *bulas*' voices, the comfort of the seating and heating/ventilating arrangements, the general ambience and so on. *Mevluds* vary greatly in these respects from those where almost everyone gets a seat to those where women are squashed together on the floor; from wealthy surroundings in which guests wear silk and fresh, white embroidered or gold-laden headscarves to those with a high proportion of old women in knitted slipper-socks and floral flannel; from those where one is served coffee, some *pita* (cheese or spinach pastry), salad and cake to those where one is regaled with six or seven courses served in relay by young women of the household.

So too does the textual content of the ritual vary. The *mevlud* may last for up to two and a half hours and is led by the *bulas* who take it in turns to recite sections of the Qur'an and passages from various different *mevlud* poems. Among the standard elements of any *mevlud* are the collective recitation of *salavats* (salutations to the Prophet) and prayers towards the end of the formal ritual, a pause for the drinking of sherbet (a cinnamon flavoured beverage) handed round to all participants after the *mevlud* poem section in which the childbed of the Prophet's mother is described (a heavenly bird offered Amina sherbet to ease her labour pains), and the collective chanting of the Serbo-Croatian 'Dobro Nam Dosao, O Pegjamber' (Welcome, O Prophet, a text from a *mevlud* poem) after the birth of Muhammed. These moments at which the guests are required to become active participants are invariable, but from the *bula's* point of view a *mevlud* involves a significant degree of judicious creativity, decision-making and intuition. Without having rehearsed and without distracting on-the-spot discussions as to whose turn it is next, each *bula* must contribute an appropriate bit or bits of recitation. The Prophet's story must be told, but who should tell which bit of it and using which section of which text is a question resolved only as the ritual unfolds.

The optional nature, flexibility and spontaneous creativity typical of *mevluds* allows for innovation and contrasts relevantly with the tone of the *mevludski* programme mentioned above. In the mid-1980s, I attended *mevludski* events organised by *medresa* students and other committed reform-style Muslims. Held in mosques and thus without hosts, the *mevludski* programmes also differed from *mevluds* in their content and tone. Carefully rehearsed Qur'anic recitations and Serbo-Croatian hymns rather than *mevlud* poems formed the textual core of the event.[1] Since there was no sherbet and no 'Dobro Nam Dosao', and since few ordinary Sarajevans can recite much of the Qur'an, and the hymns were at that time little known and somewhat suspected outside the circle of the *medresas* from whence they were being spread, the scope for active participation on the part of those attending a *mevludski* programme was limited. Rather than a collective ritual, the *mevludski* programme felt very much like a meeting between performers – the *medresa* young people who sang and recited – and the audience. While the former were the focus of the event and were congratulated on their performances, no one suggested that the attenders had acquired any *sevap*. Although they had attended a religious occasion, they had not actually done anything much that could attract *sevap*. In short, the *mevludski* programmes were controlled, didactic and self-consciously 'modern' in a way that the traditional *mevluds* were not. Four or five years later, some elements of these programmes were to be introduced to household *mevluds* in a way that was partially successful, but also a cause for unease.

A *Mevlud* in 1990

These changes were apparent during a *mevlud* which I attended at the time of my fieldwork in 1990. The house had three rooms, a kitchen and a courtyard hidden from the street and the neighbours by high walls. Perhaps a hundred women had packed themselves into the available space. Those in the drawing room, where the ten *bulas* sat, consoled themselves that while none of the courtyard breeze could reach them there, at least they were acquiring more *sevap* than their more comfortably seated companions. As the foreign guest I got a place in the drawing room where I sweltered in my jacket and headscarf until kindly told to take the jacket off and let the scarf hang over and cover my bare arms. At first I resisted the suggestion, since bare arms at a *mevlud*, even covered by a scarf, seemed completely unacceptable in the light of my prior *mevlud* experiences. But when a second woman urged me, and I looked around the room to find any number of women in short sleeves, I gratefully gave in.

We drank our coffee and gossiped until the first *bula*'s reedy voice signalled the start of the ritual. Each *bula* took her turn, while we sat and listened. I watched the company, particularly intrigued by a tall, pale young woman in a black headscarf who sat near the front, deeply involved in the proceedings and silently reciting to herself. The sherbet and the 'Dobro Nam Dosao' came and went, upon which 'black headscarf's' voice filled the room with the mournful tones of a Serbo-Croatian hymn. She had bided her time and let her seniors recite first, but the piece she chose now was a long one, each heart-rending verse followed by a heart-rending chorus. The latter was reasonably easy to pick up after a couple of hearings, and some of the assembled women began to sing along with it, encouraged by 'black headscarf' herself, whose preoccupation lifted slightly and whose eyes opened to glance at us all in the silent beat preceding the chorus. I realised that the woman must be a *bula/mu'alima*.

Not all of the old *bulas* appeared happy with this innovation to the *mevlud* ritual, and one or two began to fan themselves vigorously and to 'tut-tut'. On the other hand, some of the women present evidently

appreciated the hymn enough to join in. Part of their enjoyment probably lay in the fact that they *could* actively join in, that after sitting quiet
and cramped there was something they could rouse themselves for in
the same way that they did for 'Dobro Nam Dosao'. At the same time,
the sort of suspicious resistance to joining in that had been felt by some
attenders at *mevludski* programmes in the mid-1980s had been partially
broken down by the spreading fame of the *medresa* choir. Earlier in the
year a concert had been arranged at the Zetra sports stadium where popular, commercial singers sang *sevdalinke* (Muslim folk songs), and the
medresa choir recited religious material. This event, in which national
and religious identity were jointly celebrated, had been attended by
thousands and then widely distributed on a video cassette that almost
everyone I knew had watched.

If 'black headscarf's' success was an example of the reformed reaching the unreformed (but not all of the old *bulas*), what happened in the
courtyard after the event suggested the opposite. The formal ritual had
ended, we had all been served *pita*, salad, cake and coffee and now was
the time for mingling and conversation. I found myself in a small circle
of women, including one in her late forties and attired in a just-below-
the-knee-length, short-sleeved dress. She, like most of us, had removed
her headscarf after the formal ritual ended, but was nevertheless per-
spiring in the heat. A second woman, around 35 and smartly dressed in
long skirt, co-ordinating jacket, silk blouse and headscarf fastened with
a pearl pin, stood near her. Out of the blue the short-sleeved woman suddenly and rather aggressively enquired: 'Why are you dressed up like
that in all this heat?' There was a long uncomfortable pause before the
proud and yet more aggressive answer: 'Because of Allah!' For a split
second there was silence as the two stared at each other, then both
turned their attention to their immediate neighbours, and some moments
later, the smartly dressed woman moved off to another circle. It was a
small incident, but everyone felt the tear it had made in the fabric of an
occasion intended as one of piety and unity. The contrast between short-
sleeved comfort and headscarved elegance (neither of which had been
typical of mid-1980s *mevluds*) stands as a visual image of the strain
between reformed and non-reformed Muslims.

A Diffused Conflict

The wary relationship between the two groups had developed and
changed in the context of the new political freedom and the general
Islamic revival. Since the non-reformed felt that they had always been
proper Muslims at heart, just a bit lapsed, it seemed to them that their

current religious vigour should make up for the lapse and repair the breach between themselves and the reformed. It was certainly the case that my non-reformed acquaintances seemed to feel a new confidence and ownership of their religion. Women who had five years earlier dodged my questions about Islam, mildly teased me about my penchant for hanging around mosques and jovially presented me to each other as someone who 'knows more about Islam than you do!' no longer made these implied denials of religious knowledge, but lectured me on Islamic history and custom in a way that claimed the topics as their own. If they were reclaiming Islam there was no longer a need to feel shifty and resentful about the devout and practising reformed.

Yet from the reformed's point of view, religious observance or enthusiasm was not and never had been the only yardstick. As indicated elsewhere, devout but illiterate old women had always fallen outside the realm of those who could be criticised, but had never been included in the realm of the truly admirable. As for those who had never previously been devout but were making efforts now, they were frequently seen as jumping on a bandwagon. Thus many Muslims took pains to point out: 'I'm not one of these new Muslims who only just discovered it when it got easy, I was a Muslim years ago when the authorities disapproved'.

At stake in the dispute between the two groups of women was the personal integrity of both. For the old *bulas* both personal integrity and traditional authority were being challenged by the black headscarved *mu'alima*. Her innovative hymn had been taken up by some of the *mevlud* participants and what it stood for – reform style Islam – threatened to unhinge the old balance between *bula* and non-*bula* in which the former was revered for her piety and learning and the latter provided with religious services but not with demands for rethinking and rejuvenating Islam.

Behind such immediate threats to the person lay the uneasy feeling that, when it was most needed, religious/national unity was being threatened. All understood themselves as attending the *mevlud* for the sake of Islam, and for all Islam was intimately related to Muslim national identity and thus of relevance to the political future being debated in every cafe and newspaper and on every street corner and shop floor. All shared certain basic wishes for that future – more jobs, better wages, less corruption, more religious freedom – but the extent to which Muslim identity implied distinction from Serbs and Croats, unity with the wider Islamic world, or any other relationships, was by no means a matter of agreement. The possible political implications of stressing different aspects of Muslim identity were not articulated or debated by anyone. This was not a dispute between defined positions and aspirations (and certainly not a dispute between those wanting a secular or an Islamic state), but a diffused conflict between various far less detailed or explicit attitudes. Striking at the heart of national/religious unity as it did, it was nonetheless profoundly disturbing.

Postscript

Since this chapter was written, Bosnia-Hercegovina has been ripped apart by an extraordinarily brutal war for the creation of ethnically pure territories and polities. Its Muslims have become the target of genocide, and Sarajevo itself subjected to a full year of constant shelling. In spite of their 1990 anxieties, as this war drew closer Muslims denied its possibility with increasing vigour, widely insisting that no serious violence could disrupt Bosnia's long traditions of multi-ethnic co-existence (and failing to arm or organise for conflict). The path from summer 1990 to the beginning of the assault on Bosnia in spring 1992 has been a tortured and complex one which cannot be dealt with here. But two points should be made.

This chapter has highlighted two aspects of Muslim identity, distinction from Serbs and Croats and co-identity with the wider Muslim world, but these do not exhaust the number of ways in which Muslims have understood themselves or their situation. As war drew closer in 1991, the nature of Muslim identity as European identity and of Islam as faith in keeping with the spirit of Europe – rational, tolerant and just, as it was perceived in the pre-war period – received increasing stress. So too did the importance of multi-national Bosnian identity as opposed to the identities of Serbia and Croatia. In Sarajevo the onset of war was widely understood as an urban/rural conflict between civilised citizens and barbaric peasants (Sorabji, 1993). The European nature of Muslim Bosnian identity and the urban/rural divide were not new ideas coined for the moment, but understandings which had always been present. It is the stress placed on varying perceptions of identity that has changed over time and in response to changing contexts (and this is as true of Serbs, Croats and of all identity groups as it is of Bosnia's Muslims).

The second point concerns the route by which so bloody a war took hold. The conflict has sometimes been presented as caused and fuelled by age-old inter-ethnic hatreds which festered within families and communities until the communist lid was removed from the boiling pot. The example of the 1990 *mevluds* and their context suggests a differing scenario, pointing to fear rather than hatred and underlining communism's legacy and final collapse as significant in themselves rather than merely as the removal of a lid covering something else of decisive significance.

In the 1980s Sarajevans had generally known who was Muslim, Serb or Croat and symbolically guarded the ethnic boundaries, but this had not implied hatred. As noted, in 1990 Sarajevans were both optimistic about the future and anxious that aggressive nationalism should not blight it. This anxiety was reflected in fairly widespread support for a legal ban (later overturned) on the creation of nationally-based political parties.[2] Until the last moment, the reformed Communist Party and the Alliance of Reform Forces (multi-national parties) appeared to have political support in Sarajevo. Overall then the desire was precisely for inter-ethnic peace rather than strife. The 1990 *mevlud* expressed nationalism of a celebratory, nervous and disunited character, containing no coherent idea of how the future should be organised, merely hoping that it should be better, more prosperous, more liberated, more peaceful than the past. Nevertheless, Muslim religious activities were to become disturbing to non-Muslims, just as, for example, the increasingly heard Serbian patriotic pop songs were disturbing to Muslims.[3] Fear, liberally stoked by the media, helped pave the way for the importing of a wider Yugoslav war, brewed, supplied and originally prosecuted outside Bosnia-Hercegovina, and in this war the Muslims could only be the major targets.

1. Since the idea of 'hymns', singing and music seems anathema to scripturalistic, reformed Islam, some explanation of the term seems in order here. While the hymn was indeed classed as a type of song (*pjesmo*), specifically a *pobozno pjesmo* (a Godly song), it was not a song which one 'sang' (*pjevati*, to sing). One might sing a *narodno pjesmo* (a folk song), or a *sevdalinka* (a traditional Muslim folk song), or a pop song, but in the context of a religious gathering one was not 'singing' a Godly song but 'reciting' it (*uciti*, to learn, study or recite). Qur'anic chanting, musical recitation of *mevlud* poems and the *pobozno pjesmo* were all things that one recited rather than sang. It is interesting to note that people 'reciting' Serbo-Croatian *mevlud* poems or hymns did so in the somewhat nasal and constricted tones in which Arabic, Qur'anic texts were recited. Their voices took on a quality different from that evident in the singing of folk or pop songs.

2. A poll conducted in Sarajevo, Banja Luka and Mostar in May 1990 (see *Danas* 22 May 1990) saw 73 per cent in favour of the ruling banning nationally based parties. With 1,039 respondents, all of whom had telephones and lived in major towns, this survey cannot represent a scientific sample of Bosnian opinion in general, but does give an indication of widespread awareness of and desire to avoid the possibility of inter-ethnic hostility.

3. See D. Janjic, 1992 and Z. Slavujevic, 1992 for statistical evidence of Muslim, Serb and Croat suspicion and fears of each other.

References

Bringa, T., 1991, 'Gender, Religion and Person: The Muslim Identity in Rural Bosnia', Ph. D. Thesis, University of London.

Favret-Saada, J., 1980, *Deadly Words: Witchcraft in the Bocage*, Cambridge: Cambridge University Press.

Holden, P., ed., 1983, *Women's Religious Experience: Cross-Cultural Perspectives*, London: Croom Helm.

Janjic, D. 1992, *Gradanski Rat u Bosni i Hercegovini* (Civil War in Bosnia Hercegovina), in D. Janjic and P. Shoup, eds., *Bosnia i Hercegovini Izmedu Rata i Mira* (Bosnia Hercegovina Between War and Peace), Belgrade/Sarajevo: Forum for Ethnic Relations.

Janjic, D. and P. Shoup, eds., 1992, *Bosnia i Hercegovini Izmedu Rata i Mira* (Bosnia Hercegovina Between War and Peace), Belgrade/Sarajevo: Forum for Ethnic Relations.

Lan, D., 1985, *Guns and Rain: Guerillas and Spirit Mediums in Zimbabwe*, London: James Currey.

Lewis, I., 1971, *Ecstatic Religion*, London: Penguin.

Parkin, D., ed., 1985, *The Anthropology of Evil*, Oxford: Basil Blackwell.

Ramet, P., 1985, 'Apocalypse Culture and Social Change', in P. Ramet, ed., *Yugoslavia in the 1980s*, Boulder, Co.: Westview Press.

Ramet, P., ed., 1985, *Yugoslavia in the 1980s*, Boulder, Co.: Westview Press.

Rheubottom, D., 1985, 'The Seed of Evil Within', in D. Parkin, ed., *The Anthropology of Evil*, Oxford: Basil Blackwell.

Sorabji, C., 1988, 'Islamic Revival and Marriage in Bosnia', *Journal Institute of Muslim Minority Studies*, vol. 9, no. 2.

Sorabji, C. 1993, 'Ethnic War in Bosnia?', in *Radical Philosophy*, 63.

Tapper, N., 1983, 'Gender and Religion in a Turkish Town: A Comparison of Two Types of Women's Gatherings', in P. Holden, ed., *Women's Religious Experience: Cross-Cultural Perspectives*, London, Croom Helm.

Wilson, R., 1991, 'Machine Guns and Mountain Spirits: The Cultural Effects of State Repression Among the Q'eqch'i of Guatemala', *Critique of Anthropology*, vol. 11, no. 1.

6

'Guardians of the Faith?': Gender and Religion in an (ex) Soviet Tajik Village

Gillian Tett

Walking through a noisy political demonstration in a Tajik town recently, I caught sight of a small pamphlet. It featured two satirical cartoon drawings: on one side of the page there was a Tajik woman, dressed in Russian style clothes; on the other a 'Muslim' woman, swathed in a headscarf. Which one? asked the pamphlet, somewhat ambiguously, in Tajik, a language closely related to Persian.

The pamphlet was from one of the many new political parties that have sprung up in the Tajik republic since the collapse of the Soviet Union in 1991. Nevertheless, the images were ones that most Tajiks now share. After 70 years of being a Soviet republic, dominated by an officially atheist state, the break-up of the Soviet Union has pushed Tajikistan into independence and towards a reassessment of its Islamic identity. Correspondingly, the 'woman question' has become an emotive political issue as some recently emerged Islamic groups use their new-found freedoms to demand a more 'Muslim' model of society and female behaviour, while others (most notably those previously associated with the old communist regime) reject this.

This chapter seeks to shed some light on these issues, by looking at the relationship between women and Islam in a small Tajik village during the last months of communist rule in Tajikistan (in the year before the collapse of the Soviet Union).[1] The aim of the chapter is not to assess what Islam should or should not 'mean' for women in Tajikistan – the question that most Tajiks use to discuss the issue – but rather to look at the issue in reverse: what have women 'meant' for Islam in Tajikistan? Or, more specifically, what role have women played in the religious life and Muslim identity of a rural community?

The question of what type of roles women might play in the religious life of Muslim communities is an issue that has often been downplayed, not only in the study of Central Asian Islam, but also in the anthropology of Islam more generally. Although there is an extensive literature on male religious practices in the Muslim world, female religious practices in Muslim communities have generally attracted rather less attention – a state of affairs that reflects a prevailing perception that what women do in Islam is often less 'orthodox', less visible and less prestigious, and thus, by inference, less vital to the religious well-being of their communities. One very interesting exception to this lies in the work of the Tappers (Tapper, 1983; Tapper and Tapper, 1987), who have looked at the role women can play in the religious life of a Turkish community – a study that leads them to argue that: 'It is wrong to assume *a priori* that women's religious "work" is less important than or peripheral to that of men. Not only do women too practise the central, day-to-day rites of Islam, but in their performances they may carry a religious load often of greater transcendental importance to the community than that borne by men' (Tapper and Tapper, 1987:72).

However, as far as Central Asia is concerned, women have been notably absent from accounts of practised Islam. Western scholars who looked at the region during the Soviet period (see, for example, Carrère D'Encause, 1979; Bennigsen and Broxup, 1983; Bennigsen and Wimbush, 1985) have generally attempted to assess how far religious practices had 'survived' Soviet rule by focusing on issues such as Sufi brotherhoods, underground mosques or circumcision – all male-dominated activities. And although some interesting accounts of female religious practices can be found in the work of Soviet ethnographers (Mardonova, 1985; Taidzhanov and Ismailov, 1986; Babayeva, 1989; Mukhiddinov, 1989; to name but a few), the accounts have usually considered such practices to be 'survivals' (*perezhitki*, Russian) of 'pre-Islamic' cults,[2] and as such distinct from proper Islam – something which Soviet scholars have, like western ones, implied was primarily a male dominated activity.

This chapter, however, takes a slightly different approach. For its central thesis is that during the Soviet period, rural Tajik women were a key focus for their community's religious life and Muslim identity. Not only were they more diligent in performing their religious duties than the men, but they were also associated with the areas of life perceived as the most 'traditional', 'Tajik' and 'Muslim' – labels that were partly defined through the villagers' experience of the Soviet state. One reason for this lay, as I will explore, in the cultural and gender distinctions that were attached to space in village culture. However, another factor was the concept of female 'shame' – a concept that had taken on specific ethnic implications in Tajikistan.

Background to Obi-Safed[3]

The material that forms the basis of this chapter was gathered in a small, Tajik-speaking,[4] mountain village called Obi-Safed (population 1,200), located about 30 miles from the Tajik capital, Dushanbe (and 80 miles from the Soviet–Afghan border).[5] Before the Soviet period, the village had been a tiny, isolated herding community, which was nominally part of the emirate in distant Bukhara (which, in turn was part of the Russian empire). In practice though, its political life had centred around the mosque, the village elders (*mui-safed*, Tajik, white haired) and large land-owners (*bey*). Although accounts of the period[6] refer to the inhabitants of the region as 'Tajiks', it appears that the villagers perceived themselves primarily as being 'Muslim' and belonging to a certain region (i.e. the valley around Obi-Safed), rather than being specifically 'Tajik'. They considered themselves Sunni Muslims, and the position of women appears to have been comparable to that of most rural women in other parts of the Turkic and Persian world: women usually lacked property rights; were married young; and were secluded in the home whenever it was economically possible.

In the late 1920s[7] the area was overrun by Soviet troops, who rapidly set about establishing the basic structures of the Soviet communist state: agriculture was collectivised, political structures based around the Communist Party imposed on the valley, and the villagers informed that they were now part of the Tajik republic – a new Soviet creation. Then, in the 1940s, a mining complex was built near the village, which brought a road, shops, a hospital, a school and electricity cables into the valley. By the time I came to do my fieldwork, most villagers were earning a reliable living on the state farm, or nearby mines, or in local service industries. They supplemented this with food from their tiny kitchen plots – the only land that was legally 'theirs' under the Soviet system.

These economic changes were accompanied by a vigorous programme of cultural reform, which sought to educate the villagers into the new communist ideology and culture – a culture that was heavily infused with Russian influences. For the purposes of this chapter, there are two main strands of this which need to be considered: firstly, the drive against Islam; and secondly, the movement to 'liberate' women.

The drive against Islam began almost as soon as the communists arrived in the valley. In the 1930s, the small village mosque was destroyed, and the villagers forbidden to pray in public. During the Stalinist purges in the late 1930s, a number of villagers were arrested for so-called 'Islamic behaviour'. After the demise of the Stalinist regime in the early 1950s, these arrests ceased. Nevertheless, public displays of Islam continued to be severely curtailed. As late as 1985, for example, a local schoolteacher was threatened with dismissal if he circumcised his son too publicly. Although a few state-sponsored mosques were allowed to operate in the large Central Asian cities, the villagers had little contact with these.[8] Thus although this repression did not mean that all religious activity ceased, between the 1930s and mid-1980s (a period that corresponded to the villagers' living memories) Islam had generally been excluded from the public sphere.

Shortly before I arrived in the village, this situation had slowly begun to change. As a result of the perestroika reform campaigns that had been launched by Soviet President Mikhail Gorbachev at the end of the 1980s, most state controls on religion had been lifted. By the beginning of 1990, the villagers were being allowed to pray in public. Shortly after I arrived, the family which had traditionally provided the mullahs in the village started to rebuild the mosque. Nevertheless, these changes should not be overstated. In spite of the political turmoil that was occurring in faraway Moscow during 1990, in Obi-Safed the Communist Party was still believed to be the most powerful institution in the valley, backed up by the omnipresent KGB. The villagers remained wary of discussing their political or religious views in public. Most villagers, in short, still believed that they lived in an aggressively secular state.

The second strand of these Soviet campaigns, namely the drive to 'liberate' women, affected the villagers rather more gradually. From the mid-1920s onwards, the Communist Party in Central Asia began vigorous initiatives designed to undermine the influence of Islamic tradition on gender and family.[9] Propaganda campaigns were waged against veiling and female seclusion; legislation was passed raising the marriage age, banning polygamy and forced marriage; and efforts were made to suck women into education and employment. Initially these campaigns were fiercely resisted in villages like Obi-Safed. However, as Communist Party control was consolidated, they gradually began to have some impact (albeit at a very much slower rate than in the urban areas). By the end of the Second World War, some Obi-Safed women were working in the state farm (a change that seems to have been partly triggered by a drop in the male labour force when village men were called up to fight in the Soviet army[10]). By the 1950s most girls were receiving some schooling, and the marriage age was gradually rising.

What influence these changes had on the actual position of women is an issue that I will explore later in the chapter. However, by way of background, two points should be noted. Firstly, in comparison with many rural communities elsewhere in the Muslim world, the Obi-Safed women often had a relatively high status in the village. In 1990 and 1991, for example, all girls attended the coeducational village school to the age of 17. About a sixth of the girls (plus about a third of the boys) entered higher education. Most women had worked for wages at some point in their lives (usually in temporary agricultural work at the local state farm), and about a fifth held full-time jobs, ranging from lowly jobs as cleaners, to very prestigious posts as doctors, or accountants at the state farm. Indeed, the highest ranking communist official in the valley was a village woman. Women were expected to dress modestly in baggy trousers and long tunic, and cover their heads with a scarf, but full veiling had disappeared. Girls usually married between the ages of 18 and 22.

Nevertheless, in spite of these changes, the Obi-Safed villagers were adamant that their ideals of female behaviour were still essentially Islamic. And indeed, in many aspects of village life, attitudes towards women closely echoed patterns seen in other parts of the Muslim world. Although many individual women worked, women in general were still perceived primarily as mothers and wives. They were expected to show excessive respect to the older generation, particularly to the male elders. Most marriages were arranged, virginity was considered essential for a bride, and unmarried and recently married women were heavily chaperoned.

From this brief background description, then, it can be seen that the Obi-Safed villagers, like most Soviet Muslims,[11] lived in a world shaped by two distinct factors. On the one hand there was their experience of the Soviet state, which had dominated the political and economic institutions of the village for most of the villagers' lives. On the other hand, there was the villagers' sense of their Islamic identity, which had been sporadically repressed during the Soviet regime, but was still, as far as the villagers were concerned, not only pre-eminent, but central to their ethnic and cultural identity. In the course of day-to-day life, the villagers often expressed this ethnic identity in terms of 'being Tajik'. However, it should be noted that they still perceived themselves *primarily* as members of a distinct regional group, and then, only secondly, as members of the Tajik republic (although their sense of being 'Muslim' was fundamental to both of these territorial identities).

To an outside observer, these separate strands often seemed a strange mixture. The first time I visited the village myself, for example, it struck me as distinctly odd to spend the morning sitting in the farm offices under a portrait of Karl Marx, chatting in Russian to the local Communist Party official – and the afternoon in this same official's house talking in Tajik to his wife about pilgrimages to the local Muslim shrine.

However, this was not a reaction that was shared by the villagers. Seventy years of Soviet rule had left them adept at juggling multiple identities, and with distinct attitudes towards gender, space and religion. In the rest of the chapter, I will look at these specific points in detail. I will do this in three stages: firstly I will explore the role that women played in religious practice; then I will look at the cultural ideals that were attached to women; and lastly I will discuss the relationship between space and gender in the village – distinctions that had taken on specific cultural implications during the Soviet period.

Islam in Obi-Safed

Male and Female Religious Practices

All the villagers in Obi-Safed were adamant that they were Muslims. However, their understanding of what this meant was not clear cut. After 70 years of being largely isolated from the rest of the Muslim world, their knowledge of 'orthodox' Islamic ideologies was limited. Nevertheless, what they did know about were a set of *practices* that they believed should be performed in order to be a good Muslim. Islam, in other words, was perceived not so much as an abstract 'ideology', but as a cultural and ethnic identity and set of religious duties that Muslims should – ideally – perform.

Some of these religious ideals were seen as specifically male duties. Thus, for a man to be a good Muslim, the villagers said, he was supposed to meet and pray in the mosque, fast during Ramadan, give alms to the poor, read the Qur'an, and observe the daily prayer. He should also take part in the religious rituals associated with birth, death and circumcision – a ceremony that was considered essential for village men. Although it was recognised that men could pray at home, the best type of male religious activity was believed to be mosque based.

Other religious ideals were seen to be female duties. Most of these were associated with domestic space. Thus, although women were generally excluded from mosques, good Muslim women were supposed to observe the Ramadan fast, pray and give alms at home. In addition, they were also expected to take part in small intercessionary ritual prayer sessions, known variously as the *bibi-seshambe* (Tajik, grandmother's Tuesday) or, less commonly, as *mushkil-kusho* (Tajik, solving of problems). In cases of specific misfortune, women were also expected to stage small rituals to ward off the evil eye (Tajik, *chashm*), or make small pilgrimages to local shrines (Tajik, *mazor*) – one of the few cases when women took part in religious activity outside the household.

Out of this list of female and male religious duties, male practices were generally deemed most prestigious. If I asked the villagers a question about Islam in the village, for example, they would usually start their answer by talking about mosques, mullahs and the *mui-safed*. Women would often expand this answer by talking about their own practices, and usually stressed that these were also valuable. Nevertheless, I never heard any woman challenge the dominant view that the most prestigious type of Islam was mosque based.

But although these distinctions had implications for status, it should be stressed that this did not mean that male and female religious duties were regarded as separate religious categories, or categorised as being 'more' or 'less' Islamic. When the villagers themselves talked about their religious practices, in other words, they did not invoke the type of distinctions that outside observers are apt to apply (such as the distinction between orthodox/popular, or Islamic/pre-Islamic). Instead, both male and female practices were seen as being part of a general category of things of the 'faith' (Tajik, *dina*) – practices that Muslims should perform. Furthermore, although female practices apparently had less prestige, they were not considered unimportant. Indeed, as I will now explain, in some senses women's religious practices were often regarded as more, not less important than the men's practices.

Religion in Practice

So, how did these ideals of religious practice match reality? At this point in the discussion, a central paradox must be noted: although women's religious practices were considered less prestigious than men's, women were considerably more diligent than the men in their observance of religious duties.

During the year that I was in Obi-Safed almost all the women and girls over the age of 12 fasted during Ramadan. Most of them also took part in small ritual meals and prayer ceremonies in the evenings. And during the rest of the year most married women regularly took part in rituals like the *bibi-seshambe*. These were held both during life-cycle ceremonies (such as marriage), and when a household had a specific intercession (if a household was looking for a bride, for example). Most women also visited shrines or took part in small rituals to ward off evil spirits whenever there was any misfortune. Quite a significant proportion of the middle-aged women also observed the daily prayer at home.

The proportion of the men who observed religious duties, however, was significantly lower. Shortly before my arrival in Obi-Safed, the villagers had started work on rebuilding their mosque. And indeed, during my time in the village, the mullah was leading the Friday prayer in a makeshift mosque nearby. But although a few men, primarily the elderly, were meticulous in their religious duties, the majority (particularly the young) were lax. Only a small minority of men, for example, rigorously fasted during Ramadan in 1990 and 1991. An even smaller proportion observed the daily prayer, or read the Qur'an at home. And although most men visited the mosque on festival days like *id-i-kurbon* or *id-i-ramadan*, most did not visit the mosque regularly. To illustrate this disparity, it is perhaps useful to cite a concrete (and fairly typical) example from my fieldwork.

> Tolib was a middle-aged teacher at the local village school. A relatively wealthy man, he lived in a household with his father and mother, wife, two sons and three daughters. Tolib and his sons did not fast during the 1991 Ramadan, and only visited the mosque once. Tolib's father, a *mui-safed*, did fast, and sometimes visited the mosque once it was built. However, the people who were most diligent in the household were the women: they rigorously fasted during Ramadan, and regularly attended *bibi-seshambe*. Tolib's mother also said prayers in the evening – something she was teaching Tolib's daughter to do as well.

Furthermore, it appeared that before perestroika this bias had been even more marked. Whereas men's religious activity was perceived to have increased, women's religious activity was generally perceived to be unchanged. Women, I was told, had always fasted, or performed ceremonies like *bibi-seshambe*, even during the Stalinist years. This did not mean that it was *only* women who had been practising Islam. A few *mui-safed*, for example, claimed that they had 'quietly' said prayers at home in the past. The mullah told me that he had occasionally met in great secrecy to read the Qur'an. Nevertheless, the point to be stressed is that these male observances appear to have been limited. Whereas most women had been regularly taking part in religious rituals during the Soviet period, most men had not. And although the proportion of men participating in Islam had significantly increased during the time I did my fieldwork, they were still, overall, less than diligent in their performance than the women.

'Religious Women'?

The pattern that emerges from the material above is one where women seemed to have been doing considerably more 'religious work' than the men during the recent Soviet period. So why was this? Why, in other words, had the men been so lax? or the women so diligent?

Asking the villagers themselves these questions usually provoked two distinct replies. The first answer (usually given by men) centred around the mosque. This 'explanation' went like this: 'Our men pray in the mosque; but for 70 years we did not have a mosque; therefore we could not pray.' By losing the mosque, in other words, the men had lost the locus of their religious activities. Or, as one *mui-safed* told me: 'Before, in the time of Stalin and Breschnev we had no mosque, so we (the men) could not meet. But now – a thousand thanks to Gorbachev![12] – we have a mosque, so we can pray and fast!'

The underlying implication behind this was that because women had always performed their religious duties in the home, they had been less affected by the ban on public religious displays. Indeed, since their practices had always been marked by a considerable degree of 'privacy', they had been easier to conceal from the state – or, perhaps more accurately, the state had been more willing to turn a blind eye to them. Certainly none of the villagers could remember any instances where women had been punished for religious observance. To cite this *mui-safed* again: 'Before, if the men met together to pray, then, there would be trouble. The women though – that was different. No one saw.'

But, in addition to this, the villagers sometimes gave a second type of answer, related to women themselves. This 'explanation' (usually given by women), went like this: 'According to the Qur'an,[13] women have more sins (*ghuna*) than men; so they need to fast more and pray to cancel out their sins; otherwise, everyone would suffer.' The rationale behind this female sin varied. Men usually explained this in terms of women's alleged sexual and spiritual weakness. Women, however, usually ascribed it to the polluting effects of menstruation and childbirth. Nevertheless, the implication in both male and female explanations was that women were the spiritual 'weak link' of the community. If they did not carry out the duties that might counteract the sin the entire community could suffer. Women's religious practices, in other words, were essentially *defensive*, guarding the community from misfortune, from the result of sin, from *chashm*, or from wicked spirits (*jinn*). They were, in a sense, the minimum a household needed to do to maintain its standing *vis-à-vis* the spiritual forces that shaped the villagers' world. Or, as one female friend of mine said: 'Women have to do Ramadan and pray, because we have more sins. If we didn't do Ramadan then it would be bad for us all.'

These two explanations were based around issues that villagers considered so 'self evident' and 'natural', that they almost never mentioned them directly. Nevertheless, these assumptions clearly begged a number of questions – Why did men 'have' to pray in a mosque, for example? Why were women 'naturally' in need of religious protection? So, at this point, it is necessary to widen the discussion, and look at some of these broader attitudes towards gender and cultural identity. To do this, we need to look at two specific issues: firstly the concept of 'shame', and secondly the issue of space and gender. For, as I will suggest below, these issues not only shed light on attitudes towards women – but also suggest women's diligence in their religious duties during the Soviet period was only one facet of a wider role they played in maintaining the community's cultural and religious traditions.

Women and Shame

In common with many other Muslim (and non-Muslim) cultures, attitudes towards women were often expressed in terms of the concept of shame (*sharm*). Women were expected to behave in ways that would not bring shame on themselves, and destroy the honour of their community. Although there were instances when men could cause shame, most shame was perceived to be caused by women.

The underlying issue in the definition of shame was the sexual control of women in particular, and the younger generation in general. Any action that defied the elder generation's authority to control the sexual rights of women was deemed to be shameful. If a woman refused an arranged marriage, for example, had an affair outside marriage, flirted with men, or dressed in a provocative manner, then she caused shame. This did not merely reflect badly on her, but also on the people who were supposed to be controlling her. Thus female shame could cause male shame, since it implied that her male relatives were too weak to control or defend her.

These attitudes towards shame and the control of women appear to have been well entrenched in the region long before the arrival of the Russians. However, during the Soviet period they became overlaid with new cultural and ethnic implications. For in so far as male honour was dependent on a type of female control, the Soviet state's campaigns to liberate women came to be seen as a direct attack on the honour of the men, and the entire community.

As I explained earlier, although the Soviet state had launched campaigns for the liberation of women soon after taking control of Central Asia, the impact of these campaigns was initially fairly limited on isolated villages like Obi-Safed. Nevertheless, they seem to have left a rapid and lasting stamp on the villagers' perceptions of the 'women question'. Most of the early communists that the villagers encountered were, it seems, Russian speakers. And so, in the eyes of the villagers, the campaigns for female 'liberation' became closely associated with russification (in much the same way that campaigns for female emancipation often became synonymous with westernisation in other former European Muslim colonies; cf. Kandiyoti, 1991:7). The communists, as far as the villagers were concerned, were trying to turn 'their' women into 'loose' Russian women, who had no respect for Islam – or shame. As one elderly woman remembered:

> When I was little, the communists came. The Russians – and some Tajiks too – they used to come up from Dushanbe and say things like – you women, why are you wearing big scarves! (over your head); you girls – why aren't you going to school? . . . so my father used to hide me and other girls in the hay. He said that the communists wanted to take the women away, and turn us into Russian women. They told us that if we took off our scarves they would beat us because we had no shame!

By the time I came to do my fieldwork in 1990, the days of these direct campaigns were long gone. However, the legacy was such that informants still tended to define their models of female behaviour in opposition to their images of 'Russian' or 'communist' women. Although the villagers had gradually assimilated some of the reforms (such as female education), they were adamant their women were still 'good' Muslim women – defined in opposition to 'Russian' women. If I asked a question like 'why do you wear headscarves?' for example, I was told: 'Without a headscarf a girl has no shame – she looks like a Russian.' Similarly, on the issue of arranged marriages, I was repeatedly told that whereas the Russian girls 'had no shame' because they freely associated with men, village girls were not like that – they had 'shame'. It was common to hear the villagers commenting that urban Tajik girls were not 'real Tajiks' because they tended to wear Russian clothes and had often adopted a considerably more russified lifestyle.

Issues of honour and shame, then, had become overlaid with highly emotive cultural and ethnic meanings. Just as a woman could cause her menfolk shame by sexual misdemeanour, so too, she could cause her entire community shame by cultural misdemeanour. If a man, for example, dressed in Russian clothes, failed to keep Ramadan and indulged in behaviour that was seen by villagers as being specifically Russian and un-Islamic (e.g. eating pork, and drinking alcohol), then his behaviour was deemed regrettable, but not utterly disastrous. It was primarily his *personal* religious standing that was seen to suffer – a standing that could be put right in later life when he became a *mui-safed*. If however, a woman did the same (i.e. drank alcohol, failed to keep Ramadan, and so on) then the 'offence' was regarded as infinitely more serious. She was deemed to have not only brought shame on herself, but also her entire community. Thus any evidence that women were abandoning the community's core values was seen to threaten its entire religious and cultural identity – as in the case of Amina, a pretty, 26 year old woman from a village near Obi-Safed.

Amina worked in the mining office as a clerk. She was unmarried – something that was very unusual at that age. When I made enquiries, I was told that this was because she was a 'bad' girl, who had no shame. When studying in a teacher training college in Dushanbe, she had allegedly had a romance with a Ukrainian. Rumour of this reached the village, prompting a furious reaction. *Mui-safed* had apparently ordered her family to remove her from college, and her family had been loudly harangued for the 'shame' they had brought the village. Amina returned, but although the Ukrainian apparently vanished, no one else wanted to marry her. For five years she stayed at home, and then quietly started a job.

She left the valley to live with a sister shortly after I heard the tale, so I never knew her version of events. But six years after the event, both men and women still expressed shock. Amina, I was told, had acted 'like a Russian', not just because she had defied village norms about arranged marriages, but because (according to rumour) she had behaved 'without shame' in Dushanbe, abandoning her headscarf, cutting her hair and smoking. Even though several male members of her family were fairly 'russified' – and indeed, one cousin was reportedly married to a Tatar woman – this apparently made no difference. Her parents, I was told, had so much 'shame' that they could barely call themselves Muslims or Tajiks any more.

Space and Gender in Obi-Safed

From the material that I have discussed so far, the pattern that has emerged is one in which women not only performed more religious work than men, but were also more generally associated with the side of village life that was seen as the most 'Tajik', most 'traditional'[14] and most 'Muslim'. In this section I will look a little closer at what this meant in everyday life in the village – and, more specifically, in the villagers' perceptions of space and gender. I will do this in three stages: firstly, I will look at the separation of public and private; secondly the distinction between Soviet and Tajik, and thirdly at the way in which these distinctions were gendered.

The Public and the Private

Obi-Safed village culture maintained a strong distinction between the public and private spheres of life – or, to put it as they usually did, between space where one could be seen by 'anyone', and space where only the closest circle of kin (*khesh*) were present. This distinction usually corresponded to the boundaries of the household (*khona*): the area inside the walled courtyards of the village houses, was generally treated as private, whereas the area outside the house, was usually considered public. However, these boundaries were not rigid. For the defining factor was not simply space per se, but space *and* people.

Most places were fairly fixed in their treatment – the village school, state farm, and the roads that lead outside the village for example, were always regarded as public. Conversely, a household's kitchens were 'private.' But between these two poles, the treatment of other spaces shifted with context. If guests came into a household, for example, a subtle redefinition of space would often take place: one room, or a verandah, would be deemed a public 'guest' area; while the other rooms would be kept more private. (Families which were rich enough to have a spare room tried to smooth this redefiniton of space, by keeping one room as a permanent 'guest' room.) Conversely, if there were no strangers present, the backyard space between neighbouring households was often considered relatively private.

The distinctions were expressed in a number of ways. On the most general level, the private sphere was where the villagers relaxed, carried out domestic business, wore their oldest clothes, and ate meals without excessive ceremony or strict gender segregation. In the public sphere, however, there was a more formal type of social interaction, with a greater degree of gender segregation, and ceremony. However, these distinctions were also expressed in the movement of people – or more specifically, as I will consider below, the movement of women.

The Soviet and Tajik in Space

This spatial ordering was not, of course, particularly unusual – most other Muslim communities would appear to share similar patterns. However, during the Soviet period these distinctions took on a particular political and cultural role in villages like Obi-Safed. For, under the pressures of a forceful state and sporadic cultural repression, the private sphere came to be seen as a bastion of 'traditional' values and culture. To understand this point, however, it is necessary to briefly look at villagers' perceptions of the communist state.

As I noted earlier, during the early years of Soviet rule, many of the changes imposed on villages like Obi-Safed had seemed distinctly 'alien' to the villagers. The first communists the villagers had come into contact with had been Russian-speakers and outsiders, and the reforms they brought had been distinctly at odds with village traditions. As time went on, this sense of 'alieness' seems to have broken down, as the villagers themselves gradually got sucked into the 'system'. By the time I came to do my fieldwork, for example, the local state structures and

Communist Party were predominantly staffed by villagers. The people who were teaching Soviet dogmas in the schools were also locals.

This shift did not mean that the villagers had entirely endorsed the 'system'. In some areas of their life – like religion – they were keenly aware of discrepancies between their 'traditional', 'Muslim' values, and those espoused by the state. Nevertheless, during the time I did my fieldwork, there was not, in general, an atmosphere of open *resistance* to the Soviet 'system' – or, at least, not in public. In the public areas like the state farm, or the school, for example, the villagers generally conformed to their image of 'modern', 'Soviet' behaviour: they hung pictures of Lenin on the walls, sat on 'Russian' style chairs, dressed in European clothes, and often conducted much of their working life in Russian. Back in the more private rooms of the house, however, they maintained 'their' traditions: they sat on 'Tajik' quilts (*kurbacha*), replaced their Russian suits with 'Tajik' clothes (such as the striped robes, or *joma* that men wore), and spoke almost entirely in Tajik.

The distinctions were not entirely rigid (not least because in some areas of life the state's ideologies closely overlapped with traditional or Muslim values). Some very 'Tajik' values, such as respect for the elder generation, were observed both in the public and private sphere. Conversely, the inside of village houses were dotted with a number of 'modern' influences, such as televisions, or gas cookers. And indeed, some of the more 'communist' houses had a picture of Lenin hanging in the most public guest rooms. Nevertheless this was rare. For although villagers were prepared to pay respect to Lenin in the state farm, most were uneasy about placing his portrait on their private walls. As far as they were concerned, the household was a private realm, outside the sphere of the communist state – and as such a bastion of Tajik and Muslim values.

Women and Space

So what did this mean for women? Again, as in many Muslim cultures, the division between public and private carried distinct gender implications. Prior to the Soviet period, women had generally been excluded from the more public spheres of village life. However, during the Soviet period women had come to play a more visible role in the public sphere. Although brides (*kelin*) were secluded within the private sphere for several months after marriage, this seclusion did not apply to older (or younger) women. At the time I did my fieldwork, for example, women could be seen working in the offices of the state farm or the schools, visiting the village shop or other households, or even walking a couple of miles down the road to the nearest large administration centre.

But in spite of these changes, women were still perceived *primarily* in terms of their domestic roles and their association with the domestic sphere. The household, and the private sphere was regarded as the most 'rightful' place for women. Correspondingly, this domestic sphere was seen to be centred around women. It was not perceived *exclusively* as female space: men spent a significant part of their leisure time sitting indoors, watching television, or simply chatting, sometimes with women, sometimes in segregated groups. If a group of male guests was being entertained by the men of the household, the men would sometimes perform simple domestic tasks for themselves, like making tea. I often saw men ironing their trousers. Nevertheless, the bulk of everyday domestic tasks were still performed by women. Women were at the heart of the household, and to have a household without a woman was inconceivable, as this small example, shows.

> Rustam had been living in a house with his wife for several years, but they were childless. One day he suddenly threatened to divorce her. She left their house, and Rustam, who was left alone there, promptly moved out. Although Rustam could cook everyone agreed he could not live in a house by himself. Quoting a village proverb, he commented: 'Women are the hearth of a house. Without a woman, a house is not good to live in.'

When women did enter the public sphere, they usually did so in ways that left their traditional association with the domestic sphere unchallenged. Women who entered public areas such as the streets were expected to do so for a good reason (such as going to school, or shopping). They were not allowed to just 'hang around,' as the men were apt to do, and expected to behave with decorum and dignity. Furthermore, if a woman did hold a job outside the house, she tended to do so in ways that kept, as Dragadaze (1981:166) notes in a nearby Tajik context, 'her role *as a woman* outside and inside the house . . . separate' (author's italics). Women wore different clothes at work, were often addressed differently, and often had separate statuses at work and at home – as the following case illustrates.

> Shamsiya was a doctor at the local hospital, and a prominent member of the local Communist Party. At work she commanded great respect and responsibility, mixed with men, and was generally treated as an equal with them. She was usually addressed as *muallim* (teacher). Back at home, however, she resumed her role of mother, and wife. She was addressed by kin terms – such as *kelin* or *zan-i-Kodir* (Kodir's wife) – deferred to her father-in-law, and if guests came, sat with the women. At work she wore a mixture of European and Tajik clothes. Before she went home, she always scrambled back into Tajik clothes. On several occasions when I accompanied her up from Dushanbe, we ended up rushing into a public toilet on the way up so that she

could put on a headscarf and baggy trousers under her dress before she went home.

Soviet Men and Muslim Women?

If we tie these different threads together, then it can be seen that the issues of honour and attitudes towards space reflected and reinforced each other. In so far as men were more engaged in the public sphere and in the state than the women, they tended to be more readily associated with the 'communist' and 'modern' side of village life. Conversely, since women, in their traditional roles, were regarded as the centre of the domestic sphere, they were perceived as central to its traditional values. The traditional image of 'woman' in other words was perceived to be not simply at the 'hearth' of the house, but at the very heart of the most 'traditional', and most 'Islamic' side of village life.

These distinctions were not entirely rigid. As I have noted above, some women were involved in high profile jobs in the state sector (albeit in a manner that usually left the 'traditional' domestic role of women in general unchallenged). Similarly, some men were linked with the more private or traditional sides of village life. Once a man retired from a state job, for example, and became a *mui-safed*, he would often begin to spend more time in the house, devote more energy to religious practice, and don 'traditional' Tajik clothes, such as a scull-cap, or turban. Nevertheless, as a general pattern, these distinctions between male and female, and between Soviet and Muslim spheres, underscored most aspects of village life, setting the agenda for female behaviour. To illustrate the point, it is useful to cite the household of Bobo Jamshed, one of the communist officials in the village. Although the example is a little extreme in the degree to which Bobo Jamshed was affiliated with the Soviet state, it was not unusual.

> Bobo Jamshed held a powerful position in the state farm. He had been a member of the Communist Party for over 40 years. His favourite leader, he told me, was Stalin (followed by Margaret Thatcher!).[15] In line with his communist credentials, he and his sons eschewed public displays of Islam: they did not fast at Ramadan, or attend the mosque. Although Bobo Jamshed occasionally wore a scull-cap at home, at work he always dressed in a Russian suit, with a row of Soviet medals on his chest.
>
> His wife, and two daughters-in-law, who spent most of their time at home, however, were quite fastidious in observing the duties of 'good' Muslim women. They fasted, attended *bibi-seshambes*, and other small ritualised prayer gatherings. They always wore Tajik clothes. Although one daughter-in-law worked, at home she played the traditional role of *kelin*.

Bobo Jamshed insisted that he was both a 'communist', and a 'good Muslim'. So did he not see any contradiction in this? I asked him one day during Ramadan. Not at all, he laughed. 'I am a communist. I cannot fast or pray at work. But my wife and *kelin*, they are sitting at home, so they must fast and pray! So we will not suffer from sins. We are a Muslim home!'

Of course, the question that arises at this point is: what did women themselves make of this? Did Bobo-Jamshed's wife and *kelins* not consider it 'unfair' that they had to fast? Or, to return to the story of Amina cited earlier, did Amina's female relatives not consider it strange that Amina had been punished for her romance with a Ukrainian – while her male cousin had married a Tatar with impunity?

Broadly speaking, the answer to these questions was 'no'. The attitudes outlined in this chapter were ones that were shared by both male and female villagers. Most women, for example, said – like men – that women were more sinful, that women should be the 'hearth' of the home, or that it was 'shameful' if they acted like Russian women. Or, as Bobo-Jamshed's wife cheerfully told me later, when I related her husband's comment about fasting: 'That's just the way it is. If we [women] stopped fasting, then no one would fast – and what kind of Muslims would we be then!'

This did not mean that all women always acquiesced to this status quo. In the course of their everyday life, women often defied some of the practical details of these overriding beliefs. The case of Amina provides one very extreme example of a challenge to the concept of arranged marriage and ban on hypergamy. On a less dramatic note, young unmarried girls (and boys) would sometimes admit in private that they would prefer a 'love' marriage to an arranged one. A few girls even managed to conduct some secret and coy romances, most of which were ultimately covered up as 'arranged' marriages. Similarly, I occasionally heard young women, particularly those who had studied in Dushanbe, grumbling against wearing the headscarf, or other restrictions – as in the case of Zebi, a vivacious 26 year old.

Zebi lived in a household with her husband, Jamshed, his formidable mother, Mo-sharif, and their two children. Before marriage, Zebi had worked as a seamstress in a state workshop. After marriage she had given up work, and lead a secluded life – something she accepted as natural, in her status as a new *kelin*. But five years later, she now wanted to work again. Mo-Sharif refused, primarily because Zebi was the only *kelin* in the household. 'My *kelin* has no shame to be asking this!' Mo-Sharif shouted at me, when I raised the matter. Zebi grumbled, but did not provoke an open argument. 'Mo-sharif is crazy – it is not as if I was a new *kelin* any more. But soon she will be dead, so then it will be easier,' she told me in private.

Nevertheless, as this last example shows, when women did lodge these small challenges, they were usually directed at the older generation in particular, rather than at men in general. The people who enforced these ideas of female behaviour were not so much the men, as the elder generation of men *and* women. Furthermore, even when individual women challenged small details of the status quo, they almost never dared challenge the 'fundamentals'. Although Zebi grumbled that it was 'unfair' that her mother-in-law would not let her work, for example, she still believed that it was 'natural' that new *kelins* should stay in the house, or that her primary role was that of a *kelin* and mother. Similarly, although most teenage girls dreamt of romance, this did not mean that they approved of romance with a Ukrainian. Cases like that of Amina, which I cited earlier, were very rare – and in so far as they breached commonly held norms, provoked outrage from both men and women.

Conclusion: Woman and Islam in Obi-Safed

At the beginning of this chapter, I pointed out that studies of Soviet Central Asia – as with many other anthropological studies of Islam – have often side-stepped the role that women play in Islam and Islamic identity in the region. As the material above has shown, however, a consideration of the religious role of women is vital for any analysis of how the Obi-Safed villagers maintained their sense of Islamic identity during the Soviet period. For during the years of Soviet rule, the 'religious load' that women were carrying – to cite the Tappers' phrase again (Tapper and Tapper 1987:72) – had been crucial to the community, both in a narrowly religious sense (by warding off the threat of misfortune, the evil eye, or the consequence of sin), and in a broader ethnic and cultural sense (by ensuring that the community could still call itself 'good Muslims'). Performing the essential religious duties, wearing Tajik dress, adhering to 'Muslim' notions of sexual honour, and maintaining a beautifully kept 'traditional' home were thus all facets of the wider role that women were playing in maintaining the community's sense of its Tajik, Muslim identity.

The conditions that had shaped this pattern had, of course, been those of cultural change, under an authoritarian (and quasi colonial) state, which had curtailed public religion. The model of Islam that I have sketched, therefore, is essentially a defensive one, shaped around the need to comply with the Soviet system in public, while maintaining religious identity in private. And indeed, as such it would seem to have echoes in other communities, Muslim and non-Muslim, elsewhere in the former Soviet world.[16] Nevertheless, I would suggest that the material from Obi-Safed also has wider implications for the way in which we look at the relationship between women and Islam more generally. For the underlying theme of this chapter has been that although women may often seem to have less prestige and visibility than men in the religious life of Muslim communities, this does not always mean that their roles in practised Islam are peripheral. Indeed, faced with the type of cultural pressure that Obi-Safed had experienced during its recent history, it had been the women, rather than the men, who had been the main 'guardians' of Islam in the community.

Epilogue

When I first arrived in Obi-Safed in 1990, I had little idea that the days of the communist system in Tajikistan were numbered. However, shortly after I left the republic in the summer of 1991, the Soviet Union was rocked by an attempted coup – an event which triggered significant political changes. So, by way of epilogue I will now summarise some of the changes that I observed on two brief visits I made to the republic in the autumn of 1991, and spring of 1992.

Shortly after the attempted coup in Moscow in the summer of 1991, Tajikistan's communist leaders, like most other Soviet republics, declared the republic's independence. For about six months these 'communist'[17] leaders attempted to rule the republic through the old political system, albeit under a banner of nationalism, and greater tolerance of Islam. However, this government was soon challenged by emerging opposition groups, particularly a new Islamic Party which had formed in certain regions of the country. In the spring of 1992, a coalition of democratic and Islamic groups violently toppled the communist government. However, at the end of 1992 the communists seized power again, amid a wave of fighting across the country which has so far left hundreds dead.

To a certain extent, this conflict has been a regional one.[18] Most of the Islamic Party supporters are from the Garm and Kurgan-Tyube regions of Tajikistan, whereas most communist supporters are from the Khodjent and Kulyab regions. However, on another level, the clashes also reflect wider political and ideological disputes. Whereas most of the old communist supporters want a secular type of state in Tajikistan, most of the Islamic Party opposition favour a more obviously Islamic model of government.

These sudden changes and spiralling violence have, unsurprisingly, left the villagers in Obi-Safed shocked and bewildered. However, they have also stirred up a new type of reflectiveness. The villagers I had worked with in 1990 had generally been nervous of discussing politics or Islam. When I met them again in 1992, however, these topics dominated discussion. After months of cautious silences, this deluge of talk was extraordinary.

As a result of regional loyalties, most of the villagers vehemently supported the 'communist' side, and some of the men in the village became actively involved in demonstrations and fighting down in the valleys. However, this label 'communist' did not have any real ideological meaning: by the spring of 1992 Obi-Safed, like other villages across Tajikistan, was beginning to look markedly more 'Islamic'. Whereas Islam had only been emerging into the open in 1990, by 1992 it was extremely visible in all areas of life. The mosque had been completed, and was a landmark in the centre of the village. As more men began to attend the mosque, it was rapidly becoming the main social and political focus for the village, rivalling the state structures: the local state farm council, for example, was beginning to hold its meetings there, instead of in the school. Correspondingly, the village mullah had begun to play an increasingly prominent role in village affairs. By the spring of 1992, his outspoken criticism of vodka drinking, of wedding dancing and Indian videos was beginning to be heeded by some villagers. The farm chairman now had a Qur'an in his office – next to his pictures of Lenin and Marx. The old divisions between public and private, and Soviet and Muslim are, in other words, being reshaped.

So, what type of impact has this had on the women? In the republic as a whole, women's issues have become a highly emotive political symbol in the conflict. On the one hand those associated with the old regime have accused Islamic groups of wanting to push women back into seclusion, 'just like the women in Iran'. For them, then, the image of the veil – or *paranja* as it is locally known – sums up everything that was alleged to be 'extreme' about the Islamic Party. For its part, the Islamic Party has denied accusations that it would force women into seclusion, or impose the Shari'a. Nevertheless it has repeatedly accused the communists of being part of a regime that corrupted and dishonoured women. As far as many Islamic Party supporters are concerned, then, the hated image is that of the gaudily made-up, Russian-dressed Tajik woman – an image they equate with the corruption and dishonour that Tajikistan is perceived to have suffered during the communist period.

On the ground in Obi-Safed, however, the villagers themselves seemed rather more ambiguous about these issues. Back in 1990, when the villagers discussed the behaviour of their women, they tended to do so by defining it in opposition to their image of Russian women (e.g. Tajik women do not cut their hair – not like Russian women). On occasion, they would also define it in opposition to the 'old times' before the Soviet period and acknowledge some of the changes that had occurred (e.g. in the past women wore *paranja* – they don't now). But the dominant contrast was between behaving like a 'Muslim' woman – or not.

However, the issue of what it means to be 'a Muslim woman' is becoming more complex. The villagers were adamant that they did not want to be ruled by Islamic 'fanatics' (as they tended to call the Islamic Party), and both men and women were vocal in their opposition to the veil. At the same time, though, they insisted, as before, that their women should not behave like Russians. There were now two images to define women against: the image of the veiled woman, or Muslim 'extremist' and the image of the non-Muslim.

As far as I could tell, these debates have not yet had much impact on women's actual behaviour. In 1992, women in Obi-Safed were still working in state jobs, walking in the streets and studying in schools as they had in 1990. They were also continuing to observe the Islamic duties in much the same way as before. Nevertheless, the rapid increase in male religious activities would seem to be altering the significance of this female role. For as more and more men become involved in Islam, and Islam begins to re-enter the public sphere, it seems that it is now the men who are dominating the on-going revival of the village's Islamic identity. Meanwhile, on the streets of Dushanbe, it is also primarily men who are producing the type of satirical political pamphlet sketching out these images of 'Russian' and 'Muslim' women.

Notes

1. The fieldwork on which this chapter is based was carried out between July 1990 and 1991 and was funded by a studentship from the Wyse Fund, Trinity College, Cambridge and a stipend from the British Council Anglo-Soviet exchange scheme. Early drafts of the paper were presented at a 1992 SOAS conference on women in Central Asia, and at seminars in Birmingham and Cambridge Universities. I am grateful for the many helpful comments received on these occasions.

After Tajikistan gained its independence in the autumn of 1991 I was able to make two, very brief, further visits. An epilogue at the end of the chapter summarises some of the changes that have occurred in the republic since the collapse of the Soviet system.

2. Although I do not have the space to explore the work of Soviet ethnographers in any detail here, it should be noted that this approach partly reflected the strong political constraints they faced (Soviet ethnograhers were, after all, working under a state that was batting to lessen the influence of Islam in the region).

3. In light of the on-going political uncertainty in Tajikistan, all identities have been concealed in the chapter. Obi-Safed (literally white water) is a fictional name.

4. The Obi-Safed villagers spoke a dialect of Tajik, a language closely related to Persian. There is as yet no well-agreed system for the transliteration of Tajik into English. The republic, for example, can be spelt Tajikistan, Tadzhikistan, Tadjikistan, or Tojikistan, depending on whether a Persian, Russian or literal system of transliteration is used. In this chapter, I have aimed for simplicity, rather than complete linguistic consistency, reflecting the pronunciation in Obi-Safed (which was often distinctly different from literary Tajik).

5. Due to the tight restrictions on foreign research that were in force during the time I did fieldwork, I was not able to live permanently in Obi-Safed, but visited it for several days each week during the time I was in Tajikistan. In total, I probably spent about 3 months there.

6. For more detailed descriptions of Tajikistan's history see Barthold (1927), Pierce (1960), Wheeler (1964) or, for the post-Soviet period, Rakowska-Harmstone (1970).

7. Although the main Soviet revolution happened in 1917, it was several years before the Communists gained control of all the outlying areas of the Russian empire. In the region around Obi-Safed they faced considerable resistance from opposition groups known as the *basmachi*, led by the old Emirate of Bukhara.

8. From the early 1940s onwards the Soviet state did allow a few mosques and mullahs to operate in the Soviet Union. However, these were tightly controlled, and strictly limited in number – by the early 1980s, for example, there were two small *medressehs* (religious schools) and an estimated 400–500 working mosques for a Soviet Muslim population of about 50 million (Bennigsen and Broxup, 1983:70). None of the villagers had ever had any contact with the handful of official mosques in Tajikistan.

9. For more information on these campaigns in Central Asia see an excellent account by Massell (1974). For general background to the Soviet state's approach to women's issues, see Lapidus (1978) or Buckley (1989).

10. Although Tajikistan was far from the Soviet front during the second world war, considerable numbers of villagers in this valley were called up to fight.

11. For comparable comments about this 'dual identity' among the ex-Soviet Uzbeks see, for example, Lubin (1984:7).

12. This little interjection of thanks to Gorbachev (*hazor rakhmat ba Gorbachev!*) was a fairly common expression, that was not entirely 'phoney' – Gorbachev was fairly popular in this village because he was seen as the author of the new religious freedoms.

13. These references to the Qur'an were again essentially a linguistic expression – none of the villagers had ever managed to read the Qur'an in full.

14. My use of the word traditional here refers to a concept held by the villagers, rather than any historical reality. What the villagers perceived as being their time-honoured traditions (*rasmoin*, Tajik) was not necessarily what had happened in the past, but rather what the villagers *thought* had happened in the past – usually defined in opposition to what was modern (a concept that they usually expressed through the Russian word *sovremmenie*) and/or communist.

15. Margaret Thatcher appeared on television screens in the village when on

a trip to Moscow in the days of perestroika. She made a terrific impression on the villagers (an impression that was, of course, made more of a conversation piece by my own presence in the village).

16. For similar observations on the role that women have played as the 'guardians of tradition' under a Soviet regime see, for example, Pine on Polish women, who writes: 'When Polish national culture was forced underground in many regions, men took the more active political and social roles, while women came to represent the transmission of culture in the form of language and Catholicism in the home' (1992:73). Other examples of the link between women and the transmission of culture can be seen in Dragadze's work on the Georgians (1988:160) or Humphrey's work on the Siberian Buryat (1983:35).

17. I use this label because this was the general political label that most Tajiks used when describing those who had been part of the former Soviet regime. The label does not mean that these 'communists' were actually espousing a specifically Marxist creed (indeed, most were not).

18. Correspondingly, it should be noted that these comments are essentially about one village, and do not necessarily apply to the whole of Tajikistan. It would seem that at the moment there are growing differences between regions in the way that these issues are perceived.

References

Babaeva, N.S., 1989, 'Prizhizhennye Pominki kak Perezhitok Ritual'nogo Ubieniya Starykh Lyudei' in *Ethnografiya v Tadzhikistane*, Dushanbe: Donish Press.

Barthold, V., 1927, *Iistoriia Kul'turnoi Zhizn' Tadzhkikistana*, Leningrad.

Bennigsen, A. and M. Broxup, 1983, *The Islamic Threat to the Soviet State*, London: Croom Helm.

Bennigsen, A., and E. Wimbush, 1985, *Mystics and Commissars: Sufism in the Soviet Union*, London: C. Hurst.

Buckley, M., 1989, *Women and Ideology in the Soviet Union*, London: Harvester Wheatsheaf.

Carrore d'Encause, H., 1979, *Decline of an Empire; The Soviet Socialist Republics in Revolt*, New York: Newsweek Books.

Dragadze, T., 1981, 'The Sexual Division of Space among Two Soviet Minorities: The Georgians and the Tadjiks' in S. Ardener (ed.), *Women and Space; Ground Rules and Social Maps*, London: Croom Helm; 1993 revised edn, Providence & Oxford: Berg Publishers.

Dragadze, T., 1988, *Rural Families in Soviet Georgia*, London: Routledge.

Humphrey, C., 1983, *Karl Marx Collective; Economy, Society and Religion in a Siberian Collective Farm*, Cambridge University Press.

Kandiyoti, D. (ed.), 1991, *Women, Islam and the State*, London: Macmillan.

Lapidus, G. W., 1978, *Women in Soviet Society; Equality, Development and Social Change*, University of California Press.

Lubin, N., 1984, *Labour and Nationality in Soviet Central Asia; An Uneasy Compromise*, London: Macmillan.

Mardonova, A., 1985, 'Khna v byti tadzhikov gornogo Tadzhikistana i zirabad-skikh eroni Bukharskoi oblasti' in *Ethnografiya Tadzhkistana*, Dushanbe: Donish Press.

Massell, G. J., 1974, *The Surrogate Proletariat; Moslem Women and Revolutionary Strategies in Soviet Central Asia, 1919–1929*, Princeton University Press.

Mukhiddinov, 1989, *Relikty Doislamskikh Obychaev i Obryadov u Zemledel'tsev Zapadnogo Pamira*, Dushanbe: Donish Press.

Pierce, R., 1960, *Russian Central Asia 1867–1917; A Study in Colonial Rule*, University of California Press.

Pine, F., 1992, 'Uneven Burdens: Women in Rural Poland' in S. Rai, H. Pilkington, and A. Phizacklea (eds), *Women in the Face of Change; The Soviet Union, Eastern Europe and China*, London: Routledge.

Rakowska-Harmstone, T., 1970, *Russia and Nationalism in Central Asia: The Case of Tajikistan*, Baltimore and London: John Hopkins Press.

Rywkin, M., 1982, *Moscow's Muslim Challenge: Soviet Central Asia*, London: C. Hurst.

Taidzhanov, K., and K. H.Ismailov, 1989, 'Osobennosti Doislamsckikh Verovaniie u Uzbekov-Karamurtov' in B. Basilov, *Drevniie obryady, verovaniya i kul'ty narodov Srednei Azii*, Moscow: Nauka Press.

Tapper, N., 1983, 'Gender and Religion in a Turkish Town; A Comparison of Two Types of Formal Women's Gatherings', in P. Holden, *Women's Religious Experiences*, London: Croom Helm.

Tapper, N. and R. Tapper, 1987, 'The Birth of the Prophet: Ritual and Gender in Turkish Islam, *Man* (NS) vol. 22, 69–92.

Wheeler, G., 1964, *The Modern History of Soviet Central Asia*, London: C. Hurst.

7

Islam in Azerbaijan: The Position of Women[1]

Tamara Dragadze

In this chapter I will discuss the position of women in the Republic of Azerbaijan, which is by far the most secularised of the republics of the former Soviet Union with a Muslim majority population. The first section will briefly describe the various approaches found in the literature on women and Islam. This will be followed by some background information on the arrival of Islam in the region of the Caucasus and on Azerbaijan. Most of the discussion is based on fieldwork data gathered in Charhan village in Shemakha region in the ancient province of Shirvan.[2] I shall include by way of contrast some information on urban, upper-class women, although the focus of this chapter is the village wedding ceremony and what it can tell us about the position of women in Azerbaijani society. Finally, I shall consider whether there are any specific 'Islamic' explanations for the position of women in Azerbaijan today after 70 years of Soviet legislation and given the multifaceted nature of Azerbaijani ethnic identity.

Women and Islam

There are four approaches to the study of the position of women in Islam which are commonly encountered. The first may be called the 'apologetica' approach, of which there are two versions. Thus, it is sometimes argued that Muslim women are not as subordinate and oppressed as might appear, because they have hidden power and authority, despite the restrictions imposed on them by Islam with respect to their role and status in Muslim society. An alternative view is that Muslim women cannot be as badly off as might appear, since they do not perceive themselves as being particularly restricted, even if others do so. Thus, it is argued, western feminists are merely being patronising in their feminism, and culturally imperialist in their advocacy of what they consider to be equal rights and fair attitudes.

The second approach is the 'universalist' approach, which bases its arguments on the premiss that there is nothing intrinsically Islamic in the persecution of women. In other words, women's subordination is universal; it is men everywhere who misinterpret religious writings to oppress women. According to the followers of this approach, in the Qur'an itself there are no injunctions which are detrimental to women. Rather, it is cultural practice which has adversely affected gender relations and which favours men. This is demonstrated by the fact that Muslim women living under Islamic law in different cultures are in very different positions of subordination or dominance.

The next approach may be called the 'reluctant conclusion' approach. Those who adhere to this argue that, without any prejudice and based entirely on factual evidence, it is an undeniable fact that Islam takes a particularly harsh line against women and advocates their segregation and oppression.

In a book on dance in the Arab world, Wendy Buonaventura (1989) writes that since Islam drew heavily on Judaism and Christianity, two male-centred faiths which both distrusted women because of their dangerous sexuality, Islam also perceived women as a disruptive force. Furthermore, there is the assumption that men cannot resist women's lure, which offers another justification for controlling their sexuality. She observes that the word in Arabic for chaos (*fitna*) is the same as that for a beautiful woman which carries, she states, all the connotations of a 'femme fatale' as defined in western culture and societies. Consequently, according to Buonaventura:

> The solution to the problem of what is seen by Muslim men as woman's disruptive sexual power is threefold: to define her sphere of influence as the home; to confine her presence to the harem, where children are reared and the daily business of the household is carried out; and to enforce the use of the veil (1989:83).

In support of this argument, for example, it is often pointed out that before the advent of Islam in Persia women had high status and freedom and even fought in battle, as found in the sixteenth-century epic poem Shahnameh (the Book of Kings) by Ferdosi. In cases where women in Muslim societies have succeeded in retaining a significant amount of equality with men, as is the case in some rural societies, this tends to be explained by the fact that the influence of Islam has in fact been superficial in those areas.

Finally, there is the 'Orientalist' approach which, oblivious to the connotations of oppression which might derive from it, asserts that women brought up in Islam are quite different in character from other women, and particularly from European women, since within their prison walls and behind their veils, they are bursting with lasciviousness and sensuality. Kept apart from the world of men, they are closer to nature, which not all Orientalist writers necessarily regarded as negative (cf. Mabro, 1991). For example, the French painter Eugène Delacroix wrote of Moroccan Muslim women in 1832: 'They are closer to nature in a thousand ways – their dress, the form of their shoes . . . As for us in our corsets, our tight shoes, our ridiculous pinching clothes, we are pitiful' (quoted in Buonaventura, 1989: 55).

This approach might be considered as simply a variant of the first, the 'apologetica' approach. However, this would not be correct, for in that approach it is asserted that Muslim women in fact have as much power and freedom as women of other religions, the difference being that the power is not the same and is not always visible to the untrained eye. By contrast, those who follow the 'orientalist' approach are not actually concerned with the position of Muslim women, but more with their identity, almost suggesting that they belong to a different species.

It is certainly the case that in the literature by native scholars on women in Azerbaijan, all four approaches are found. Though these sources have yet to be published in English, the very fact that the approaches defining women in Islam are under discussion is indicative of an on-going debate within Azerbaijan society on this issue.[3]

'Islam' in Perspective

An attempt was made recently to define the use of the term 'Islam' in population studies where the unity in Islamic space expressed in the *hajj* (pilgrimage to Mecca) and in time (continuity of the faith) is understood as a 'total way of life' (Rowley, 1984). Furthermore, the basis of the faith is a religion based on the 'five pillars' in their most formal sense, that is not only the recognition of the unity of God and the recognition of Mohammad as the final Prophet, but also the practice of prayer five times daily, the *zakat* (charity tax), fasting during Ramadan and making a pilgrimage to Mecca.

By and large, unlike some other Muslim republics of the former Soviet Union, the population of the Republic of Azerbaijan does not conform to these obligations since, after 70 years of coercive, atheist Bolshevism, the last three practices – prayer, charity tax and fasting – are rarely followed even in the most rural areas. However, it should be kept in mind that my use of the term 'Muslim' conforms to the self-identity of the majority populations in the Central Asian, Volga Tatar, North Caucasian and Azerbaijani republics.

Islam first came to the region of the Caucasus with the Arab conquest in the eighth century when small city centres were created that later were overtaken by Persian and then Turkish rulers. During a century of Russian imperial rule, Azerbaijanis were referred to by officials either as 'Turks', 'Mountain Tatars' or 'Muslims'. The question of identity for the national liberation movement in Azerbaijan at the turn of the century, culminating in an independent republic from 1918 to 1920, became extremely important. While the promotion of modernisation was regarded as very necessary for the movement, at the same time Muslim identity was emphasised in order to combat Russification and to co-opt the conservative rural population (cf. Swietochowski, 1985). Then, as today with the contemporary Popular Front of Azerbaijan, 'Muslim' identity is presented as a cultural heritage, a spiritual idea, but hardly a 'way of life' embracing the five pillars of Islam.

It is interesting to note that Azerbaijani women were the first Muslim women in the world to get the vote in 1918 (before women in England) and also that women's education was seen as an important factor in the building of the nation (cf. Swietochowski, 1985). Indeed, this point is not lost on the Azerbaijanis, and they are very proud of their 'progressive' status. At the time of writing, the Deputy Minister of Defence is a woman, Leila Yunusova. In the previous communist government, Elmira Kafarova was Chair of the Supreme Council and foreigners were surprised that such a forceful public speaker who protested at the massacre of Baku residents by Russian troops[4] was a woman in a republic which Gorbachev had said was in danger of being absorbed by 'Islamic fundamentalism'. Another woman who had been in public life was Academician Pusta Azizbekova who not only was a communist deputy and director of a museum but was also known to have had seven husbands. Nevertheless, it must be added that there are no more women in political power in Azerbaijan than there are in either the other Caucasian states or indeed elsewhere in the world.

In Azerbaijan today there are few people who are well informed about Islam. This fact is often used by the urban elite to prove their 'progressiveness' in the face of accusations about their Islamic fanaticism – which they believe originate from the political aims of Russia and Armenia. They eat pork and drink alcohol and are often quite ignorant about religious holidays. Novruz Bairam, the main annual festival celebrated in Azerbaijan by Shi'a and Sunni alike was not allowed to be acknowledged publicly until the Gorbachev era.

In order to reorientate people who are living in a vacuum after the demise of the ubiquitous communist ideology, members of the political elite are promoting the idea of 'the spirituality of Islam' which by and large is limited to the idea of national identity and positive attitudes to charity. On the other hand, there is a form of 'lay Islam', for want of a better word, which focuses around worship at holy shrines (*pir*)[5] and rites of passage.

Under the coercive rule of militant atheist communism, religion of all kinds was discouraged and most mosques were destroyed. Elsewhere I have described what followed as the 'domestication of religion' whereby religious worship was brought into the domestic orbit (Dragadze, forthcoming). During this period lay people felt capable of taking on the roles of the religious ritual specialists who were being persecuted. As a result of these events women were able to play a significant role. Although they had always been practitioners of domestic religious rituals, the importance of these rituals grew under Soviet rule as they were the only ones available. Similarly, at the graves of the Holy Men which had become shrines, it was their female descendants who assumed the task of attending to them and to the worshipping public.

The Rural Scene

In discussions on the role of women in Islam it is frequently argued that although the urban elite might be 'emancipated', in the rural areas it is quite a different matter. Here, so it is generally argued, the oppressive nature of Islam is revealed in the country under study, an assumption which takes little account of the influence of customary law and traditions.

In most cross-cultural studies it is recognised that data on the availability of education and healthcare for women is necessary in order to assess their position in society. In Azerbaijan both of these are at the same level as in most parts of the former Soviet Union, that is women have equal access to health and education as men. As in the rest of the former Soviet Union, however, career opportunities for women are dogged by many inequalities. In order to achieve a more meaningful understanding and qualitative assessment of women's position, however, it is in the gift of anthropologists to be able to present ethnographic material which gives an insight into women's roles as perceived by the society itself, often in symbolic form. An example of this are weddings where the rich detail provides the researcher with much valuable data.

Charhan Village, where I carried out my fieldwork, is relatively large (population around 4,000) and is situated about three hours drive from the capital, Baku. At the time of my research it had a large state farm with a wine and cognac distillery on the premises. Although many villagers were employed by the farm, others worked in Shemakha, the regional capital of Shirvan province which is only eight kilometres distant. The province is traditionally Sunni, as are the villagers I studied, although there are also Shi'a families living in the area. The extent of differences expressed between them was limited to banter and jokes about each other. The mosque in the regional capital Shemakha served the needs of both groups. This is a further reflection of the lack of barriers between the sects, a pattern not easily found in other parts of the Muslim world.

Relevant to wedding practices in rural areas is the fact that the school leaving age is normally around 17 years, and it is rare for girls to marry before then. Boys do military service and it would be common for them to marry when they have completed it. Village girls, whose virginity is considered to be paramount before marriage, as in the rest of the Caucasus, generally marry earlier than boys. The usual way for village pairs to meet is at school or work. Most marriages take place within the village and region although some young men will marry elsewhere if that is where they work and live – thus acquiring residence and a new circle of kin through their wife.

The only legal requirements for marriage in Azerbaijan are civic and secular. This involves registering the intent to marry at the local registry office where proof of single status is required (bigamy is outlawed), and the legal age is 18 for both partners. A law passed in the 1970s, however, has permitted marriage at age 17 in the Caucasian republics if there are extenuating circumstances, however these may be defined. The status of bridewealth and dowry are entirely informal, and except for the undertaking to respect each other for better or for worse, no other formal undertakings are required to be made at a legal level.

Negotiations start with the sending of relatives to a potential bride's home. The usual practice is for these negotiations to be carried out initially by women. As in Georgia, women act as mediators in village social life in various ways (cf. Dragadze, 1988). The main interest is to achieve an agreement on dowry and bridewealth. These essentially include from the boy's family gold jewellery, sums of money, clothes and cloth, shoes and the wedding dress ensemble (as in Georgia). Women in village society are virtually obsessed with their dowry which will consist of mattresses made with wool (half a dozen at least), quilts and cushions and, above all, their main 'insurance' – a full set of bedroom furniture with display cabinets for crockery and glassware which they are expected to bring when they enter the marital home. The groom's contribution to the bride is brought in two stages and it is at the second one, the *buyuk nisan* (big sign) that the *kiz toy* (women's wedding festivities) takes place. These are very jolly affairs, with usually 100 to 200 people present, although this may vary of course from family to family. The musicians are males, the same as at the men's wedding celebration, but they play different, less solemn, music. The bride is brought out into the women's presence and is enticed to dance. She has to resist but will eventually do one or two steps, covered in scarves that the guests throw around her. It is a blessing to dance around the bride, and women of all ages take part. Afterwards the bride is taken away and the feasting continues.

When a week or so later the groom's family comes to collect the bride, both families dance in her courtyard, men dancing with men and women with women although both groups do so at the same time. Then the bride is taken away by the groom's family in a procession with music and drums and dancing. On arrival at the groom's home a sheep is sacrificed literally at the bride's feet. She puts her right foot for a moment on the slaughtered sheep, which is said to symbolise the respect in which she is held by her husband and his family. She then withdraws to a separate room with close female relatives.

The men have their wedding feast, the *oglan toy*, which will be less light-hearted and humorous than the earlier women's feast, but there is often much drinking of vodka among the young men. Later in the night, after all the guests have gone home, throughout the village the sound of gunfire will be heard, signifying that the marriage has been consummated.

Local women say that their social position is demonstrated in the wedding ceremony because it shows that they themselves are treasures, that they bring joy and wealth to their families and that around them alone is the family centred. And of course through kinship the whole village is linked. Although in the home there is a certain spatial division among the sexes, nevertheless men do help with domestic chores. No single decision of significance is likely to be taken by any young man without his mother's advice. It is often she who guards the family's wealth in hidden wads of rouble notes.

One of my concerns in this chapter is to consider to what extent Islam is responsible for women's position. If women symbolise treasure, wealth and a source of joy in the village, is this because of Islam? And if they must also maintain their good reputation through discreet skirt lengths (no slacks or jeans are ever worn), discreet sex (with husband only) and, as already mentioned, virginity before marriage, is that because of Islam? This question is posed rhetorically, since the answer, which would force me to distinguish between national and religious culture, would be a contrived one.

With the active suppression of religion by a militant atheist Bolshevik state, men were inhibited from practising their religion. By contrast, because women were able to carry out religious rituals away from public view, they could more easily avoid the attention of the authorities (Dragadze, forthcoming). While it is true that before the Sovietisation of the region women in villages had been considered the ritual specialists, thereafter their importance increased as did the frequency with which they were called upon to perform rituals such as those surrounding life cycle events or against illness. In Azerbaijani villages there are commonly several women to be found who are referred to as 'mullahs'. It is only in the official town mosques that a woman is made to feel apart. While there are no explicit prohibitions against women attending the mosque, the general feeling is that they are better off praying at home.[6]

As in Georgia, the role of women is important in mediating in disputes (cf. Dragadze, forthcoming). Azerbaijani women are even known to have acted to prevent some of the assaults and murders of Armenians during the recent conflict in Baku. In the villages, they intervene in disputes in the family and with neighbours and also counsel young couples who are having problems in their marriage. However, their influence is not confined to domestic matters alone.

Nearly all adult women in Azerbaijan work at salaried jobs. In the rural areas some women were able to rise to relatively powerful positions through the Communist Party networks, although the Party Chairman and the First Secretary were invariably men. Again, this pattern does not differ significantly from that found in other parts of the Soviet Union. This leads to the conclusion that the absence of total equality in the job market cannot be laid at the feet of Islam, but needs to be assessed in relation to the way other variables will affect women's position in society.

A common cause of concern to women is that all their children, male and female, be able to acquire an adequate post-school education or training which will enable them to earn their living. This is also important for widows since it is less usual now for them to remarry compared with the past. (Women themselves indicate that the reason is that husbands are perceived to be a burden which they feel they can do without!) In villages women dress modestly with skirts mid-shin length but women of 30 and under are unlikely to wear a headscarf at all times as the previous generation did.

If asked, people will say it is 'Islam' that insists that women have a joyful time at weddings, that they should study, that they should have authority in their home and so on. If asked whether this is also 'Azerbaijani' they will insist that 'it is the same thing.' People are appalled at the restrictions placed on women in other Muslim countries such as Iran and I have heard village women saying that it is not 'Islamic' that it should be so. Thus it becomes necessary to define what is 'Islam' – the villagers' or the scholars' definition? In the case of Azerbaijan, it is clearly the former, though the influence of the Islamic resurgence sweeping across much of the Muslim world remains to be seen.

Urban Contrasts

Baku, the capital of Azerbaijan, contains strong social divisions: the population consists of unskilled and semi-skilled labourers and their families who have recently settled there from the villages; a traditional industrial working-class population which is one of the oldest in the Caucasus because of the development of the oil industry since the nineteenth century; and, finally, an educated urban elite. All these groups have tried to maintain their links with the countryside in some way, even if it is only possible to manage an annual summer visit to a country dacha or ancestral village. The manner in which this attempted continuity spills over into marriage and the position of women is a fluid one. There are, by and large, significant similarities and the differences are usually attributed to educational and income levels.

There are appreciable nuances in such issues as expectations of financial support by husbands. Most urban women – and indeed this is also true of village women – think that if you are married a strong premium should be put on your husband being the main breadwinner. Divorcées (and widows) in the capital, where the rate of divorce is higher than elsewhere, are less happy than village women about being single. However, it is rare for divorced women in the town to remarry, because an urban male divorcé will experience no difficulty in finding a young girl to be his bride if he can provide good material conditions.

In an attempt to demonstrate the high level of enlightenment in their country, Azerbaijani patriots can point to successful and prestigious women, particularly in Baku. Women are certainly prominent in the performing arts today and in literature their pedigree stretches back to the eighteenth and nineteenth centuries. In scholarship women are well represented in publications and academic posts. So far so good, but there are nevertheless just as few women in significant positions of power and authority in Azerbaijan as in the rest of the former Soviet Union and indeed in most of the world at large. This is indicative of the reality that, as is the case among women cross-culturally, Azerbaijani women are confronted by a number of structural barriers which affect their position in society and their relationship with men.

Some General Points

From the Azerbaijani case it must be acknowledged that 70 years of Soviet legislation has had its effects, the most positive being the insistence on universal education, universal suffrage and the obligation for all adults to work. However, it should be noted that universal suffrage and education had already been promoted by the independent government before Sovietisation. In the present political climate, therefore, Azerbaijanis will claim that these laws were manifestations of their advanced level of humanitarian and national policy orientations rather than an imported Russian Bolshevik model. Although, as elsewhere, women have carried a 'double burden' because they have invariably assumed more responsibility than men for their homes and family welfare, it must be recognised that the vision and independence that basic legislation has afforded women has undoubtedly ameliorated their position in society.

As mentioned earlier, Azerbaijan is by far the most secularised of the former Soviet republics. Once again, this is not only a result of Soviet policies but arises also from the flourishing of secular thought in the nineteenth century. This in turn can be attributed both to the presence in Baku of a large number of foreign residents at that time and also perhaps to the nature of this Caucasian society. With its egalitarian ethos and its system of kinship and marriage, this particular society into which Islam has been integrated has possibly been more capable of adapting to secular norms and ideals than, for example, the more feudally organised societies in parts of Central Asia where Bolshevik militant atheism was forcibly imposed.

Another important factor is the multifaceted nature of the Azerbaijani ethnic identity – with Caucasian, Turkik (Turkik broadly speaking and not Turkish as in the republic of Turkey), East European and both Shi'a and Sunni Muslim components. Islam today is certainly not the principal element in this ethnic identity. The culture in which women hold their position is described by them above all as Azerbaijani and it would be rare, except in jest, that their subordinate position should be attributed to religious rather than ethnic reasons.

There has been a tendency recently to use Islam to attack the nationalist movements in Azerbaijan and this is deeply resented. Russian politicians such as Galina Staravoitova and Mikhail Gorbachev, as well as Armenians with whose country Azerbaijan is at war, have used scaremongering in an attempt to raise fears of another Iran by referring to the 'Muslim fundamentalist' threat of the nationalists.

However, from my personal research into the economy, society and politics of Azerbaijan I would suggest that while the chance in the future of an upsurge of 'Islamic fundamentalism' (of the Iranian type, for example) is indeed there, it is only equal in probability to there being an upsurge into the government of fundamentalist Evangelism in the United States of America.

The sensitivity of Azerbaijanis to claims of extremism on their part is such that they are very cautious in their discussions on the position of women in case their words should be used as evidence of their fanatic backwardness. It is worth pointing out that at recent state banquets given by the Azerbaijani government in honour of two British official guests, the wives of most of the high-ranking officials were present. This public female presence should help improve the image of Azerbaijani women in the wake of negative 'Islamic' descriptions, especially in view of the fact that there is little specifically 'Muslim' either about the Republic of Azerbaijan or the position of women there.

Conclusion

The aim of this chapter has been to examine the premiss that Islam ordains women to be subordinate and oppressed, by looking at the specific situation of Azerbaijani women. In the Soviet Union, the accepted view was that nationalism in Azerbaijan should be equated with Islamic extremism and this was in turn equated with the oppression of women. In the official militant atheist propaganda, religion was targeted, it was claimed, in order to improve the position of women in Soviet society. In recent times a similar approach was used by Soviet officials when the union was disintegrating. They announced that human rights in Azerbaijan would be violated, including those of women, because of the rise of nationalism (along with its alleged Muslim extremism).

It must be emphasised, however, that Azerbaijani nationalism is not specifically Islamic but rather economic and cultural. The crescent and other Islamic symbols which have been resuscitated for the flag and other uses come from the short-lived independent republic of 1918–20. In Azerbaijani culture and society today, Islam is not a more important component than its other attributes – Caucasian, Near Eastern, East European, formerly Soviet and so on. Finally, it is clear that Azerbaijani women have achieved the same rights and advantages that they would have done in any country in the world with similar legislation. Where they are discriminated against, as in the villages, for example, this can be attributed as much to the inbalances which usually occur in favour of men when there is poverty and backwardness in transport and communications as it can be to Islam. None the less, Islam has undoubtedly provided Azerbaijan with a singular hue in its traditions and culture, reflected particularly in its splendid art, literature and music. And the role of women in this cultural life has been noteworthy for a considerable time.

Notes

1. Much of my research in Azerbaijan was funded by the ESRC. I would also like to thank my research partner Dr Attiga Izmailova, the Institute of History of Azerbaijan and the editors of the present volume for their valuable help and encouragement.

2. The fieldwork on which this chapter is based was gathered between 1989 and 1991.

3. To my knowledge, one such attempt has been made in the West. At the University of Oslo, Hulya Demirderek is preparing a Ph.D. thesis on professional women in Azerbaijan.

4. On 20 January, 1990 (Black January) around 200 people were killed indiscriminately in Baku by Soviet Army troops sent by the Moscow government. At the funeral for the victims, the Sheikh al Islam was joined by the Chief Rabbi and the Russian Orthodox priest.

5. Fuller information on this can be found in T. Dragadze, forthcoming.

6. Indeed, during my fieldwork I visited a mosque with another woman and we were told that although we were invited most cordially to visit, we would be more effective if we prayed at home.

References

Buonaventura, W., 1989, *Serpents of the Nile*, London: Saqi Books.

Dragadze, T. 1988, *Rural Families in Soviet Georgia*, London: Routledge.

Dragadze, T. (forthcoming), 'The Domestication of Religion under Communism' in C. Hann (ed.), ASA monographs.

Mabro, J., 1991, *Veiled Half-Truths: Western Travellers' Perceptions of Middle Eastern Women*, London: I.B. Tauris.

Rowley, G., 1984 paper delivered at the Population Geography Study Group Conference, 'The Unity of Islam – Implications for a Population Geography', 5 January, University of Sheffield.

Swietochowski, T., 1985, *Russian Azerbaijan, 1905–1920; The Shaping of National Identity in a Muslim Community*: Cambridge: Cambridge University Press.

8

Women's Labour in the Bangladesh Garment Industry: Choice and Constraints*

Naila Kabeer

This chapter examines some of the processes underlying the massive influx of women workers into export-oriented garment factories in Bangladesh. Bangladesh has long been characterised as an underdeveloped economy, where Islam operates in a conservative fashion, particularly in determining permissible modes of behaviour for women. Socially sanctioned norms of purdah (female seclusion) have enforced women's absence from public employment for most of its known history. Yet within a relatively short space of time, several thousands of women have entered a highly visible form of employment in factory production. The explanation of this phenomenon can be undertaken at a number of levels, and the broader contexts are dealt with very briefly in the following section. However, the main substance of this chapter is based on the self-explanation offered by women workers themselves of their labour supply behaviour. It draws on material from semi-structured, informal interviews conducted in Dhaka in 1987/88 with 60 female garment workers from different social categories: educated and illiterate, married and non-married.

The International Restructuring of the Garment Industry

Over the last three decades there has been a global restructuring of garment production, accompanied by a geographical recomposition of its labour force. The earlier phases of this restructuring saw the opening up of successful new production sites in the low-wage, newly-industrialising countries of South-East Asia. However, massive import penetration of western markets, coupled with growing world recession in the early

*This is an edited version of an article published in *The European Journal of Development Research*, vol., 3, no.1; see Kabeer, 1991c.

1970s, led to the imposition of protective quotas on textile imports from the major Third World producers. As a consequence, quota-free countries like Bangladesh with large supplies of cheap labour became attractive new locations for labour-intensive stages of garment production intended for the markets of Europe and the USA. With the active encouragement of the government, a spectacular growth of garment factories took place in Bangladesh, mainly in the cities of Dhaka and Chittagong – from around four or five in 1976 to over 600 by 1985.[1]

Even more remarkable was the category of labour drawn in during this expansion. The garment factories have helped to create a first-generation female industrial work-force in a society where purdah was long believed to constitute an almost impenetrable barrier to the flow of female labour into the public sphere of factory work – except among the very poorest.[2]

There is an extensive literature attempting to explain the remarkable female-intensiveness of the labour force in garment production internationally, and indeed in many other industries prone to relocation or subcontracting (cf. Lim, 1978; UNIDO, 1980; Elson and Pearson, 1981; Chapkis and Enloe, 1983; Nash and Fernandez-Kelly, 1983; Mitter, 1986; Joekes, 1987). These studies generally concur that the 'footloose' industries have a number of features in common: they tend to be highly labour intensive and therefore have to reduce their labour costs to be able to compete in international markets. They are also concentrated in sectors which are particularly prone to unstable conditions of demand. Employers seeking to tailor their labour recruitment strategies to the needs of profit maximisation, demonstrate a preference for certain characteristics in their workforce – cheapness, docility and dispensability. The ascription of secondary-earner status to women in many cultures gives them a competitive edge for these jobs, a phenomenon described as 'the comparative advantage of women's disadvantage' (Aranda and Arizpe, 1981).

Garment Production in Bangladesh

The predominance of female labour in Bangladesh's export-oriented garment industry can also be analysed along these lines: women can be paid less than men, they appear more acquiescent to enforced periods of overtime work, and they can also be laid off in the absence of orders without too much protest. There is, in particular, a demand for young, single women – 'unencumbered women' in the words of one employer – who are willing to give 'undivided attention to their work without the constant anxieties about their husbands, their in-laws or their children', and, for the same reason, will be more willing to work overtime in peak seasons. Women form over 85 per cent of production workers in the Bangladeshi garment factories, working mainly as helpers, machinists and, less frequently, as line supervisors and quality controllers. A very small minority of men work on the factory floor as machinists. The rest are responsible for packing, pressing, cutting and loading. Men also dominate at administrative and management levels – clerical work in Bangladesh is predominantly male.

While these explanations account for employer preferences for a female work-force in Bangladesh's garment factories, they offer no insights into the circumstances, choices, and constraints of the women who came into factory production, despite the existence of strong cultural proscriptions on public forms of female labour. After all, employment patterns are not purely artefacts of the drive for profit maximisation; they also represent the responses of different categories of workers to the perceived range of opportunities and constraints facing them.

Two dominant explanatory paradigms can be distinguished in social science accounts of women's labour supply patterns: those which point to cultural constraints and those which stress economic choice. The choice theoretic model favoured by liberal economists sees the process of decision-making within households as the allocation of resources such as members' labour time in accordance with the basic principle of rational behaviour, namely maximisation of the household's joint welfare function.[3] The culturalist paradigm gives analytical weight to cultural constructions of masculinity and femininity in explaining gender differences in labour supply behaviour. Muslim women have attracted considerable attention within this paradigm because of the powerful and pervasive character of Islamic ideologies in general, and the constraints of purdah on women's mobility and visibility in particular. While cultural interpretations of purdah have varied, there has been a general consensus that it plays an important role in constraining women's employment options (cf. Jeffries, 1979; Papanek and Minault, 1982; Mernissi, 1985). At the core of the institution is the notion that the *izzat* (honour) of the family resides in the virtue of its women; constant surveillance is necessary to ensure that women do nothing to bring *sharam* (shame) on their kin. Female seclusion effectively cements the syndrome of family honour and female virtue.

In the specific context of Bangladesh, the Islamic content of purdah is interwoven with local notions of female propriety, based on separate spheres for women and men, and on the social ideal of male breadwinner/female dependent. The focus on culturally-generated structures as the explanation for women's general absence from public forms of employment abound in the academic field (cf. Cain et al., 1979; Greely, 1983; Kabeer, 1985). However, the emphasis of this approach on compiling 'cultural inventories' (Connell, 1987: 98) of gender relations in Bangladesh makes it relatively inflexible in dealing with forms of behaviour which appear to go against the established culture. It tends to treat women and men as passive occupants, rather than active negotiators, of socially prescribed roles. Thus, the culturalist paradigm offers limited scope for dealing with the ways in which women have responded to changing material realities (except, for instance, in terms of 'extreme economic pressures', 'destitution' and 'desperation'; cf. Huq, 1979). The reformulation of this paradigm does not imply that individual choices escape constraining structures which continue to define what is possible. But it does suggest the possibility for human action to affect structural conditions and hence engender social change.

In the following I shall use some of the accounts given by Bangladeshi women workers in the Dhaka garment industry to re-conceptualise household decision-making through an analysis of the concrete decision-making processes described by them. The discussion aims to demonstrate how constraining cultural norms are being challenged through the women's responses to changing material incentives, but also to point to the way in which these changing forms of culture continue to enter and shape decision-making processes.

The Historical Context

Prior to presenting the case study material, it is essential to point out that, while the expansion of female labour in the Dhaka garment industry has been unexpectedly rapid, it is part of a process of social change which began some time ago (cf. Kabeer, 1991a).

Briefly, the post-colonial history of Bangladesh has been one of growing impoverishment and landlessness on the one hand, and growing dependence on foreign aid on the other. The growth of the export-oriented garment industry itself can to some extent be seen as a response to the pressures of international donors.[4] As in other patriarchally-organised societies, growing impoverishment has had particular implications for women in Bangladesh (cf. Feldman and McCarthy, 1984; Kabeer, 1991a). Research over the years has helped to document increasing trends of female-headed households among the landless, resulting from male migration to the cities, or the breakdown of family structures and male desertion. The appearance of women from impoverished households in rural public works was noted for the first time in the early 1970s (cf. Chen and Ghuznavi, 1979). However, this form of employment continued to be associated with destitute women – 'the poorest of the poor' – so that women's presence in public forms of manual labour was taken as a signal of extreme economic distress.

Among the lower middle classes, inflation and the erosion of living standards also led to increased labour force participation among educated women, primarily in the 'respectable' occupations of teaching and, more recently, in the public sector health and family planning programmes. Both forms of employment are seen as female occupations, entailing working with other women in female spheres of responsibility, so that some semblance of purdah could be maintained.

Declining economic standards have been one element in the broader climate of change, encouraging a rise in female income-earning activities. The other has been the commitment professed by the state to the cause of women and development. Although successive military regimes have sought to promote an Islamic identity for Bangladesh, with some of the attendant rhetoric of female seclusion and propriety, they have also simultaneously sought to champion women and development programmes, with its very different rhetoric of women's emancipation (cf. Guhathakurtha, 1985; Kabeer, 1991b).

These contradictory policies have had contradictory outcomes. On the one hand there has been a resurgence in religious consciousness, expanded membership of Islamic fundamentalist parties and growing numbers of mosques and *madrassas* (religious schools). At the same time, income-generating projects for women have proliferated, women's organisations have become more active and self-confident, and the monopoly of archaic ideological preconceptions about women's place in society is being challenged. Although the costs of development continue to fall disproportionately on women, an ideological space has also been opened up for them to consider new strategies and opportunities. It is in this sense that the preconditions which allowed for the incorporation of female labour into factory employment were laid in the course of broader social changes that have been occurring over the past few decades.

Labour Market Strategies: An Economic Perspective

A striking feature which emerged from the interviews with women workers was that the overwhelming majority appeared to have taken the initiative themselves to enter the garment factories. In many cases, this entailed overcoming the initial resistance of male guardians. Male resistance to female family members entering factory production is hardly unexpected, given the link between female seclusion and male honour in Bangladeshi society. More unexpected is the fact that women were able to override these objections. In some cases, women did not inform their guardians of their decision until they had already secured a job so that they could negotiate from a position of *fait accompli*.

The resistance of husbands was particularly acute and often protracted. The marital contract in Bangladesh is based on the norm of male breadwinner/guardian and its corollary, female dependence and seclusion, and forms a key social relationship in the lives of adult men and women. An earning wife threatens the balance of power within marriage by her routine daily contacts with strange men (and attendant sexual connotations), by impugning the breadwinning ability of her husband, and consequently, by undermining the foundations on which his sense of masculine selfhood rests.

In effect, the women interviewed represent those who had been successful in persuading their male guardians through a variety of arguments that their moral character would not be compromised by factory work, along with a minority who had defied their guardians' wishes. In this sense, they constitute a biased sample and we have no way of knowing how many women's preferences were overridden by male authority or even male violence, and who therefore did not succeed in implementing their 'choice' to take up factory employment. It is thus important to bear in mind that the ensuing account of female labour supply behaviour focuses only on 'successful' female decision-makers. Nevertheless, the accounts are valuable in throwing light on how such success is effected when it entails a departure from norms of female propriety.

As far as the immediate reasons which propelled women into factory employment are concerned, they can as a first approximation be summarised as economic ones; quite simply, the need for some, or additional, income. In the context of Bangladeshi society, where female factory employment would still be regarded as a cultural anomaly, economic need may be considered (in actual fact as well as in *ex post* rationalisations) the only reason compelling enough to justify a break with purdah norms.[5]

However, within the broad category of economic need, there was a variety of motivations which reflect the class, marital and social backgrounds of the women involved. The garment labour force is by no means a homogeneous group, comprising entirely impoverished and abandoned women. Most of the women are currently not married, many are single, others deserted, divorced or widowed. Many live with their families rather than on their own. There is also a significant minority of married women.

Furthermore, since entry qualifications often include a literacy requirement, the labour force includes many women who have completed some formal education. These women are therefore not necessarily the poorest of the poor, driven by the imperatives of survival into 'distress' sales of labour in an unconventional form of employment. Disaggregating the concept of 'economic' needs will help to distinguish further the kinds of motivation which lay behind the labour supply decisions of different social categories of women.

First, there were those for whom employment was, in fact, simply a survival strategy for themselves and their dependents. While the issue of *choosing* to work was not a meaningful one for this group, some degree of choice over *type* of occupation was apparent. For those who had already been working – as domestic servants, prostitutes or in casualised home-based piece work – the garment factories offered a preferred form of employment. Others in this group had been precipitated into the labour market for the first time in their lives by a sudden catastrophe within the family – the death of a breadwinner, the loss of a guardian's land, the collapse of a business – and garment employment represented one (or perhaps the only) acceptable option in their distressed circumstances.

A second category of economic need comprised those cases where women's earnings were a part of the broader income-earning strategy of the household. In these households, there was usually another breadwinner, male or female. Whether the women contributed their earnings to a common household fund, or used it to finance all or some of their own daily needs, their employment helped to ease the financial constraints of their families.

A third group of women used their wages to improve their household's standard of living. Many of this group considered themselves middle class, and sought additional income to ensure a fit between their social aspirations and their financial means. A motive frequently reported by this group for entering employment was to finance their children's education, an eminently acceptable and respectable goal among middle-class families.

Finally, there was a small proportion of women who worked in order to secure an income for personal expenditure. These were mainly young unmarried girls from reasonably well-off families, living with their parents, whose status as daughters of the house meant that they were not required to contribute to the family budget, or even to account for their earnings. They used their incomes to save for their dowries, or to spend on clothes and leisure activities.

Whatever the complex reasons behind the decision to enter factory employment, once the decision had been implemented, most women workers appeared to behave like rational economic agents in order to improve their situation. They used their lunch hours to improve their speed on the machines, and then negotiated for higher pay with their supervisors. If they failed, they presented themselves at another factory, citing their new speed as the basis for an upgraded scale of pay. Turnover was therefore reported to be high as women moved between factories, seeking the most favourable terms for themselves, and employers complained of having their best workers poached by their rivals. For some women, proximity to their homes or the availability of cheap public transport, also entered into their choice of factory. If there were non-economic factors influencing this decision, it was most apparent among middle-class women, particularly married ones, who made a distinction between factories which had a 'decent atmosphere', and those which did not. This group expressed reluctance to take up higher paid jobs in factories where the managers did not have impeccable reputations, or where the behaviour between male and female workers was considered too free and easy.

The Cultural Dimension of Labour Market Strategies

While economic needs were clearly a primary factor propelling women into factory employment, the labour supply decision-making processes described by the women were by no means as transparent as suggested by rational choice theory, namely, the straightforward comparison of returns to different uses of their time. Some women had responded to the 'pull' of new incentives in the female segment of the labour market, while others were 'pushed' into it by the failure of the 'patriarchal bargain' (cf. Kandiyoti, 1988), and loss of male guardianship. But nearly all of them sought to justify their decision in the light of existing cultural norms of female propriety and virtue, rather than appearing to regard economic need as a sufficient and self-explanatory rationale on its own. The concept of cultural strategies refers here to the adoption of modes of behaviour or the profession of opinions and interpretations which permitted women to explain and justify their actions, when these actions seemed to contradict the dominant traditions of female propriety. Before going on to discuss these strategies as they emerged out of the accounts of women workers, a number of general points can be made concerning the nature of purdah norms in Bengali society as revealed by these accounts.

One important point was that purdah operates at a number of different levels. At one level, it exists as part of their belief systems, internalised in the course of their lives and shaping everyday practice. At another level, however, it operates as an external social control, exercised by the *samaj* (community) through modalities which vary considerably between its different sub-groups: the face-to-face community (the immediate family, the extended family, village society, the *mohalla* (neighbourhood), the workplace), and the wider 'imagined' community (cf. Anderson, 1983) of religious leaders and influential figures, whom the women might not personally encounter, but whose influence in shaping public opinion and monitoring public morality they were well aware of.

One consequence of the diversity of sub-groups making up 'the community' was that the cultural strategies through which women workers sought to gain acceptance for their apparent break with purdah norms were also characterised by diversity rather than uniformity. Their behaviour and explanations varied according to the section of the community which was perceived to impinge most directly upon their choices and behaviour. Paradoxically, however, through their attempts to reconcile their practice with prevailing norms, it became clear that the workers were, often unintentionally, helping to transform the very norms they invoked to justify their practice.

A second point to note was that the institution of *samaj* – as guardian of social norms and values – is most viable and effective within the tightly-knit context of village life. This *samaj* - based on close kinship support, surveillance and face-to-face contact – has been replaced in the women's lives by the more dispersed and impersonal *samaj* of the city neighbourhood. Urban anonymity protected the workers and their families from the opinions and judgements of their neighbours, and the interpretation of *uchit* (norms) and *niyom* (customs) consequently took on greater malleability. While those interviewed made frequent references to the idea of *samaj*, it was to an abstract and impersonal notion of the community, rather than to the personalised and familiar *samaj* of village life. In fact, some rejected its relevance to their own lives, in a way that might not have been possible in the more tightly integrated context of village society: 'Who is *samaj*? *Samaj* is made up of people who are educated, who own houses and cars and work in government jobs. *Samaj* is for them, not for us.'

The final point to make at this stage is that women's accounts of their behaviour also helped to reveal other meanings of purdah hidden behind the hitherto received idea of purdah as female seclusion within the four walls of the home. The narrow view of purdah, which had been the dominant one in earlier times, was summarised very concisely by one of the women workers:

> No man, other than my husband, should see the hair of my head. Even my
> sons become 'other men' when they reach adolescence. All this is in the

Hadith-Qur'an. Allah does not want women to mix with men. He asks us to remain within four walls, wear a *dosh-hather* (ten feet long) sari, and a *burkah* (a concealing tent-like garment) if we have to go outside.

However, this idea of purdah is clearly proving unsustainable in the face of new economic realities. While women referred to it in their accounts, it was to challenge its relevance to their own lives. In this process, new interpretations of purdah became apparent as working women drew upon the rules and resources latent within apparently monolithic cultural belief systems in order to negotiate the boundaries of permissible female behaviour.

The cultural strategies described below are classified broadly according to the notion of 'the community' that figures, explicitly or implicitly, as the source of sanctions over women's behaviour in specific contexts. The different strategies should not be seen as mutually exclusive; they frequently co-existed, overlapped or contradicted each other within the same account. But taken together, they offer a valuable insight into the processes by which cultural constraints are reshaped in the face of economic exigency.

Purdah and Exceptional Necessity: The Community as Guardian of Cultural Norms

While there have always been women who were forced outside the acceptable boundaries of purdah, they tended to be seen as a destitute minority. Until the coming of the garment factories, the roads, markets and public places in Dhaka were rarely frequented by women, unless accompanied by men. The presence of large numbers of unaccompanied women today on buses and in the streets continues to excite more or less disapproving comments in the popular press, in research reports and in the mosques. A local newspaper description of 'the garment girls' is fairly typical:

> A group of girls ... with faces in cheap makeup, gaudy ribbons adorning their oily braids and draped in psychedelic coloured sarees with tiffin carriers in their hands are a common sight (these) days during the morning and evening hours. These are the garment workers, (a) new class of employees.[6]

One of the factories visited had been subjected to a *waz* (religious meeting) that had lasted two days and two nights, during which various *mullahs* had, through the use of loudspeakers, denounced to the entire neighbourhood the 'shameless' women who walked 'boldly' down the streets in groups, their heads uncovered, unaccompanied by male guardians.

Women workers were aware of this generalised social disapproval of their conduct. Their responses varied between anger, bitterness and shame, but they generally defended their actions by pointing to the failure of *samaj* in general, and its moral guardians in particular, to give them the protection and provision that are part of women's cultural entitlements.

Many of the workers felt that purdah norms were conditional, rather than absolute, and that in exceptional situations, their violation did not reflect on the morality of the women involved. Their arguments concerning what constituted acceptable exceptions relied on both social and religious rationales, and were directed at those who represented the forces of convention in the community.

An example of religious-based exceptions came from those who claimed that the Qur'an itself recognised legitimate cases of 'exceptional need'. Women who entered the public sphere because of exceptional need could thus still be regarded as faithful to the spirit of Qur'anic injunctions. Others felt that if those sections of the community responsible for upholding moral standards cared so much about women's virtue, it was their duty to come forward with more proper forms of economic assistance. Given their failure to do so, exceptional need justified exceptional solutions. The following quotes illustrate how this set of rationales was expressed:

> Rahela: People say that working violates purdah. The *mullahs* say it most; they are bringing out cassettes which say that women no longer remain in purdah and are getting spoiled. But they only say it to keep women down. How can we be breaking purdah when we work to fill our stomachs?
>
> Hanufa: According to the Qur'an, one has to keep one's purdah. But it also says that you are responsible for your own survival. This is a *faraz* (a must). If I don't work, I will die and God will ask me why I did not take more care of my family and my husband.
>
> Naseema: The Qur'an says it is one's duty to preserve oneself. So even if we are breaking the Qur'an by coming outside to work, we are not breaking it fully. It cannot be sinful to work when one has to earn a living. It is said in the Qur'an that when one's survival is at stake, one can eat anything, even that which is forbidden by the Qur'an.

'A Woman Carries Her Purdah With Her': Street Encounters with the Male Community

While women workers can shrug off the generalised social approval of *samaj*, it is less easy to do so in other more immediate encounters with the community, ones they experience daily, and which serve as a constant face-to-face reminder that they are women transgressing in what is still regarded as 'male' space. This is with the *achena purush* (male strangers) whom they pass on their way to work – on the streets, in the buses and rickshaws; men who frequently make abusive catcalls and suggestive comments to the women workers, sometimes following them to make threatening sexual overtures. Women coming home late at night are particularly fearful since, in addition to the 'normal' quota of harassment, they can also be picked up by the police on suspicion of prostitution. Many factories issue their women workers with identification cards so that they can show legitimate grounds for being out on the streets after dark. While a small minority of women wear *burkahs* on the streets as a way of making themselves invisible, these are expensive and often get stolen at work. Others seek to counter these constant reminders of their *bepurdah* (purdahless) condition by shifting the emphasis in their accounts of purdah from seclusion as external control and physical seclusion to purdah as individual responsibility and personal morality. Time and again, they stressed that purdah was in the mind; that every woman carried her purdah with her; that the important distinction was not between staying within four walls and appearing on the streets, but between authentic morality and inauthentic purdah. Others resisted purdah definitions which laid the blame for men's behaviour at women's door. By their modesty of deportment, by lowering their gaze and covering their heads, by ignoring the comments and catcalls, the women maintained that they carried their purdah with them as they moved through public space.

The idiom in which the women spoke often conjured up an image of an invisible protected corridor stretching from the threshold of their homes to the factory gates. There were limits to the 'elasticity' of purdah, however, and for many it only applied to the journey between home and work. Aside from this journey, most women stressed that they rarely went out unless accompanied by an adult male relative. Married women also mentioned that if they had to go out, they often took their children with them as a form of protection, since it declared their status as mothers and therefore demanded respect from men on the streets. The following examples depict this clearly:

> Zobeida: Even if men try to behave badly with other women, as long as I am virtuous, no one will misbehave with me. People respond to you as they perceive you. My relatives say Zobeida's honour is in Zobeida's hands. If she remains virtuous, no one can take it.
>
> Hanufa: As for purdah, that sort of purdah is no good. Those who are bad can be bad at home. A person can be bad anywhere, it depends on her character.

Afifa: If I remain good and behave decently, why should I care what other people have to say? It is a good thing to wear a *burkah*, but if one wears a *burkah* and does not have a good character, then there is no sense in wearing it. That is not observing purdah. It is possible to walk down the street without wearing purdah and still stay virtuous.

De-Sexualising the Factory Floor: The Workplace Community

Although male co-workers in the factory did not generally subject women to the overt sexual harassment they faced on the streets, their presence alongside women workers was another factor which had to be reconciled with norms of purdah and propriety. Among more religious sections of the local community, the breakdown of the 'natural' principle of sex-segregation represented by factory work was denounced in the strongest terms. Not only was it seen as taking work away from unemployed men – the breadwinners of their families – but, more fundamentally, as a threat to the very fabric of the moral community.

However, from the way in which factory space was represented in the accounts of women workers, it was clear that they sought to de-emphasise the sexual connotations of male–female proximity and thus defuse the threat to their reputations. A very common metaphor employed in this context was the familial one. This creation of fictive kinship is by no means unique to factory life; it is employed in a variety of circumstances in Bengali society to permit forms of cross-gender interactions between non-related people which both de-sexualise the encounter, and, through choice of kinship terms, also acknowledge the hierarchy of age and gender. In the factory context, it clearly played an important role in defining acceptable forms of relationships between women and men who were by and large strangers to each other, but who spent a significant proportion of the day in close proximity.

Frequent references were made by women workers to the 'brother –sister' character of the relationship between male and female co-workers, and to the 'respect and affection' between them. Kinship terms were sometimes used to address members of the same as well as the opposite sex. Thus, female supervisors would be referred to as *apa* (older sister), while male ones would be called *bhai* (older brother), and older men such as the gatekeeper or the master tailor would be referred to as *chacha* (uncle). In many cases, the employer would be referred to as the women's guardian, replacing their familial guardians in the context of the factory, and held to be responsible for their reputations and for protecting them from the predatory attentions of outsiders. If a male factory worker developed an attraction for a female co-worker, the employer was frequently considered to be the proper channel through which a marriage proposal could be put forward. Employers themselves often assumed the role of guardian of their workers' morals, since few wanted their factories to get a reputation for 'immoral and scandalous affairs', thereby scaring off their supply of labour.

The de-sexualisation of the workplace was also affected by stressing the discipline, pace and noise of the production process. The factory gates were generally kept locked and guarded throughout the working day. The main reason for this was to prevent the smuggling out of clothing, particularly since export-garment production used high-quality imported textiles which were exempt from normal import taxes. However, the locked gates were also symbolic of the strict regulations which characterised factory life, and permitted the workers – in their accounts – to reconstitute the inside/outside cultural divide, this time between the factory and the streets. Frequent reference was also made to the way the production process was organised, which left no time for frivolous chatter between women and men. A woman indulging in chatter would be immediately identifiable through the hold-ups she would cause in the production stages.

In many ways, the division of labour within the factory mirrored in microcosm the hierarchy of social differences outside. Class and gender were key principles in organising the assignment of workers to different jobs. As management correctly recognised, the reproduction of wider class-based patterns of authority and deference within the factory floor could be mobilised for the benefit of factory discipline, since their production workers fell easily into taking orders from the small group of higher educated women they deemed their social superiors.

Similarly, the potential discomfort over male and female proximity in the factory was partly minimised by a spatial segregation and partly by the division of labour. During the lunch hour, women and men tended to eat in separate groups. There was little chance of flirtatious interaction between them, particularly with the constant surveillance of co-workers. In most factories, the proportion of men working side by side with women was very small. More commonly, a physical gender segregation was effected by placing those stages of production where men predominated (ironing, packing, cutting, supervision, timekeepers, security guards, administration) in a different room or on a different floor.

Men often (though not always) earned more than women, and their tasks were considered more 'masculine' in that it was heavier and dirtier work, requiring more movement than those tasks where women were concentrated. The reconstitution of gender norms in the factory division of labour was reflected in a male worker's explanation that women were not employed in the ironing section because of their 'inability to deal with electricity'. It was also reflected in a female worker's sense of shame in doing the unfeminine job of 'ironman'.

Thus the practices and norms that governed factory life attempted, as far as possible, to reproduce those of the outside world, in order to protect factory culture from any perceptions of impropriety or departure from convention in either class or gender norms of behaviour. The following quote aptly illustrates this:

> Sathi: Some men and women like to flirt. Men who are married, but go after other women and behave like lovers should not work here; nor should such women. But women like myself, who have come to work, not flirt, will have no problems working in garments. They will regard men like brothers, or fathers, or uncles.

Transforming Ideologies of Women's Roles: The Familial Context

Members of the women workers' families are the group that impinge most immediately on women's ability to make decisions. Obviously, many of the arguments put forward to counter resistance from the wider community also helped to persuade workers' family members to assent to their entry into the garment factories. In addition, however, cultural norms about altruistic mothers and dutiful daughters were given new meanings in order to justify the break with conventions about 'women's place'. This strategy figured particularly prominently in the women's attempts to persuade their families to allow them to work in the factories.

Women with children, whether or not currently married, argued that the need to provide for their children was a sufficiently laudable motive to justify their emergence from the confines of the home. The argument was that they were, in a way, simply fulfilling their motherhood roles in the context of changing times. Education, in particular, occupied a prominent place in these explanations. Frequently, the desire to educate children – girls as well as boys – was expressed in conjunction with women's deep regret and resentment that their own parents had not done the same for them. Education, especially for daughters, was seen as a precondition for becoming *manush* (fully human), meaning to command respect rather than being subject to the wishes and whims of others. Women wanted to educate their children so that they would have a future, so that their daughters would not have to submit to the same restricted life chances as their mothers, and also to ensure their children's support in their old age.

[handwritten margin note: Identity also lay with the prospects of their children in education but also of marriage partners.]

However, motherhood responsibilities were not the only form of familial ideologies appealed to. Thus, children would cite the need to support their parents as justification for their employment. Here it was the convention of the dutiful daughter which was undergoing a reinterpretation in the context of new times. Such women presented their financial contributions in terms of easing the pressures on ageing fathers or widowed mothers by supporting younger siblings, by saving for future dowries, or simply by helping meet their family's daily survival needs:

> Afifa: My father is the only earning member. We are four sisters and two brothers, both of whom are younger than me. He has worked all his life for us, and now he is getting old and finding it difficult to make ends meet. So my elder sister and I both took factory jobs to help him out.
>
> Hanufa: I saw that women who worked can run the family better, so I decided to work as well. I want to be able to save money. I have a daughter, she has her whole future ahead. Given my husband is not educated and the kind of work he and I do, I want my daughter to study as much as we can afford – at least until the school-leaving examinations. Then she will get a proposal from a good family. But I want her to marry only when she has the understanding and capacity to decide what is good for her own future interests.

Concluding Comments: 'Keeping in Step with the Rhythm of Change'

It is clear from these accounts that, while economic motivations explain women's entry into the labour market, the processes by which labour supply decisions were made entailed a close interaction between economic incentives and cultural norms. The accounts of the women interviewed highlight the complex considerations that come into play when response to market incentives requires a break with cultural routine, particularly when such a break appears to impinge upon such subjective dimensions of individual experience: gender identities, sexual codes and inter-personal power relations within marriage and family. Women have justified their decision to break with convention by challenging the moral authority of those who uphold it, by renegotiating the meanings of purdah and morality in the light of changing circumstances, and by reinterpreting their roles and responsibilities within the family.

In the light of our empirical analysis, a number of modifications to household decision-making can be suggested which allow the interaction between cultural and economic factors to be considered more explicitly.

The first point to make is that while households do pursue economic objectives, 'welfare maximisation' is a rather tautologous description and merely serves to disguise their specific and differing content. It becomes evident from this brief account of female garment workers in Bangladesh that household labour supply strategies can be shaped by a variety of individual and collective goals, such as basic survival needs, the profitable use of free time, acquisition of status-improving accoutrements, desire for independent purchasing power, security seeking, human capital accumulation. A better understanding of these goals, who holds them and in what circumstances they can be implemented will improve our understanding of household supply behaviour, including that of women in these households.

The second point is that while labour supply decisions reflected the material conditions of the household, they are also shaped by cultural considerations. Cultural ideals and practices serve to differentiate different members of the household in such a way that each enters the market on specific terms, depending on age, gender, marital status and so on.

Therefore, while changes in market signals may induce changes in individual/household behaviour, the relationship between market signals and final outcomes is likely to be mediated by a complex set of deliberations which weigh the material and non-material costs of responses by different individuals. Adjustments to market signals are likely to be most painful and problematic when they entail changes in those aspects of behaviour which are most severely and prescriptively governed by religious/cultural beliefs. These costs may also be very differently experienced within the household, and thus entail conflicting interpretations of what constitutes household welfare maximisation.

Finally, cultural constraints will themselves have to be reconceptualised. Purdah is clearly not a monolithic and immutable fact of life, eternally constraining women's economic options. Like other forms of cultural ideology, it is historically constituted, internally complex, often contradictory and lends itself to multiple interpretations. Culture is both structure and practice, constraints and opportunities (cf. Giddens, 1979). It shapes the conditions in which individual practices take place, but individual practice also determines the forms in which culture is reproduced. What we are perhaps witnessing in Bangladesh is a situation where the current practices of women workers – in both the ideological and material senses of the word – are pushing up against the boundaries of old structures and helping to reconstitute them in more enabling ways. Women may not have managed to escape culture – purdah and other gender ideologies continue to impinge upon their choices and behaviour – but they are in the process of redefining it through their accounts and their practices.[7]

The women workers themselves appear to be under no illusion that Bangladesh has been undergoing a social transformation, and that they are part of it. One saying which has gained common currency among them was: 'You have to keep in step with the rhythm of change.' Such change refers to the political upheavals of recent decades, the rising cost of living, rising rural–urban migration, increased landlessness, the gradual disintegration of extended family networks, and the growing significance of education as a means to economic improvement. In particular, there is acute awareness among women of the unreliability of marriage as a way of assuring security and protection in their adult lives, particularly since so many are casualties of the death of, or divorce and abandonment by, male providers. While marriage remains the primary option for most women, they also seek other forms of security through greater investment in their children and greater reliance on themselves.

Social transformation has therefore brought new insecurities in its wake, but also new potentials and opportunities. The women workers interviewed appeared to be abandoning the old perceptions of women as passive occupants of predestined roles, and increasingly behaving as active agents who sought to anticipate the new insecurities, and to exploit the new opportunities.

Notes

1. See *The Economist*, 23 September 1989: 46.

2. In 1980, it was estimated that there were around 50,000 female garment workers (World Bank, 1990:101). By 1989, the Bangladesh Garment Manufacturers and Exporters Association estimated this number at 225,000, employed in 667 manufacturing units.

3. For a detailed discussion of the economic paradigms, see Kabeer, 1991c: 135–8.

4. In fact, the New Industrial Policy of 1982, which gave state backing to export-oriented economic growth, merely helped to formalise aspects of earlier IMF/World Bank aid conditionalities in Bangladesh by further liberalising industrial policies, promoting private sector participation, easing investment sanctioning procedures and opening up the economy to international trade.

5. In this, the Bangladeshi women workers interviewed differ from those studied, for instance, by Wolf in Central Java (1990), and by Standing in Calcutta (1991) who mention, in addition to economic reasons, more socially-motivated ones, such as wanting to make use of their education, or wanting the company of friends.

6. See *New Nation*, 22 December 1986.

7. This serves as a timely reminder that women's income-generating activities promoted by governmental and non-governmental agencies reveal that the latter are often so steeped in the prevailing cultural preconceptions that they find it difficult to separate norms from practice, ideology from reality.

References

Anderson, B., 1983, *Imagined Communities*, London: Verso.

Aranda, J. and I. Arizpe, 1981, 'The "Comparative Advantages" of Women's Disadvantages: Women Workers in the Strawberry Export Agribusiness in Mexico', in *Signs*, vol. 7, no.2.

Cain, M., et al., 1979, 'Class, Patriarchy and Women's Work in Bangladesh' in *Population and Development* Review, vol. 5, no.3.

Chapkis, W. and C. Enloe, (eds), 1983, *Of Common Cloth: Women in the Global Textile Industry*, Amsterdam: Transnational Institute.

Chen, M. and R. Ghuznavi, 1979, *Women in Food-For-Work: The Bangladesh Experience*, Rome: World Food Programme.

Connell, R. W., 1987, *Gender and Power*, London: Polity Press.

Elson, D. and R. Pearson, 1981, 'The Subordination of Women and the Internationalisation of Factory Production', in K. Young et al., (eds), *Of Marriage and the Market: Women's Subordination in International Perspective*, London: CSE Books.

Feldman, S. and F. McCarthy, 1984, *Rural Women and Development: Selected Issues*, Oslo: NORAD.

Giddens, A., 1979, *Central Problems of Social Theory*, London: Macmillan.

Greely, M., 1983, 'Patriarchy and Poverty: A Bangladesh Case Study", in *South Asia Research*, vol. 3, no. 1.

Guhathakurtha, M., 1985, 'Gender Violence in Bangladesh: the Role of the State', in *Journal of Social Studies*, no. 30.

Huq, J., 1979, 'Women in the Economic Sphere', in *Situation of Women in Bangladesh*, Women for Women Research and Study Group, Dhaka, Bangladesh.

Jeffries, P., 1979, *Frogs in a Well: Indian Women in Purdah*, London: Zed Press.

Joekes, S., 1987, *Women in the World Economy*, New York: INSTRAW; Oxford: Oxford University Press.

Kabeer, N., 1985, 'Do Women Gain From High Fertility?', in H. Afshar, ed., *Women, Work and Ideology in the Third World*, London: Tavistock Press.

Kabeer, N., 1991a, 'Monitoring Poverty as if Gender Mattered: A Methodology for Rural Bangladesh', in *Journal of Peasant Studies*, vol. 18, no. 2.

Kabeer, N., 1991b, 'Women, Islam and the State: The Quest for National Identity in Bangladesh', in D. Kandiyoti, ed., *Women, Islam and the State*, London: Macmillan.

Kabeer, N., 1991c, 'Cultural Dopes or Rational Fools? Women and Labour Supply in the Bangladesh Garment Industry', in *The European Journal of Development Research*, vol.3, no.1.

Kandiyoti, D., 1988, 'Bargaining with Patriarchy', in *Gender and Society*, vol. 2, no. 3.

Lim, L., 1978, 'Women Workers in Multinational Corporations: The Case of the Electronics Industry in Malaysia and Singapore', in *Michigan Occasional Paper*, no. 9, University of Michigan.

Mernissi, F., 1985, *Beyond the Veil: Male-Female Dynamics in a Modern Mus-*

lim Society, Rabat: Al-Saqi Books.

Mitter, S., 1986, *Common Fate, Common Bond: Women in the Global Economy*, London: Pluto Press.

Nash, J. and M. P. Fernandez-Kelly, (eds), 1983, *Women, Men and the International Division of Labour*, Albany: State University of New York Press.

Papanek, H. and G. Minault, eds., 1982, *Separate Worlds: Studies of Purdah in South Asia*, New Delhi: Chanakya Publications.

UNIDO, 1980, 'Women in the Redeployment of Manufacturing Industry to Developing Countries', *UNIDO Working Papers on Structural Change*, no. 18, UNIDO/ICIS.

9

Gender Relations and Islamic Resurgence in Mindanao, Southern Philippines

Jacqueline Siapno

In 1989, a Conference on Women, Development and Aid took place in Manila, the Philippines, to identify the most urgent needs of women's organisations at the grassroots level, with the aim of improving the efficiency of aid distribution by western development agencies. Though the meeting was attended by representatives of more than 100 women's organisations, there were only two Muslim women delegates from Mindanao in the southern Philippines (the country's second largest island).

Attending the meeting, I was struck by how these two women appeared to be relatively marginalised during the conference proceedings. In a way, this reflected the prejudices which even progressive Christian Filipino women have internalised about their female Muslim compatriots, a prejudice coloured by a more or less unconscious bias towards Islam. But their marginalisation appeared to be also inadvertently reinforced by the way they identified the problems faced by their communities, more specifically the way in which they spelt out their needs in terms which indicated that feminist concerns – such as polygamy, arranged marriage and female circumcision – were more or less at the bottom of their agenda. Instead, they made a point of stressing that their more pressing problems were the on-going civil war, poverty, and the exploitation of their region's natural resources by multinational corporations. The raising of these concerns triggered my interest in the political developments in the southern Philippines, and eventually led me to write a dissertation on Islamic resurgence in this region, from which this chapter is drawn (Siapno, 1990).[1]

The interviews which I conducted during my fieldwork took place in Marawi City in the province of Lanao del Sur, with men and women of the Maranao ethno-linguistic group. Though I was an 'outsider' in the sense of being non-Muslim and not from the region, I did not find it unduly difficult to establish the contacts necessary to my study. Very

184

probably my research was perceived as a means of informing other out-siders, i.e. 'Northerners' like myself, about the situation in Muslim Mindanao and the justice of the separatist cause.

In order to establish the context of the Islamic resurgence in Min-danao and some of its effect on gender relations, I shall first provide some historical background to its emergence in the southern Philip-pines.

Origins of the Separatist Movement

The present-day Islamic insurgence in Mindanao is not a recent phe-nomenon, but can be traced back over 400 years to the arrival of the Spanish in 1521. Islam had begun to make its presence felt in the Philip-pines a century or more earlier, spreading from India, then Malaysia and Indonesia largely through trade and through contact with Muslim preachers (Holt et. al., 1977: 128–30). While the Spaniards succeeded in Christianising much of the country, Muslims remained entrenched in the southern islands from where they fiercely resisted the invaders. The infamous 'Moro wars' date back to the seventeenth century when the Spanish colonial administration waged battles against the Muslims of Mindanao who refused to be Christianised, hence the designation of the present-day conflict in the southern Philippines as the 'Moro question'.

The three main interpretations of the origins of the present-day sepa-ratist movement centre either on religious differences, economic exploitation or the continuation of political warlordism. Although Mus-lim nationalists acknowledge the relevance of economic exploitation and warlordism, they generally argue that religion is at the root of all conflict in Mindanao. In this vein, their analysis tends to focus on the long history of suffering of Muslim Filipinos dating back to the wars waged against the Spaniards, followed by the period of American rule (1890–1945), the hostile integration policies of the Marcos regime and the discriminatory policies pursued by the present government in Mani-la (cf. George, 1980). The emphasis is on the difference between Mus-lims in the South and Christians in the North, the most recurrent themes being that of a minority challenging an oppressive majority, and an 'unconquered' society confronting one with a deeply ingrained colonial mentality and westernised social values.

The prevalence of this interpretation has among other things led to the proliferation of studies in music, art, literature and religion, all of which highlight the uniqueness of Muslim Filipino culture untainted by US imperialism, Spanish colonialism or Christianity.[2] Perhaps the most notable aspects of this nationalist literature on Muslim Mindanao is that, firstly, it was mainly written during the seventies; and, secondly, it is written by Muslims from a particular social class. Just as the writings of Frantz Fanon on Algeria and Edward Said on Palestine powerfully expressed the hopes and aspirations of an oppressed people, so did these Muslim nationalists in the southern Philippines attempt to bring their struggle to the attention of the international community, in particular other Muslim countries from whom they hoped to receive moral and material support for their cause. But what many of these writings by Muslim Filipinos neglect to take sufficiently into consideration is the structural injustices which ensure that some Muslims in the southern Philippines suffer more hardship than others, such as economic exploitation and traditional alliances which perpetuate the tenant-landowner and patron-client relationships (cf. Siapno, 1990: 13–16).

Islamic Resurgence in Muslim Mindanao

The designation 'Muslim Mindanao' is misleading, for the reality is that Muslims only comprise around one third, while Christians make up some 66 per cent of the Mindanao population.[3] From the first decades of the twentieth century onwards, and particularly during the Second World War, there has been an influx of Christian settlers in the southern Philippines coming from the northern and central parts of the country. In fact, by the 1970s, Muslims had become a minority in many of their traditional homelands, and only remained a majority in five of the 23 provinces of Mindanao and Sulu. Elsewhere I discuss these demographic realities and their implications for the perpetuation of an 'imagined community' and the separatist movement in the southern Philippines (Siapno, 1990: 2–3). It is sufficient here to point out that this Christian immigration, which led to the loss of land and political power, was to become one of the main causes of social unrest in Mindanao. More importantly, this unrest largely coincided with a surging sense of Muslim identity. The latter, though it has its roots in the Islamic renaissance fed by 'Muslim reformism and modernism' at the end of the nineteenth century (Holt et. al., 1977: 183), was particularly affected by the world-wide Islamic resurgence which had begun to make its mark by the early 1970s (cf. May, 1991).

Surprisingly, very little has been written on the *balik islam* (Islamic resurgence) in Mindanao as a religious movement. Except for occasional media articles, the bulk of publications on this separatist movement is concerned with its political impacts rather than its religious dimensions. This behaviouralist approach is somewhat problematic, since religious ideas and beliefs are given no independent status (cf. McVey, 1980).

Rather, they are subsumed under categories such as 'politics' and 'psychology', for which social scientists have a comprehensive analytical vocabulary.

The relative neglect of the religious dimension in analyses of the separatist movement in the southern Philippines is mainly related to the formerly muted role which Islam as a creed played in the consciousness of Muslim Filipinos in general. As Peter Gowing, a Philippines historian, has written, before the resurgence of Islam in the late 1960s, an estimated 80 per cent of the Muslims in the Philippines were more or less ignorant of their religion. He further observed that most of their knowledge about Islam has been handed down to them through oral traditions connected with folk beliefs; that 'adat (customary law) is strong and departs markedly from the Shari'a; that animism and animist rituals abound; that the five pillars of Islam (proclamation of the faith, prayer, fast, giving of alms and the pilgrimage) are only arbitrarily observed; and that there is a general ignorance of the Qur'an and even the rudimentary teachings of Islam (1969).

If this was the case before the seventies, how then did the present conflict between the so-called traditionalist and modernist Muslims in Mindanao come about? Did it occur coincidently or simultaneously with the emergence of the separatist movement? Which movement preceded the other? Is the Islamic resurgence a consequence of the separatist movement? It is certainly the case that this conflict has implications not only for the unity of the movement, but also for gender relations and conventional ideas about women's role and status in Muslim Filipino society.

Three major interpretations tend to be proffered for the resurgence of Islam in Mindanao. One interpretation is that Islam is utilised as a symbol of coherence by the factionalised separatist movement; another that it is part of the larger international movement of Islamic resurgence; while a third interpretation believes that it emerged as an alternative to, and a critique of, the demoralised leadership of the secular elite. Prior to the escalation of the conflict in Mindanao, Muslims in the Philippines generally did not define themselves in terms of their religion, but according to their ethno-linguistic group (e.g. as Maranao, Tausug or Maguindanao).[4] The 13 different Muslim tribes have a long history of rivalry that can be dated back to the nineteenth century if not earlier. The ethno-linguistic differences among Muslims were fundamental enough to sustain serious rivalries even in times of common danger (cf. Siapno, 1990: 18–19). When the Moro National Liberation Front (MNLF) was first formed in the late 1960s, the founding leaders were aware that these differences would pose a vast hurdle in keeping the different factions united. Moreover, from the very beginning, Nur Misuari (Chairman of the MNLF) and the younger group of Muslim radicals appear to have been conscious of the fact that an alliance with the conservative traditional royalty would be particularly problematic. If traditionally they had been enemies, what common ground could possibly keep them together?

In any nationalist movement, a symbol of commonality is important in order to cement co-operation among factions and to mitigate the possible hostility between them. To the nationalists of Mindanao, Islam came to serve as a symbol for transcending rivalries and reinforcing loyalties in order to foster the commonly aspired goal of national independence. Moro, which derives from the term 'moor' used in connection with the inhabitants of North Africa and southern Spain, and which was used as a pejorative term by the Spaniards when they colonised the Philippines, was given a subversive meaning by the MNLF. It became a symbol of community cohesion, and was subsequently attached to the names of all the splinter groups which emerged after the creation of the MNLF.

In addition to names, the Islamic dress came to be adopted as an important symbol of unity. The traditional elite, which previously had preferred to wear western-style attire, was now reverting to a type of dress identified as 'Islamic'. The traditional royalty, aware that the reformist 'ulemas exert a great deal of influence over the people, and careful not to cause any alienation which could lead to the erosion of their own political power, have also become more conscious of the need to signal their adherence to a Muslim identity by adopting a dress style identified as Islamic. Some among the secular elites, convinced that it is in their own interest to accommodate the Islamic resurgence, have also resorted to adopting visible manifestations of a Muslim identity such as dress and rhetoric.

However, the adoption of these Islamic symbols did not have the desired effect, and the alliance holding the different factions together did not last long. In 1977, four separate factions emerged on the political scene: the MNLF which consists mostly of Tausugs, and operates mainly in Sulu, remains the most radical and influential of these groupings; the Moro Islamic Liberation Front (MILF) composed mainly of Minguindanaoans from North Cotabato; the so-called MNLF Reformist Group which is active in Lanao provinces populated predominantly by Maranaos; and the Bagsa Moro Liberation Organisation (BMLO) based in Jeddah, Saudi Arabia and supported mainly by the conservative royalty (mostly Maranaos). In their bid to become the 'true representatives' of the aspirations of Muslim Filipinos, each faction has waged bitter campaigns against the others, thus reflecting not only the pervasiveness of the ethnic factor, but also undermining the very credibility of a legitimate separatist movement. For example, the Organisation of the Islamic Conference (OIC, based in Jeddah, Saudi Arabia) has repeatedly rejected the MNLF's application to become a member because of the factionalism and disunity of the movement (cf. May, 1991).

Islamic Resurgence as an International Movement

The situation of Muslims in the Philippines became an issue of concern to the international Islamic community in the late 1960s, following the infamous Jabidah massacre and other human rights violations against Muslims.[5] In 1969, MNLF guerrillas began training in Malaysia. By the early 1970s, the chief minister of Sabah in Malaysia, Tun Mustapha, had become an open supporter of the MNLF, channelling arms and other assistance into Mindanao and Sulu. From around this time onwards, Libya's President Qaddafi began to openly identify with the cause of Moro nationalism, supplying arms and financial aid to the MNLF and supporting its efforts to be recognised by the Islamic Conference of Foreign Ministers.

More significant than military or material aid, however, is the intellectual and religious influence of the Islamic resurgence sweeping through other Muslim countries. Like most of the leaders of the Dakwah Movement in Malaysia (cf. Anwar, 1987), for example, many among the new generation of 'ulemas in Muslim Mindanao have received their education in Al-Azhar University in Cairo, Egypt, renowned for its intellectual influence on the worldwide movement of Islamic reformism. The teachings of the Egyptian philosopher, Muhammad Abduh, who led the reformist movement in Cairo at the beginning of the present century, and who influenced a generation of intellectual nationalists, was to become an inspiration to the 'ulemas and Muslim political figures in Mindanao (cf. Gowing, 1988).

Saudi Arabia in particular has provided scholarships for study in a number of Muslim countries, as well as economic support which has enabled 'ulemas in Mindanao to expand existing and build new madrasas (religious schools).[6] These sectarian schools, which originally only offered a year's course in Islamic exegesis, prayers and rituals, were now upgraded to meet the changing needs of Muslims and to provide an alternative education system to that instituted by the Philippines government. This has been welcomed by many Muslim parents suspicious of secular schools which they perceive to be a means of Christianising their children. In effect, this means that there are now two parallel educational systems in Mindanao: the *madrasa* which is similar to the school system in parts of the Arab Middle East, and which aims to provide spiritual guidance and a religious education based on Islam; and the Philippine system which is oriented towards western cultural values, and is by this very fact associated with Christianity. Needless to add, this development has served to encourage a further wedge between Christians and Muslims in the Philippines.

In addition to the increasing spread of Islamic schools, the resurgence of Islam in Mindanao can be attributed to the following factors which have not failed to have an impact: increased contact with Muslim visiting scholars from the Arab world, which has served to shorten the geographical and cultural gulf separating Muslim Filipinos from the wider world of Islam; increasing numbers of Filipino Muslims going on the *hajj* (pilgrimage to Mecca) and returning with a reinforced sense of Muslim identity; visits to Mindanao by officials and government representatives from the Muslim world (particularly from Pakistan, Libya and Malaysia); and international press coverage of the on-going war in Mindanao and the human rights abuses committed by the Philippine military personnel in the region, which has served to ensure that the Muslim minority in the Philippines has found a place on the stage of international affairs.

While all these factors undoubtedly play a role, based on the interviews I conducted during my research, I would argue that enthusiasm for the Islamic resurgence is also determined by the individual's socio-economic background as well as age-group. In this respect, one may broadly distinguish between religious and political groups. Among the former, one needs to differentiate between the modernists and the traditionalists. The latter are mainly composed of the older generation who cling to the *andang sa mona* (the way of the ancestors), and perceive any changes in religious ritual as a threat to the heritage they treasure. In fact, they are the practitioners of folk Islam (a syncretism of animist beliefs and Islamic inspired custom handed down through the generations), and prefer women to wear the *malong* (traditional Maranao dress) rather than the *kumbong* (the veil). Few of them will have the means to make the pilgrimage to Mecca, and they are mainly of modest backgrounds, clustered in occupations such as weavers and vendors. The modernists, who generally belong to the younger generation, call for a distinction to be made between *'adat* and 'pure' Islam, and tend to be critical of any rituals unrelated to the Qur'an or the Hadith. They belong mainly to the middle class, and are often teachers or civil servants who have the opportunity to live and study abroad, and to make the pilgrimage. They will thus tend to be exposed to Islamic reformist ideology. In contrast to the traditionalists, they encourage their women to wear the Arab-style Islamic dress and veil.

Among the political groups, there is a distinction between radical and conservative leaders. The former, deemed radical because they advocate secession (and not because they advocate any radical ideology in the Marxist sense) belong to a younger generation of middle-class intellectuals, some of whom see the separatist struggle in terms of ensuring social justice. The more conservative politicians, on the other hand, belong to the old elite families or to royalty who have lost their traditional political power, as well as to formerly secular groups who became Islamised during the 1970s. They believe that genuine equality for Muslims can be achieved not through guerrilla warfare, but through institutional reforms carried out by the state itself. However, regardless of what may separate them, radicals and conservatives of both genders are as vehemently critical of western civilisation associated with 'the North', i.e. the seat of political power, as they are of any communist ideology.

Islamic Resurgence and Gender Relations

The arena of society where the separatist movement and resurgence of Islam in Mindanao have had their most visible impact is that of gender relations. This visibility is not only due to such external symbols as the veil. More important perhaps is the fact that Muslim women have been drawn into activities from which they had hitherto been barred by custom and tradition. In effect, it is the 'abnormal' conditions related to the political insurgency in Mindanao which have propelled them into a more publicly visible role. But has this development breached the traditional boundaries between the sexes, and has it led to more equality between men and women?

Much has been written about the Moro National Liberation Front and the role played by the 'ulemas, the traditional elite and intellectuals, but very little about women's role in this separatist movement. Studies on Muslim women in Mindanao have tended to focus on fertility patterns, motherhood, marriage, child-rearing practices and other behavioural accounts of the Maranao Muslim family, a focus which seeks to 'improve' women's lot but which generally neglects to relate their situation to the wider socio-political context. These accounts leave one with the impression that while men go to war against the central government in Manila, women are waiting at home, living a harmonious and static life (cf. Moore, 1981).

As my research findings indicate, this image does not necessarily fit the reality of Muslim women's way of life in Mindanao. In fact, women have become involved in several ways in the separatist struggle for autonomy. Here I shall single out two particular aspects of this involvement – the active and the symbolic – and attempt to assess the implications they have had for gender relations in particular and the separatist movement in general.

The first aspect, namely women's active participation in the struggle, is reflected in the pressure groups they have formed in order to exert pressure on government officials to explain the disappearance of their male kin, a pattern emulating women's collectives in other parts of the world which have suffered human rights abuses.[7] A more important dimension of this active participation is women's direct involvement in the MNLF. Thus, women have their own military sub-organisation within the movement – the Bangsa Bai – which was founded in the early 1970s during the intensification of the militarisation of Mindanao. Women receive training in military camps not only as first-aiders (i.e. the role with which they have historically been associated during warfare), but also as combatants and intelligence agents. None the less, while this involvement is officially welcomed as part of women's participation in the struggle, it needs to be seen in relation to the increasing government repression. As the latter became more severe and more effective, and men had to go underground to escape capture, they turned over to women tasks which they could no longer carry out. According to a male commander I interviewed, the separatist movement quickly realised that one of the most effective tasks for women was that of information agent, since the government military authorities (who were predominantly Christian) believed that Muslim women were too bound by tradition to be involved in such activities. This enabled female MNLF members to move around relatively freely, and to provide their male counterparts with valuable information on the movements of government troops.

On the face of it, the direct involvement of Muslim women in combat – indeed some were killed in military action – can be interpreted as a particular sign of progressive change in definitions of women's role in society, a change which has taken women out of the traditional sphere of the home and into the quintessential male arena of warfare. In reality, while it is true that women combatants are now perceived to be 'equal' with men in terms of the importance of their contribution to the separatist struggle, most of the conventional ideas of patriarchal control have remained untouched. For example, though women may receive the same type of military training, they are subject to the unwritten rule that they may only be trained by male relatives 'whom they can trust', thus perpetuating the ideal of spatial segregation between the sexes. In effect, while the importance of women's physical contribution to the struggle is acknowledged, this participation is not permitted to question the boundaries which mark off gender roles from one another. This reality is well reflected in the words of a male MNLF commander who, when asked whether there were any woman commanders, answered:

> Some could qualify as commanders, but we don't encourage it. They are more visible as representatives to social and community gatherings. If there are dialogues and male leaders cannot attend, we usually send women. Even if there were, we don't really make them famous because of security reasons.

Moreover, women's assumption of the traditionally male combatant role has had little impact on notions of honour, more specifically women's responsibility for upholding it and the concomitant belief in men's responsibility for protecting their womenfolk. This was explicitly expressed by the above quoted male MNLF commander, who, when asked why no women in the MNLF have surrendered to the government forces over the past 20 years, replied: 'We will never allow our women to suffer the humiliation of surrender. Men are allowed, but not women. Love, care, protection – protection is the most important thing that a Maranao man must do for his wife.'

It would thus appear to be a mistake to assume that the mobilisation of women in times of abnormal conditions in the southern Philippines has necessarily led to the re-definition of women's gender role in terms of greater equality with men. Rather, women are seen in terms of a supportive role and are permitted to assume functions traditionally associated with the male gender role almost by default. The experiences of women in countries that have undergone a comparable military struggle are in this respect instructive. For example, in Algeria, women were utilised to carry out tasks for the Algerian Liberation Front (FLN) only when men encountered difficulties (cf. Minces, 1978). Thus Algerian women's participation in the struggle was born out of necessity, rather than out of conviction that women's equality with men in society should be ensured. Once independence from France was achieved in 1962, the post-independence state relegated women's social liberation to the backburner, and the conventional patriarchal attitudes regained the upper hand.

The second aspect pertaining to women's involvement in the struggle for independence in Mindanao involves symbolic forms of resistance, of which veiling is perhaps the most important precisely because it is the most visible. Muslim women scholars have accused western feminists of 'veil-centrism', i.e. the tendency to uncritically focus on the veil as the most unambivalent sign of Muslim women's oppression (cf.

Ahmed, 1982). The simplistic equation of women + Islam + veil = oppression is perceived as being indicative of an ethnocentric tendency which attributes undue importance to such visible symbols as the veil, while neglecting to adequately analyse the context in which men and women relate to one another in the different spheres in which their roles intersect. It would seem that precisely because it is such a visible symbol, western feminists have tended to focus inordinately on the veil, particularly when studying Islamic revivalism. But perhaps what is more relevant is how feminists have tended to interpret the phenomenon of returning to the veil. While some see it simply as a passive maintenance of convention, others judge it in terms of a positive and conscious act by women to express their resistance to an external enemy.

In southern Mindanao, where women have always worn the *malong* (traditional Maranao dress), the adoption of Islamic, Arab-style dress beginning in the mid-1970s was indeed noticeable. A number of interpretations have been suggested for this change. One such interpretation, offered in explanation of the specific case of Muslim women in southern Thailand, maintains that women will tend to wear Islamic dress and attempt to uphold their Muslim ethnic identity more than men for the following reasons. Firstly, Muslim women are more isolated from the metropolitan culture than men. They are thus less integrated into Thai institutions in terms of their proficiency in the official language, in education and modern occupations. As a result they are more inclined to maintain cultural symbols such as dress. By contrast, men are by the nature of their activities more susceptible to change and will be more inclined to adopt the symbols of the dominant group. Secondly, women much more than men are expected to maintain the rule against marrying outside their community, thus ensuring that they maintain their role as the guardians of the community's honour and traditions (cf. Prachuab-moh, 1989).

While the interpretation of veiling as a symbol of maintenance of convention may be true for Muslim women in southern Thailand, it is not necessarily the case in Mindanao. Here the veil is not only a recent phenomenon, but, more importantly perhaps, those women who have resorted to wearing it are far from being isolated from the metropolitan culture. On the contrary, they will tend to be relatively the most educated, and are furthermore closely integrated into the international Islamic community. By contrast, Muslim women in the southern Philippines who are relatively isolated from the dominant metropolitan culture, mainly due to lack of education and employment opportunities which, in turn, isolate them from the wider Muslim community, are far more likely to wear the traditional *malong* than the veil.

The experiences of Algeria and Iran are perhaps particularly instructive to the adoption of the veil in Muslim Mindanao. Frantz Fanon has argued that in Algeria, veiling was used as a symbol of resistance to French colonial rule. Instead of a conservative symbol of maintenance of tradition, the veil actually represented a conscious act of resistance (1967). Similarly, in Iran, the *chador* became the symbol of resistance to the western-supported ruling elite, and to the authoritarian rule which attempted to abolish it by force, though there would appear to also be the parallel aim of enforcing the image of the 'proper' Muslim woman (cf. Yeganeh, 1982). Because colonial governments have often used the alleged 'oppressed status of native women' as one reason to colonise the natives, nationalist governments and liberation movements have tended to reclaim these so-called 'oppressive' traditions even more vehemently as an act of defiance against the colonisers (cf. Kandiyoti, 1991).

In Muslim Mindanao, here too the adoption of the veil has come to be perceived by some people in positive terms, and as a conscious decision to express resistance to the Philippine government. However, there is also an element of enforcing the image of the 'proper' Muslim woman: when asked whether or not the veil is a good sign, a male former MNLF commander replied:

> Well, yes! It is a healthy sign that we are now aware of who we are. We are forced to be aware of who we are and what we should be. We see this as a revolutionary act, being spear-headed by the *'ulemas* and the *datus* (warlords). Also, we have observed that wearing mini-skirts is too much for our women. There was a time when mini-skirts were in vogue in Marawi City, until the *'ulemas* and the *datus* stopped our women from wearing these bare clothes.

Yet, interestingly, women themselves may feel ambiguous about the veil. For example, when asked for her opinion on veiling, a Muslim woman professor at the Mindanao State University[8] replied: 'More and more women are identifying themselves with the Arab dress. What we are witnessing in Marawi is an Islamic renaissance. Now the trend is that even if she does not wear a veil, at least she has a head-dress.' However, when asked the same question, a Maranao housewife replied:

> If you ask me, I don't like it. They (i.e. veiled women) look like Ninjas. I also believe strongly in Islam, but to us the black veil is impractical. The climate is too hot. We prefer to wear the *malong*. However, if you're a *hajji* (i.e. have gone to the pilgrimage), then you have to wear the *kumbong*. It's just a cloth to cover your hair, not the whole black veil that covers the entire body.

While this woman's answer does not negate the importance of the veil as an expression of piousness or of symbolic resistance to political oppression, it does reveal that men and women in Muslim Filipino society will tend to differ as to the *type* of veil deemed appropriate and physically comfortable to wear.

Equally important is the fact that the interpretation of veiling as a symbolic act of resistance may be valid only up to a certain point, i.e. the particular circumstances during which it carries an explicit political message. Again the case of Algeria is instructive: when independence from the French was achieved, veiling became a symbol of reversion to conventional norms enforced by the newly independent state and its new political and religious elite. Similarly, in Iran, the brutal enforcement of the Shah's legal abolition of the veil in 1936 was an important reason for the pro-veil backlash enforced by the Khomeini regime after the Iranian revolution in 1979. It thus remains to be seen how attitudes towards the veil as a symbol of resistance will develop among Muslim communities in the southern Philippines if and when this resistance is resolved.

Perhaps what is paradoxical about veiling is that, on the one hand, it is perceived as a private issue concerning which women can seemingly have freedom of choice on whether or not to adopt it. Yet, on the other hand, it is not subject to the woman's individual decision at all, but is a public one enforced by patriarchal institutions (i.e. religious leadership, the state, family and community). As a form of resistance, the veil is perhaps the most accessible expression of rebellion to women in societies where they have been allowed to participate in the political struggle. Accordingly, Muslim women in Mindanao see the veil as a physical boundary which separates them from the westernised Christians, and the immorality and materialism associated with the (Christian) North. It is only when veiling is no longer voluntary but becomes mandatory – such as in Iran, for example – that women will tend to question the right of patriarchal institutions to interfere in their freedom of dress, and to perceive it in terms of oppression.

What Muslim and Christian Filipino do have in common is that both belong to a strongly patriarchal society where the only kind of expression of honour open to them is modesty. In a society such as Muslim Mindanao which is almost obsessed with morality, and which overzealously adheres to the ideology of honour, a woman who wants to gain/retain respect in her community has to hide any indication of her sexuality, which is seen as the most potent threat to the patriarchal system (cf. Bouhdiba, 1985; Mernissi, 1985). Those women who seek the freedom to express views critical of this system are at best harassed, and at worst ostracised.

This reality is well expressed by a Maranao man who, when asked what would happen to a Muslim woman who contemplated the perhaps ultimate act of defiance, namely that of marrying outside her community, replied:

> Two things can happen: the more lenient one is that she is ostracised by her family. She must separate because she has brought disgrace. But there is a harsher way – the man can get killed or sent away. A lady Maranao should not get married without the approval of her family. She is educated along that line. She should always uphold the dignity of her family. She cannot violate this.

Conclusion

In a recent study of patriarchy in Iran, Afghanistan and Pakistan during the late 1970s and up to the 1980s, Valentine Moghadam argues that 'the politics of gender may be especially strong in patriarchal societies undergoing development and social change; gender becomes politicised during periods of transition and restructuring, when social groups and values clash' (1992: 4). This has been witnessed in Mindanao, where there is an on-going separatist struggle in which women have been actively involved, but where the call for cultural authenticity fed by the Islamic resurgence has set limits to the breaching of boundaries between traditional gender roles.

Many writers have observed that in countries engaged in a nationalist struggle, the fight has often been for independence only, and has generally not aspired to create a different society, one in which both class and gender inequalities would be removed. It is also true that, in general, feminist movements have tended to postpone the questioning of patriarchal social structures and to give priority to the nationalist struggle (cf. Jayawardena, 1986). Indeed, this was the case in earlier struggles by the (Christian) Filipinos against Spanish domination. Women played an active and supportive role but 'their involvement did not induce them to question the general pattern of family and social structures which relegated them to a secondary role', a pattern reinforced by the Catholic Spanish culture (ibid: 166). When the Philippines became independent in 1946, it remained within the American sphere of influence. The Filipino women's movement succumbed to the 'strength of the prevailing ideology', and focused its energies on attaining legal equality for women, rather than questioning 'their subordinate role within the family and society (influenced by) the strong religious bias of the education system' (ibid: 166).

Among the Muslim women of Mindanao today, the struggle for independence is of over-riding importance. As indicated earlier, all the factions of the separatist movement use Islam as a symbol of cohesion. But women will tend to experience Islam differently according to their class origin, their age group, whether they live in an urban or a rural setting, and above all, the extent to which they are involved in the armed struggle. Women combatants who have breached the traditional boundaries between the sexes have been careful not to go beyond what is culturally permissible, and – as did previous generations of women involved in nationalist movements – appear to accept their relegation to a supportive rather than an equal role. Older and less educated women are more likely to practise folk Islam, and are perhaps bewildered by the younger generation of women who strive for an 'Islamic way of life'. These younger educated women are more likely to adopt the Islamic-style dress and to distinguish between *'adat* and orthodox Islam. Describing the tension between the two, a woman professor in Mindanao State University explained that 'the contradiction comes when the traditional culture clashes with Islamic teachings. Islam is a complete way of life. Even in education, we are striving to Islamise, to inject Islamic guidance in whatever we do in this world.'

The reality that an 'Islamic way of life' may have contradictory implications for women's equal status in society appears to be overlooked or, at best, given only secondary consideration. This is well reflected in the response of a female member of the traditional royalty, who had previously held the post of governor of Lanao del Sur. Questioned on her personal vision for an autonomous Muslim Mindanao, she replied: 'I want the next generation to keep the tradition that women have limitations in social functions. It is this practice that will preserve the Islamic tradition'.

The horrific events in Mindanao in the past two decades have intensified the already violent prejudices of Christians against Muslims. Interestingly, however, it is argued by some scholars of Philippine literature that in the Mindanao epics, legends and folklore, Muslims and Christians did not have an antagonistic relationship. Indeed, there is one legend that is still close to Filipino Muslims and Christians alike – the legend of Urduja. Urduja was a Muslim *bai labi* (female sultan) who is said to have ruled the Kingdom of Tawalisi during the fourteenth century with an army of 'free women, slave girls, and female captives, who fought just like men' (Ibn Batuta, 1983: 280). Possibly her legend has survived because it gives a sense of self-identity to Filipinos, whether Muslim or Christian, who desperately need an indigenous history that pre-dates Spanish and American colonisation (cf. Burton, 1988).

Whether Urduja is fact or fiction, or a delicate mixture of both, to Muslim and Christian women who have achieved varying degrees of freedom but remain in the subservience typical of patriarchal social structures, she represents a time when women are considered to have held a high status in society, and to have possessed civil and political rights. In the case of the Muslim women of Mindanao who are the focus of this chapter, it remains to be seen whether this legend will encourage them to ensure that their gender interests do not remain subservient to the wider social and political interests of their communities.

Notes

1. I would like to thank Minang Dirampatan-Sharief, Medaylin Acraman, Benasing Macarambon, Jr, Salivia Macarambon, Raquel Tiglao and Margaret Herbig whose generosity and courageous hospitality made my trip to Marawi possible. I would also like to thank Judy Mabro and Camillia Fawzi El-Solh without whose enthusiasm and editorial support this essay would not have been possible.

2. See, for example, the writings of Muslim nationalists such as Datu Michael Mastura, Carmen Abubakr, Nagasura Madale, Senator Santanina Rasul, and Senator Domocao Alonto.

3. Population estimates from Ministry of Muslim Affairs. See *An Overview on Muslim Development in the Philippines*, Plans and Policy Service, Manila 1983, p.4.

4. In fact, the study of 'Muslim Mindanao' is a fairly recent phenomenon. Most historical research has focused on ethno-linguistic groups and tribes rather than on Muslims as a minority group in the southern Philippines (cf. Majul, 1985; Loyre, 1989).

5. In March 1968, about 30 young Muslim soldiers were summarily executed on the island of Corregidor, following an alleged mutiny. They formed part of a group of about 180 Muslims secretly recruited by the military (with the knowledge if not instruction of former President Marcos) in a secret operation called 'Jabidah' for training in jungle warfare, sabotage and guerrilla tactics. The recruits believed that the purpose of their mission was to infiltrate Sabah (Malaysia).

6. Apart from providing funds for *madrasas*, Saudi Arabia is reputed to have given millions of dollars to projects such as the construction of mosques, libraries and offices.

7. In Palestine, Chile, Argentina, Brazil, South Africa, Sri Lanka, and the Philippines in general, women's collectives have initially come about as a result of human rights violations (cf. Jayawardena, 1986; Warnock, 1990).

8. Mindanao State University is government funded. It was created in 1955, one of the various government development projects for Muslim Mindanao.

References

Ahmed, L., 1982, 'Western Ethnocentrism and Perceptions of the Harem', in *Feminist Studies*, vol. 8, no. 3.

Anwar, Z., 1987, *Islamic Revivalism in Malaysia: Dakwah Among the Students*, Kuala Lumpur: Pelanduk Publications.

Beck, L. and N. Keddie, eds., 1978, *Women in the Muslim World*, Cambridge, Mass.: Harvard University Press.

Bouhdiba, A., 1985, *Sexuality in Islam*, London: Routledge & Kegan Paul.

Burton, J. W., 1988, 'The Legend of Urduja', in *Solidarity*, no. 120.

Fanon, F., 1963, *The Wretched of The Earth*, New York: Grove Press, Inc.

Fanon, F., 1967, *A Dying Colonialism*, New York: Grove Press.

George, T. J. S., 1980, *Revolt in Mindanao: The Rise of Islam in Philippine Politics*, Kuala Lumpur: Oxford University Press.

Gowing, P., 1969, 'How Muslim are the Muslim Filipinos?', in *Solidarity*, no. 8.

Gowing, P., ed., 1988, *Understanding Islam and Muslims in the Philippines*, Qezon City: New Day.

Holt, P. M. et. al., 1977, *The Cambridge History of Islam*, vol. 2, A, Cambridge: Cambridge University Press.

Ibn Batuta, 1983, *Travels in Asia and Africa 1325-1354*, London: Routledge & Kegan Paul.

Jayawardena, K., 1986, *Feminism and Nationalism in the Third World*, London: Zed Books.

Kandiyoti, D., 1991, *Women, Islam and the State*, London: Macmillan.

Loyre, G., 1989, *A la Recherche de l'Islam Philippin: La Communauté Maranao*, Paris: L'Harmattan.

Majul, C. A., 1985, *The Contemporary Muslim Movement in the Philippines*, Berkeley: Mizan Press.

May, R. J., 1991, 'The Religious Factor in Three Minority Movements: The Moro of the Philippines, the Malays of Thailand and Indonesia's West Papuans', in *Journal Institute of Muslim Minority Affairs*, vol. xii, no. 2.

McVey, R., 1981, 'Islam Explained', in *Pacific Affairs*, vol. 54, no. 2.

Mernissi, F., 1975, *Beyond the Veil: Male-Female Dynamics in Modern Muslim Society*, New York & London: Schenkman Publishing Company.

Minces, J., 1978, 'Women in Algeria', in L. Beck and N. Keddie, eds., *Women in the Muslim World*, Cambridge, Mass.: Harvard University Press.

Moghadam, V., 1992, 'Patriarchy and the Politics of Gender in Modernising Societies: Iran, Pakistan and Afghanistan', in *International Sociology*, vol.7, no.1.

Moore, R. L. P., 1981, 'Women and Warriors: Defending Islam in the Southern Philippines'. Unpublished Ph.D., University of California, San Diego.

Prachuabmoh, C., 1989, 'The Role of Women in Maintaining Ethnic Identity and Boundaries: A Case of Thai Muslims in South Thailand', in *South East Asian Review*, vol. xiv, nos. 1-2.

Said, E., 1980, *The Question of Palestine*, London: Routledge & Kegan Paul.

Siapno, J., 1990, 'The Separatist Movement and Islamic Resurgence in Mindanao, Philippines: 1970-1990'. Unpublished M.A. thesis, School of Oriental and African Studies, University of London.

Tabari, A. and N. Yeganeh, eds., 1982, *In the Shadow of Islam: The Women's Movement in Iran*, London: Zed Press.

Warnock, K., 1990, *Land Before Honour: Palestinian Women in Occupied Territories*, London: Macmillan.

Yeganeh, N., 1982, 'Women's Struggles in the Islamic Republic of Iran', in A. Tabari and N. Yeganeh, eds., *In the Shadow of Islam: The Women's Movement in Iran*, London: Zed Press.

INDEX

UNIVERSITY OF WOLVERHAMPTON
LIBRARY